Occasional Papers Series

No. 29

The Basque Moment
Egalitarianism and Traditional Basque Society

Edited by
Xabier Arregi Gordoa and Andreas Hess

Center for Basque Studies
University of Nevada, Reno

This book was published with the generous financial assistance of the Basque government

Center for Basque Studies
University of Nevada, Reno
Reno, Nevada, USA
basque.unr.edu

Occasional Papers Series, no. 29
Series editor: Joseba Zulaika

Library of Congress Cataloging-in-Publication Data

Names: Arregi Gordoa, Xabier, editor of compilation. | Hess,
    Andreas, editor of compilation.
Title: The Basque moment : egalitarianism and traditional
    Basque society / edited by Andreas Hess and Xabier Arregi
    Gordoa.
Other titles: Egalitarianism and traditional Basque society
Description: Reno, NV : University of Nevada, Reno, [2017] |
    Series: Occasional papers series no. 29 | Includes bibliographical
    references and index.
Identifiers: LCCN 2016054353 | ISBN 9781935709732 (pbk. : alk.
    paper)
Subjects: LCSH: Pais Vasco (Spain)--Civilization. | Pais Vasco
    (Spain)--Social conditions. | Basques--Social conditions. |
    Equality.
Classification: LCC DP302.B467 B42 2017 | DDC 946/.6--dc23 LC
    record available at https://lccn.loc.gov/2016054353

Contents

Introduction

Xabier Arregi Gordoa and Andreas Hess

In his book *La société des égaux* (*The Society of Equals*) the renowned French historian of ideas Pierre Rosanvallon comments on the rich tradition of egalitarian ideas that runs like a thread through the history of Western society, starting with egalitarian aspirations in predemocratic and precapitalist times, the demands for political and social equality to which the American and French Revolutions tried to provide an answer, and to the fissures and pathologies that characterize modern Western societies (Rosanvallon 2011). Political theoretical discussions of equality, just like notions of individual liberty, were part and parcel of the developments sketched out by Rosanvallon. For example, a liberal thinker like Benjamin Constant showed that the notion of freedom in the ancient world differed from that of the modern world, while Alexis de Tocqueville was one of the first to reflect systematically on a new democratic phenomenon: the tyranny of the majority. This entailed a new danger of uniform thinking that had emerged with the idea of equality for all. Attempts to introduce total social equality culminated in an even more dramatic historical turning point. The fall of the Berlin Wall in 1989 symbolized that the largest human experiment ever undertaken—the communist attempt to create an equal society—had failed. However, while capitalist democracy celebrated its victory over communism, only two and a half decades later it appears to have been a somewhat Pyrrhic victory. Over the last few years capitalist democracies have been experiencing the deepest systemic crisis since the economic downturn of the 1920s and 1930s.

Yet, the idea of equality that currently still prevails seems to be one that centers on a one-dimensional, atomistic notion, more often than not regarded as an expression of a universal tendency. The development of humanity is seen as developing in unilinear and deterministic historical fashion. We are confronted with a reading of equality that still stems very much from the Enlightenment and the French and American Revolutions. From such hegemonic interpretation and discourse derives a somewhat fixed notion of the course of history, even though we should know better after all the crises that capitalist democracies have been through in the last one hundred years. Pre-Enlightenment societies, ancien régimes or precursors of republican ideas and their ideas of equality and freedom, are still all-too easily dismissed as having been simpleminded forerunners that needed to be surpassed. Until today most contemporary social practices and political ideas are still interpreted along such one-dimensional, unilinear notions of equality and freedom. Rosanvallon hardly differs in this respect.

From the second half of the twentieth century onward some intellectual historians, historical sociologists, and political philosophers have begun to question unilinear perceptions and one-dimensional readings of history and have offered alternative readings. Unreflected universalist and unilinear accounts of egalitarian ideas have come under scrutiny. It has been suggested, alternatively, that it is more fruitful to look at the specific social, political, and cultural contexts in which egalitarian ideas and notions of freedom have emerged. In terms of excavation some of the best historical contributions have come from the Cambridge School, and most prominently within that paradigm, from Quentin Skinner and John G. A. Pocock. Having said that, other contributions, for example from political philosophy, Michael Walzer or Michael Sandel come to mind here, have also shed light on other undervalued civic notions of liberty and equality.

The title of our collection, *The Basque Moment*, pays tribute to Pocock's classic *The Machiavellian Moment: Florentine Political Thought and the Atlantic Republican Tradition* (1975). Pocock attempted to follow the intellectual history that connects the political thinking of some of the northern Italian city states in the fifteenth century with the founding of the American Republic in the 1770s. It is in many ways an underground story in which the oppositional thought of English republicans plays a major mediating role. Pocock limits himself to studying only one possible thread—that of the Anglophone world and its Atlantic connection. Very little is said about other republican traditions outside the Anglophone world, including their own Atlantic connections.

Just three hundred meters separate the statue of the second president of the United States, John Adams, in front of Bilbao's Diputación Foral/Foru Aldundia (Provincial Council) from the statue of José Antonio Aguirre (also spelled Agirre), the first democratically elected Lehendakari or Basque president, next to the Hotel Carlton at the Plaza Moyua in the heart of the city. It is less than a five-minute walk from one statue to the other; however, one could also argue that the space between the two statutes also encapsulates some crucial 150 years, which marked the transition from a traditional "democratical republic"—that is how Adams described Biscay (Bizkaia, Vizcaya in Spanish) in 1787— to that modern political entity that almost gained independence in 1936 but that had the most tragic of outcomes. As is known, the Aguirre government only survived the bombing of Gernika for a few weeks more until the insurrectionist Mola troops,[1] with the support of Italian battalions and air support from Nazi Germany, pushed through the Iron Ring defense line of Bilbao and forced the democratically elected Aguirre government into exile—an exile that would eventually lead him to the United States. The statues of Adams and Aguirre are reminders not only of two statesmen and patriots who thought about the historical roots of

---

1. Together with Generals Francisco Franco (1892–1975) and José Sanjurjo (1872–1936), General Emilio Mola (1887–1937) plotted and led the military uprising against the democratically elected Spanish government in 1936 from his base in Pamplona-Iruñea, Navarre. The premature deaths of both Sanjurjo and Mola in the early stages of the Spanish Civil War left Franco in sole control of the rebellion.

their republic but also what it practically entails to defend and fight for the republic's very existence and survival. To discuss Adams, Aguirre, and American and Basque republicanism and to interpret the connections between them in greater detail would take considerable space, space we do not have in this introduction. However, it seems appropriate to reflect at least briefly here in this introduction on the deeper meaning of that connection, particularly since it ties in with the central theme of our book: egalitarianism and its political, social, and cultural dimensions.

On January 13, 1780, John Adams, accompanied by his son, entered the Basque Country on horseback. They had been forced to travel overland from Galicia to Paris since their ship, which should have taken them directly to France where Adams was to serve as the representative of the new American Congress, had to anchor in A Coruña for urgent repairs. Approaching Biscay from the West, at Puente de la Rada (today known as Larrazubi in Basque/Puentelarrá in Spanish, in the province of Araba/Álava) they had to produce their passport crossing from Castile into Biscay. Adams and his son stayed in the "republick of Bilbao" for almost a week before continuing their journey to Baiona (Bayonne) in Iparralde, the northern, French part of the Basque Country. During his time in Bilbao, Adams observed the differences between the Basque province and the rest of Spain. In his diary he writes that

> it may seem surprising, to hear of free Provinces in Spain: But such is a Fact, that the High and independent Spirit of the People, so essentially different form the other Provinces, that a Traveller perceives it even in their Countenances, their Dress, their Air, and ordinary manner of Speech, has induced the Spanish Nation and their kings to respect the Ancient Liberties of these people, so far that each Monarch, at his Accession to the Throne, has taken an Oath, to observe the Laws of Biscay. The Government here, is therefore dramatically opposite to that of Gallicia, and the other Provinces. The King of Spain has never assumed any higher Title than that of Lord of Biscay. He has no Troops of any sort in the Lordship. (Adams in Butterfield 1961)

While Adams was impressed with some of the trade aspects of Bilbao—it looked to him much better than anything else he had seen in Spain—he saw no signs of thriving commerce or industry that would compare to the East Coast ports of the United States. Communications, especially roads, remained poor and as somebody who was of Protestant and dissenter background, he was also taken aback by the omnipresent Catholicism of the Basque province. He speculated as to whether the lack of enlightened self-interest was due to the fact that he had encountered no universities. Apart from the academy of Bergara in Gipuzkoa (Guipúzcoa), it seemed that there was little in terms of educational infrastructure.

A few years later, in 1787, while writing his *Defence of the Constitutions of Government of the United States of America*, Adams reflected again on his journey and Basque conditions. He acknowledged the peculiar customs and political traditions but also critically observed that they had not been renewed: "After those people in Europe who have had the skill, courage, and fortune, to preserve a voice in the government, Biscay, in Spain, ought by no means to be omitted. While their neighbours have long since resigned all their pretensions into the hands of kings and priests, this extraordinary people have preserved their ancient language, genius, laws, government, and manners *without innovation*, longer than any other nation of Europe. . . . It is a republic; and one of the privileges they have most insisted on is not to have a king: another was, that every new lord, at his accession, should come into the country in person, with one of his legs bare, and take an oath to preserve the privilleges of the lordship" (Adams 1787 [1797], 16–20; italics by the editors; the following quotes are all from the same source). Adams also noted local variations when it came to political institutions, which differed greatly when compared to America's large compound republic. The Basque Country consisted of smaller republics, each with its specific arrangements: "Although the government is called a democracy, we cannot find all authority collected into one center; there are, on the contrary, as many distinct governments as there are cities and merindades [counties or districts]." Adams liked what he had seen but he also remained somewhat skeptical if not reserved as to the beneficial effects of what he called the "contracted aristocracy." By that he meant the Basque *jauntxos* who helped to represent the "three branches of power of the one, the few, and the many" but who seemed to do very little to develop trade and commerce or contribute otherwise to innovation. While Adams obviously sympathized with the democratic republics of the Basque Country, he concluded with a warning: "We see the people themselves have established by law a contracted aristocracy, under the appearance of a liberal democracy. Americans, beware!"

The long nineteenth century brought competing demands to the Basque Country and in its course Adams's warning came true—although not exactly in a way that he originally foresaw. The two Carlist Wars (1833–1840 and 1872–1876) are notoriously hard to comprehend, even for historians. This is the case mainly because there were so many layers of conflict—political, economic, and cultural. On one side we encounter the more liberal, enlightened, secular, anti-royal, and urban influences that in the Basque context were particularly strong in Bilbao, demanding not only economic and social modernization but also political reform. These forces wanted to update the old rights and customs as enshrined in the fueros.[2] On the other side we have the rural areas of the Basque provinces and Navarre—dominated by the Carlists—defending religion and the longstanding autonomy based on old rights, privileges, and economic arrangements with the Crown of Castile. The Carlists defended a rural world that functioned relatively well, at least when compared to some of the other regions of Spain. True, the Carlists were certainly not radical modernizers; however, it would be wrong to describe them as simply backward or reactionary. They maybe had a valid point in holding on to and defending their traditional way of life, which by all accounts seemed to have worked rather well for that rural world that made up a big part of the Basque Country and Navarre, in particular those parts untouched by industrial development (as Bilbao surely had been). Officially, the conflict ended with the victory of the modernizers and the abolition of the fueros. However, it is not really possible to identify with certainty the winners and losers in this conflict. In the Carlist conflict we find Spanish

---

2.   This is a key term for this work that requires a brief introduction. The fueros were consuetudinary laws, guaranteeing a far-reaching level of provincial political and economic decision-making authority, by which the Basque provinces remained outside the common governmental structures of both the Spanish and French Kingdoms. The term can be rendered orthographically in different ways: foru (singular)/foruak (plural) in Basque; fuero/fueros in Spanish; and for/fors in French; a result of the linguistic flexibility that defines the geographical and cultural reality of the Basque Country. The adjective would be foral.

and Basque liberals fighting together against Spanish, Navarrese, and Basque Carlists. The underlying cultural conflict was also to continue and would reemerge in the twentieth century, particularly with Franco's coup d'état in 1936. The Carlist Wars never fully settled the latent and lingering conflict between the traditional rural and small-town world and the expanding urban and industrial environment, mainly of Bilbao. While the liberals gained access to power and, consecutively, introduced economic and legal reforms, it would turn out to be a Pyrrhic victory. In the last two decades of the nineteenth century the political, social, and economic conditions began to change dramatically, particularly in the urban zone around Bilbao. Within twenty years Bilbao became transformed and was turned into a giant industrial magnet. To maintain its productivity and labor force it needed massive immigration. Tens of thousands of immigrants followed the call and migrated from the poorer areas of Spain and also from the rural areas of the Basque Country to Bilbao. A true demographic revolution was the result. The liberal modernizers had won—but only to encounter a demographically explosive and politically volatile constellation.

It was only late, in 1936, that in order to find regional allies, the Cortes (the parliament of Spain) and the Spanish government decided to grant the three Basque provinces of Bizkaia, Gipuzkoa, and Araba more than the statute argued for unsuccessfully in 1931—namely an improved autonomy status that fell just short of full sovereignty. Navarre was not part of this new political framework and neither was Iparralde. A government was formed consisting of a coalition of Basque nationalist, republican, socialist, and communist parties under the Lehendakari José Antonio Aguirre. Finding itself under enormous military pressure by the insurgents, Aguirre's administration spent most of its time organizing the defense of the Basque provinces. It is at this point that the unresolved tensions with the Carlists came again to the forefront. The Carlists were particularly strong in the northern part of Navarre and in Araba. What had brought them to join the insurgents was the promise of a continuation of their traditional, that is, mostly rural and small-town way of life, defending their special rights and remaining fervent Catholics. After the fall of Bilbao for a short period a few Basque republican soldiers, the *gudariak*, escaped and continued with their resistance farther west in Cantabria until they surrendered. Following the defeat the Aguirre government took refuge in Barcelona before it was finally forced to leave Spain after the fall of Catalonia and Valencia. Its exile history is a true odyssey. It took the government's leading members first to Paris and London, and finally to New York. Aguirre would die in his Paris exile in 1960 and never saw his beloved Bilbao again.

The 150 years that separate Adams and the old Basque republics on one side and the tragic outcome of the short-lived, quasi independent Basque Country, which sided with the equally doomed Spanish Republic, on the other seemed to have marked the beginning of the end of Basque republicanism—at least in terms of widespread local acceptance and support. In the wake of Franco's death in 1975, the long transition from dictatorship to some form of constitutional monarchy and formal democracy in the late 1970s and 1980s never regained that lost republican momentum. There were reasons for this. First of all, there was obviously no chance of ever returning to a precapitalist state in which everyone lived in small communities and was considered a nobleman and lived under political arrangements just like Adams has described it, that is, with a contracted aristocracy safeguarded by special laws and *jauntxo* elites.

Second, during the transition there seemed to have been no great political support to revert back to the Basque Country's autonomous status under the Second Spanish Republic. That experience of de facto Basque independence and whatever republican notions, pockets, or ideological undercurrents remained thereof, were associated with a historical futile attempt, including defeat and exile—not an impressive success in terms of final outcomes, despite the heroic circumstances of Basque resistance. While no easy return to previous republican models seemed possible, there was obviously even less enthusiasm and support for the 1970s and 1980s "democratic" transition itself, particularly not in Hegoalde, the southern part of the Basque Country. The reasons were obvious: the constitutional design that emerged was that of a constitutional monarchy in which everything politically and institutionally important was decided by Madrid. (Navarre saw the situation in a more favorable light and managed to come to a separate political settlement with the new Spanish democracy.)

Today it is even more challenging to envision a new republican agenda, including revised notions of equality and freedom. Any future republican vision that favors egalitarian structures has to face the fact that the Basque Country has experienced massive social change in the intervening period. Old ideas of equality and freedom have been replaced by formal rules and constitutions. Most of these new democratic arrangements necessarily have to abstract from historical notions, apparently a prerequisite for entering the modern orbit of capitalist democracy. It may be a sign of the times that even nowadays, in the early twenty-first century, with the end of ETA's violent campaign and at the beginning of a new historical cycle for the Basque lands, no new common republican language has emerged. At a recent, well-publicized launch of a new book (Insausti Ugarriza 2011) in the Basque Country, in which Basque intellectuals and politicians reflected about a new raison d'être for the Basque Country, and in which we find, among others, contributions from the philosopher Joxe Azurmendi, the ex-Lehendakari Juan José Ibarretxe, the writer Pako Aristi, and the social anthropologist Joseba Zulaika, it was noticeable that nobody favored republican notions of liberty and equality. All the writers involved preferred their own agenda while a common political language remained elusive—despite the readily available republican rhetoric to which the Basque Country had contributed so much, even though some of it appears to be a history of undercurrent, often oppositional thought and practice. It seemed as if postmodernism and the pressure of the demands of the day had also destroyed the political imagination.

Our book serves as a reminder of that Basque undercurrent that occasionally managed to break through to the surface to establish lasting cultural practices. It is the attempt to take a closer look at some Basque notions of equality and egalitarianism and to situate them in their proper historical context. The idea is to approach the topic of Basque egalitarianism from a broader perspective, including social and contemporary history, sociology, political science, social anthropology, and political philosophy. Thus, our book brings together scholars and researchers from different disciplinary backgrounds. In the first instance, our book wants to be a primer for an English-speaking audience and readership. Some readers interested in egalitarian ideas might have heard about universal nobility (*hidalguía*) in the Basque Country, about the peasants from Bizkaia who were described by Rousseau as gathering under the oak tree in Gernika always taking wise decisions, while enjoying the special rights (fueros) that had guaranteed some form of local and provincial self-government for centuries. Equally, the name of the Mondragon cooperatives, one of the biggest modern attempts to work and produce in a different way to the dominant model of production, has surely resonated among those who think that there must be alternatives to making a living and working.

Our edited collection will look into some of the political social and cultural conditions that made such practices possible. However, we will also attempt to differentiate. We are not interested in creating or prolonging myths about the Basque egalitarian tradition. This collection of essays is therefore, secondly, also an attempt to take stock and thus appeal to a wider readership. In this vein we will try to find answers to such questions as: Is the notion of Basque egalitarianism reconcilable with modern notions of equality and justice? How does Basque egalitarianism fit into the history of social and political thought more generally speaking? Even if it were true that egalitarianism served those in power, are other notions or practices thereby automatically excluded? What exactly does Basque egalitarianism mean today? Where and how is it practiced? How does the notion of egalitarianism sit with other concepts such as more liberal notions of individual freedom? Are there any gender aspects to notions of Basque egalitarianism?

In his overview chapter, "Equality, Status, Recognition: Civic Humanism in the Basque Country," Xabier Arregi Gordoa introduces the reader to the specific egalitarian philosophical discourse and the specific Basque context in which this philosophical discourse makes sense. In "Liberties and Equality in a Catholic Republic," José Angel Achón Insausti goes a step further by identifying some of the classical republic rhetoric in early modern Gipuzkoa. Maïté Lafourcade's "Egalitarianism in Traditional Basque Society" attempts to provide an overview of how the idea of egalitarianism took hold in traditional Basque society. Oihane Oliveri Korta's "Nobles from Known Lineages: Universal Nobility in Gipuzkoa" focusses on the same topic and looks specifically at Gipuzkoa practices between the fourteenth and the eighteenth century. Coro Rubio Pobes's "The Idea of Basque Egalitarianism in the Nineteenth Century" also deals with the question of common nobility but shows that the situation resulted in increasingly oligarchic structures in the course of the nineteenth century. Anne-Marie Lagarde's "Egalitarianism and Gender in Traditional Basque Society" takes J.L. Austin's question of how to do things with words seriously by looking into sociolinguistic practices and how they relate to, and express sexual identities in rural Iparralde. In contrast, although not necessarily in opposition to Largarde's contribution, Margaret Bullen and Jone Miren Hernández's "Cracks in the Wall: Breaking Down the Myths of Egalitarianism and Matriarchy in the Basque Country" is an attempt to distinguish between myth and actual practice and to discuss the complex relationship between nation and gender. Paco (Francisco) Garmendia and Patxi Juaristi's "Notions of, and Attitudes to, Property in the Basque Country" is the attempt to study the nature of social relations in more general terms. As in Lagarde's article, the authors also take a closer look into sociolinguistic practices. Joseba Azkarraga Etxagibel's "Slaying the Dragon Together: Modern Basque Co-Operativism as a Transmutation of Traditional Society" shows how traditional egalitarian values were transformed and found expression in modern cooperative movements such as Mondragon. Finally, Andreas Hess's "Plebeian Culture, Moral Economy, Reluctant Modernization: An Attempt to Understand Basque Egalitarianism Differently" provides a view from afar. He suggests that egalitarian practices might best be studied and understood through a change of theoretical perspective and the way sociological concepts are applied.

We would like to thank Daniel Montero and Cameron Watson for helping us to get this edited volume into shape, no easy undertaking when one has to deal with texts that were originally written in four different languages, including their unique notions and concepts, usage of terms, not to mention many other special aspects that often appear hard to translate from one language and context to another.

We dedicate this book to the memory of Francisco Garmendia who passed away before being able to see the finished product.

References

Adams, J. 1787 [1794]. *A Defence of the Constitutions of Government of the United States*, vol. 1. London: John Stockdale

Butterfield, L. H., ed. 1961. *Diary and Autobiography of John Adams*, Vol. 4. Cambridge, MA: Harvard University Press. An electronic version is available from the Massachusetts Historical Society at www.masshist.org/digitaladams/.

Insausti Ugarriza, Xabier. 2011. *Euskal Herria: Errelitate eta utopia.* Donostia: Elkar.

Pocock, J. G. A. 1975. *The Machiavellian Moment: Florentine Political Thought and the Atlantic Republican Tradition*. Princeton, NJ: Princeton University Press.

Rosanvallon, Pierre. 2011. *La Société des égaux*. Paris: Seuil. In English: *The Society of Equals*. Translated by Arthur Goldhammer. Cambridge, MA: Harvard University Press, 2013.za.

1

Equality, Status, Recognition: Civic Humanism in the Basque Country

Xabier Arregi Gordoa

Apology versus Ideology in Basque Historiography

In the late twentieth century an intellectual movement emerged that saw itself as a transgressor. It maintained that traditional Basque historiography had been characterized by a lack of rigor and had been used in defense of traditional Basque society by painting a rather idealized picture of its past, while in fact not just hinting at its potential rescue but also aiming at a kind of radical political *Aufhebung*. According to the critics, that paradigm's main aim was to support the Basque nationalist political project. While it is true that there was a movement that often interpreted the *foru* (fuero) model in a protective light, it is also worthwhile pointing out that such a position seemed a legitimate answer to attacks to which the foru-republican model had long been subjected.[1]

---

1. The Basque and Navarrese foru system is a common law system based not on previously established universal "truths," privileged people, or noble lineages but on a specific people, their territoriality, undeniable origins, and historical rights. In the foru system society, social conditions and customs are usually regarded as being more important than law and political structure. The foru system is one of the strongest historical links that binds the four territories

I would argue that complimentary approaches do not necessarily devalue any model, nor should the foru approach itself become invalid or illegitimate. If that were the case, we would not be able to give any credence to Leonardo Bruni, Girolamo Savonarola, and many others who wrote about Florence and defended and praised its republican aspirations. The same applies to texts written by Dutch authors during the Dutch Revolt in the fifteenth century.[2] Today, scholars around the world discuss the substance and continuous relevance of the classical works of republicanism in the early modern period. Is it too much to demand an equally balanced scholarship when it comes to such classic Basque authors as Andrés de Poza,[3] Manuel Larramendi, Bernabé Egaña, and others?

In *La otra nobleza* José Ramón Díaz de Durana maintains that the "critical" revisionists should be regarded as innovators since they worked very hard to remove "old myths" once and for all. Methodologically, these revisionists were indebted to French historiography, particularly its Marxist stream as it developed from the 1970s, in the work of authors from, for example, the *Annales* school (Díaz de Durana 2004, 59).

However, we are all the result of the times we live in, and this necessarily applies also to the authors who Díaz de Durana

---

(the three Spanish Basque provinces plus Navarre) to each other and gives its people a strong sense of common identity. First recognized in the early thirteenth century the foru system endured until it was abolished in the course of the nineteenth century. The foru territories fought together to defend their traditional political system against attempts to integrate them under a single Spanish constitution. In this chapter I interpret the foru system as expressing the values and customs associated with humanist republicanism, in the first instance because I believe that this is the manner in which the foru communities and their people prefer to see themselves; second, because foru practice is inspired by republican humanist principles; and third because the republican tradition has been repeatedly claimed by authors, texts, and documents in order to defend the foru system against abolitionists' attempts to get rid of them.

2. For an assessment of that tradition see Van Gelderen (1993).

3. Andrés de Poza was born in the early sixteenth century into a Basque family in Antwerp, where he studied and lived for different periods in his life. He is considered the first Basque author to articulate the foru-republican culture from a legal and political view in his *Fuero de hidalguia ad Pragmaticas de Toro & Tordesillas*, which began to take shape in 1588. See Carmen Muñoz's edition (1997).

celebrates as transgressors. As he himself points out, from the 1970s onward this so-called innovation in history had less to do with being precise and trustworthy than with the application of what Quentin Skinner has called the "mythology of doctrines" (Skinner 2002, 64–72). Seen in this light, it appears strange that those who consider themselves to be true transgressors can look down on all the other scholars and traditions from the throne of objectivity and neutrality or, equally, the watchtower of civilization, and identify or try to shun "deplorable" "old-fashioned" myths, or condemn "ethnicity" and "millenarianism."

In fact, the "innovative" movement itself could be charged with showing outrage and an exclusionary vision. Its representatives often made statements that were far from precise, the very kinds of statements that they proclaimed to protect us from. For example, Alfonso Otazu's work about egalitarianism, which is regarded by many as a milestone, is in itself in parts highly ideological and polemical:

> So much work has gone into making the Basque "case" seem like something unique that, when you read a history of the country, it gives the impression that one is reading the history of a beautiful green country with many shepherds who played the flute in the morning and danced to the sound of the drum at night. . . . Everything appears democratic, everything has its origins in atavistic impulses, to such an extent that you get the sensation—even if you are not a historian but only possess some intellectual curiosity—that these are "histories" written for the mentally deficient or, at least, for people who have long ago given up thinking about anything from time to time. (Otazu 1973, 11)

Such rhetoric and history writing are indeed not far from those views that Skinner criticized as being ideologically loaded. In other words, those writers, who intended to get rid of "retrograde historiography," have themselves become slaves to modern ideological rhetoric, including its mythological and doctrinaire content. To be more precise, their ideological component consists in treating equality in absolute and universal terms and in a truly ideological sense (the latter pretty much in line with what Michael Walzer has in mind when he speaks in his *Spheres of Justice* of "simple equality"). The net effect of such ideological commitment has been to question or undermine the credibility of any author, foreigner or autochthonous, who defends some kind of egalitarian practices in traditional Basque society, by charging them with being slaves to romantic pathologies, or with making up an idyllic, rural, society that never existed. No contextualizing effort is made; even worse, such an attempt is being denounced as being intellectually unworthy.

The Complex and Dynamic Character of the Basque Foru Republican Model

The theoretical paradigm change suggested by J. G. A. Pocock and Skinner regarding the history of political ideas, and by Walzer and others regarding political theory[4] and philosophy, allows us to consider the rhetoric of equality and liberty, not as part of an ideological framework, but in their proper context. Working with such an approach helps us to study society in terms of its inner principles and to place it in its proper historical context. If we approach traditional Basque society from such a point of view, it becomes clear that we are looking at a community with republican characteristics, which has strong foundations in the Renaissance. Perceived that way, it is possible to detect links with humanist republicanism that developed in Europe between the thirteenth and seventeenth centuries, while at the same time allowing for a discussion of its own unique needs, historical dynamics, cultural connotations, particular circumstances, and communitarian aspects. It would also provide an answer to the limits placed on it to date by seeing Basque society solely through the French and Spanish eyes and vantage points. As I will argue, republican rhetoric was applied to different areas in Europe, but took on specific characteristics particular to each community's conditions, for instance, in the Pyrenees and parts of the Basque Country in the Kingdom of Navarre; in Great Britain, where it impacted on oppositional thought and politics; and in the Low Countries, where it helped to establish the Dutch Republic.

As far as traditional Basque society is concerned I will examine some of the arguments that were made in support of the republican character of the foru while also taking a closer look at the Basque legal tradition and the relevant literature linked to it.

---

4. I refer here and in what follows particularly to Pocock (1975), Skinner (2002), and Walzer (1983).

With regards to those who have pointed to the republican quality of the Basque lands there exists a good number of references from both friends and foes. Those who thought its republican aspects worth a discussion were Wilhelm von Humboldt, Jean-Jacques Rousseau, and John Adams; while among its enemies Pierre de Lancre and Juan Antonio Llorente are worth mentioning.

Wentworth Webster's work (1901) is perhaps the most detailed account of this issue, for nowhere else in relation to the Basque lands does republicanism enjoy such a prominent place. Wentworth Webster lived in the Basque Country at the beginning of the twentieth century. Looking at the local conditions from the political tradition of the United Kingdom, he suggested that the Basque foru system should be included in the debates about the pros and cons of the republican framework. In the British Isles debates about republicanism and absolute monarchy had never abated, particularly not in oppositional thought, despite the failed republican experiment under Oliver Cromwell in the seventeenth century. So it was not unusual for Webster to point toward the republican features of the Basque lands. According to him, the word "republic" had appeared frequently in political discussions, particularly in the western part of the Pyrenees (Webster 1901, 136). Continuous reference had been made even by the Spanish King and Crown to mutual obligations laid out and regulated in the foru system. Similarly, in the Kingdom of Navarre the word "republic" was referred to time and again in the kings' decrees, the court's debates, and other legal foru institutions. There was, for him, "a real differentiation in the way the governance of the province was considered, both by the king and by the Basques themselves" (Webster 1901, 137). In both cases the subjects did not submit to the king or his representatives' direct control; rather they organized themselves and possessed their own recognized form of association that then negotiated with the king. The king was accepted after that as a lord (or as the main prince) but only as long as he first accepted the Basque *foruak* (that is, the republic) and promised to defend them.

In all these accords the rhetoric of humanist republicanism played a role. The republican character can be traced in a number of documents, not least in the foru texts themselves, and in associated texts and interpretations. The works of Poza,[5] Larramendi, and Egaña are testimonies and proof to republican notions, most prominently expressed in the *batzarre* (assembly) system in every Basque and Navarrese town. Practice and text(s) constantly interplay and it is sometimes not easy to decipher which came first. It is important, however, to acknowledge that over the course of more than four centuries there developed a specific institutional system that created its own form of organizing participation, stressing particularly self-government and equal recognition—a system that was obstinately concerned with avoiding anything that resembled tyranny. It is not too farfetched to see in this an encounter between what has been called "mountain republicanism" and humanist republican positions.[6]

We must understand such a form neither as monolithic nor as static, but as having developed in complex, dynamic ways. The complexity involved has been noted in the works of many authors who have addressed the subject. Maïté Lafourcade's contribution has been exceptional on this subject. In *La société basque traditional* (2011), which is a synthesis of her main work, she examines the entire Basque Country and stresses not only the originality of its political organizations but also their systematic, yet not always uniform, nature or character, as there were many towns and republics.

Similarly, Adrian Celaya takes a closer look at the foru system in order to find out what makes it so unique. His answer is that it is the decentralization of power that includes, and at the same

---

5.   Poza notes for the sixteenth century that "we are federated peoples, preserving the original state of our republics and [are], therefore, free." Andrés de Poza (1997, 30).

6.   For Maïté Lafourcade, "The whole Basque Country, north and south, was organized as mountainous countries are." And in a note Fourcade stresses: "This type of organization is not unique to the Basque Country." In mountainous areas such as the Briançonese (Briançonnais/Brianzonese) region around Mount Viso on what is today the Franco-Italian border, where the inhabitants of the valleys met to manage common land and to defend their collective interests in assemblies called *escartons* in which there were no organizational levels, it was rather a meeting of free men, all equal, managing their own affairs; these *escartons* send representatives to the Briançonese General Escarton that, in turn, sent representatives to the États du Dauphiné; their main role was to distribute taxes (2011, 95).

time protects, different levels of territoriality. Provinces, local areas, towns, municipalities, and households were bound together and protected by an elaborate legal system (Celaya 2009, 71).

According to Celaya the complex and dynamic nature of the foru model is based on the coming together of two main ideas: First, the legislation established under the foru system is always dynamically conceived, since it has to meet changing conditions and needs. Second, the legitimacy of its practice is grounded in the community's own understanding and practice, that is, its own moral concerns provide the basis from which everything else flows. It is thus not an abstract positivism form that the system aims at, but a political and legal structure that responds to and caters for the flexible needs of the community. Neither laws nor foruak create communities; neither individuals nor society are subservient to the foru model. The foru system does not give any priority to political power, or worse, derive laws from it. Instead, the foru system derives its legitimacy from the fact that at its base is a moral community, based on a system of mutual recognition, linked to precedents but also a system in which individuals are recognized as holders of rights (Celaya 2009, 205). Such a model does not arise as if it sprang from some sacred text, but rather it is created by a community that wishes to live in harmony, yet is open enough to be molded according to different places and circumstances.

Larramendi's text ([1754] 1950) serves as a classic demonstration of such a view. Writing in the eighteenth century he distinguishes between two levels of foru, both of which give it strength: on the one hand the acceptance of precedent, that is, what was original, the roots, that which did not change, such as its connection with territoriality and common ties; on the other hand, he discovers a willingness or openness to adapt, which takes into account changing circumstances down the centuries. He has no doubt though about its historical origins; for him the foru existed before the Kingdoms of Castile and Navarre. He writes:

> The Gipuzkoa Foru is primordial, original, and from the roots, and is referred to in those documents that declare the whole of Gipuzkoa and all its children to be noble, and they always have been; a free country for local people and foreigners too; free on the sea and on land in every sense; free of poll taxes, tithes,

and taxes. The strength of the Gipuzkoa foru derives from its population. It was not granted or conceded as a favor. Gipuzkoa had its original foru before Castile and Navarre had laws. At one time Gipuzkoa was an independent republic. (Larramendi [1754] 1950, 98)

Larramendi suggests here that the communitarian republic came first. Second, Larramendi's account implies that originally there were no social contracts, no leaders, no founding charters. Thus, the foru system was not founded as a consequence of some preexisting political structure; rather, the original inhabitants created it, without relying on founding Elders, nobles, or other selected individuals. Third, such a founding process hints at egalitarian notions and notions of rights such as the freedom of movement for all, the right to be engaged in trade, and not having to pay taxes imposed from without. The result is that there is a basic recognition that is given to all members of the community, qua belonging to it.

It is worth noting that Poza, similarly, places the conditions for equality and recognition in a system of nobility with *dignitas* (Poza [1588?] 1997, 17). This idea of universal nobility with *dignitas* must be seen in its wider historical and geographical context. Nobility with *dignitas* for Poza means noble by birth, a category deeply rooted in Renaissance humanist republicanism. In his commentary on *Laudatio florentinae urbis* (Praise of the City of Florence, c. 1403–4) by Florentine humanist, historian, and statesman Leonardo Bruni, Hans Baron reminds us that its aim was to show that the objective of the laws of Florence was to guarantee the freedom and equality of all citizens.[7] For that reason Bruni makes every effort to argue that the Florentines were Rome's successors, which meant that they were all "of sufficiently noble birth," a status that in turn guaranteed equality before the law and the right to get involved in communal affairs.[8]

---

7. It is the freedom of the Florentine citizen that is at the core of the panegyric of 1428. Florentine laws, says Bruni, "aim, above all, at the liberty and equality of all citizens"; the Florentine constitution, therefore, falls under the "forma popularis" of government (Baron 1966, 418).
8. "Whoever has these qualifications is thought to be of sufficiently noble birth to participate in the government of the republic . . . not to have to fear violence or wrong-doing from anybody, and to enjoy equality among citizens

If we understand being noble by birth in that humanist republican way, then the Basque foru system certainly shows some interesting parallels. Nobility is then not a privilege and not an excuse for creating a relationship of subjugation among individuals, but on the contrary nobility means that all members of the community are subject to law and protection and have the right not to be governed by tyranny.

Universal nobility (Celaya 2009, 205) must be understood as basic status recognition, which includes all the territory's offspring, and which is highly practical. In particular, the following specific traits should be highlighted: (1) In the neighboring monarchies of Castile and France the nobility system provided no opportunity for manual workers ever to become part of it; instead, such exclusion led to the creation of diverse statuses and ranks. In contrast, recognition in the republican foru model included shoemakers and seamstresses. Such differences in status and rank allowed writers like Cervantes and Carlos Osorio to make fun of the Basque people. Osorio laughed at the Basques because their nobility included such humble professions (writing ironically about the "noble shoemaker" and "noble dressmaker" to poke fun at the Gipuzkoans). (2) On the other side, ownership should not be understood in post-Marxian terms as alienation, but, on the contrary, as the only way to preserve the Basque territories and their people from tyranny and submission and for them to be free and equally recognized. Furthermore, there existed different notions and usages of property in traditional Basque society, such as communal property, property held by the church, buildings belonging to the people of a town, farmsteads, ancestral property, rented farmsteads, and so on.[9] In any case, owning a house, whether in a town or a single farmstead in the countryside, was central to the system. Not only did it mean economic status, but pertaining to a house was the crucial component of the mutual recognition system. (3) There were limits

---

before the law and in the participation in the public office" (Baron 1966, 419).
9.   Owning property was in the context of an economic model that was worked in very particular, often quite discrete ways. There were changes in terms of ownership, sales, and loans; nobles' land could be bought and become common land; the rent, according to Julio Caro Baroja, was usually low and agreements and contracts often inherited. See Caro Baroja (1974). Similar patterns were identified by Justo Garate (1980, 64).

in terms of the taxes that authorities could raise, as noted in the Larramendi quote earlier ("free on the sea and on land in every sense; free of poll taxes, tithes, and taxes"). Celaya emphasizes that the only way to accept taxes was if they were agreed on by the foru institutions (Celaya 2009, 205). (4) Citizens benefited from strong legal protection that often extended in remarkable ways and included economically poorer segments of Basque society. As Lafourcade points out:

> By tradition and under their foru, the Basques had important legal guarantees. . . . The Basques had a system of habeas corpus that guaranteed people suspected of crimes freedom until the crime that they had been accused of was proven, long before English law, before the French declarations, and before the American Rights of Man. . . . It was above all in the Bizkaia foru, dating from 1452 and 1526, that a remarkable system of legal guarantees was drawn up. (Lafourcade 2011, 37)

All of this does not mean that the Basques were living in an ideal world; there can be no doubt, however, that it was a community that managed to maintain itself. It will be hard for us to ever understand such republican arrangements if we examine social practices and political arrangements only from the perspective of the modern state. This modern state was, as Hans Baron reminds us, the successor to absolutism—not the direct successor of the Renaissance humanist republican model.

The Basque foru system had its own ups and downs, but it is justified to say that over time it became a strong point of identification for the people of the four foru-republican territories. It is perhaps best described as an independent, functioning, non-state form of political self-government. Francisco Calatrava sums it up clearly: "The Spanish nation is a single, harmonious group, as befits its geographical limits, with two very clear exceptions. One is Portugal. . . . The other exception is the Basque provinces [and] Navarre. . . . It is true that they have always been somewhat separate. . . .They have hardly been influenced by outside influences. . . . They are free of strange mixtures and civilizing currents" (Calatrava 1876, 220).

The Basque Foru System in the European Republican Humanist Context

The humanist republican model of organization in the Basque Country was not an isolated experiment. On the contrary, in early modern Europe similarities can be detected in other parts of the continent, which connected to a significant political tradition that has long been undervalued. Considerable effort has gone into recovering this hidden European heritage during recent decades. Indeed, the rediscovery of the humanist republican tradition has facilitated a new interpretation of both history and political theory.[10]

The origins of this republican model are to be found in the changes that became manifest in Europe at the end of Middle Ages and that created a juxtaposition between absolute monarchies and humanist republicanism. As Baron states, both took shape in northern Italy, the former in Milan and the latter in Florence. Milan opted for the route of tyranny and monarchy; its main features were that its government tended to be expansive and authoritarian in character. Its rulers stemmed mainly from a lineage system that no longer cared for its citizens' freedom (Baron 1966, 12). In contrast, freedom and equality were still very much valued and recognized in the Florentine republican model. The citizens there had decided to pursue republican ideals, to oppose the monarchic model, and to experiment with new ideas as long as their pursuit did not contradict liberty and equality.

The Basque foru system fits fully into that republican tradition and it must be understood as a variant of the political practices that spread across Europe. However, it had to respond to specific challenges and conditions, develop its own particular characteristics, and, therefore, make its own unique contribution to the European republican tradition. In what follows I will take a closer look particularly at Aquinas's political theory and English Common Law.

Aquinas made a point that would later be reiterated by Larramendi, Egaña, and other defenders of the Basque model,

---

10. Here special mention should be made of van Gelderen and Skinner (2005).

namely that law was connected to and was an expression of tradition and custom.[11] Aquinas saw freedom as interwoven with community membership: each community is the creator of its own
laws.

> There can be two kinds of community into which the custom
> is introduced. For if it is a free community which may make
> its own laws, the consent of the whole community expressed
> through custom counts in favour of a particular observance
> far more than does the authority of a prince, who has not the
> power to make laws except as representing the community.
> (Aquinas 2002, 155)

In practice, this means that the community itself is the legitimate subject for deciding laws, not some powerful individual.
The prince, for example, does not have any legitimacy to decide
over laws. In fact, the prince will be freedom's biggest enemy
if he intends to impose himself as the main source of legitimacy. In Aquinas's view, legitimacy derives from the community's
customs and order; this implies that legitimacy derived from
a prince or king is regarded as unacceptable. Laws can only be
passed based on customs and to the extent to which the people
who promulgate them in that community accept those customs.
This in turn means that daily life is the context in which answers
to problems should be found. It is this embeddedness that gives
law its legitimacy.

Perusing Pocock's *The Machiavellian Moment* (1975) we see
similar parallels between the author's treatment of common
law and Larramendi's examination of the original foru model.
Pocock shows that sixteenth-century common law gave importance to the same two aspects: the priority of the community's
tradition and the possibility of adapting the legal framework to

---

11.   "Nevertheless in such a community a prevailing custom obtains the force
of law in so far as it is tolerated by those whose business it is to make laws for
that community, since by the very fact of tolerating it they seem to approve
of that which the custom has introduced" (Aquinas 2002, 155). It is true that
Aquinas also has divine law and natural law in mind, and the legitimacy of customs, in the end, is so to the extent that it agrees with divine law, but he does
accept, even if kings have received their authority from God, that they would
lose their legitimacy and deserve rebellion if they did not respect customs, and
the community's will and activities.

the times and changing needs. Particularly with respect to the second point he notes: "Nothing could be more misleading than to picture the vehement assertion of the antiquity of English law and liberties as an inert acceptance of 'traditional society.' It was rather traditionalist than traditional—to adopt a distinction of Levenson's—an assertion of conservatism; and conservation is a mode of action" (Pocock 1975, 341).

All major institutions, parliament included, were in agreement with original customs. Their main aim was to conserve and thereby to protect liberty and to serve as a bulwark against tyranny: "All English law was common law, common law was custom, custom rested on the presumption of immemoriality; property, social structure and government existed as defined by the law and were therefore presumed to be immemorial" (Pocock 1975, 340–41).

Like the foru, common law was not considered as being static, or as a backward looking operation, as something created at one particular time and set to last forever (which is often another myth created by the universally retrograde nature of ancient regimes), but rather as something dynamic, able to adapt to new circumstances, and able to renew itself.[12]

In Europe, such forms of legitimizing and managing political structures lasted for a long time, often side by side and in competition with the absolutist option. The discussion surrounding Swiss, Dutch, and other political structures and national traditions are a case in point. It would be an oversimplification to label such traditions and others that came before the French Revolution as all just "old regimes." To do so would diminish the role that the plurality of social organization and its political institutionalization played in Europe for a considerable time. In fact, a republican notion of liberty existed before liberalism, as Skinner persuasively demonstrates.

Context and Equality

I started this chapter by referring to an intellectual movement that became somewhat influential in the last quarter of the twentieth century, particularly since it appealed to a certain way of

---

12.   As Pocock observes, freedom itself is linked to custom and tradition: "liberty [is] rooted in a fabric of immemorial custom" (1975, 340).

conceiving and writing Basque history. That approach was deeply indebted to the presumed model nature of the French Revolution. Its universalist tone and ideological claims explain perhaps why it became not only popular in France, but also in the rest of Europe.

However, such an approach runs into trouble when applied to analyzing traditional forms of governance, because of its simplified take on equality and status. These simplified views of equality and status are related to two complementary views of human nature that have become prominent in both political theory and practice: collectivist and atomistic individualism. The former puts the equal distribution of wealth as the only criterion for equality. The aim of the collectivist point of view (often referred to but not limited to communism or socialism in its various possible disguises) is a society without property, not only any type of private property, but also any type of communitarian ownership. At the end of history, property and dominance by property (particularly property in terms of the means of production) would be removed to allow and make the space for all individuals to develop freely and under equal conditions. All differences arising from ownership would cease to exist; individuals would become masters of their own future and would turn into truly autonomous human beings. In contrast, the second (somewhat more Hobbesian) viewpoint puts the individual at the center of its attention. Individual human beings, so goes the assumption, are representative of and already characterize human nature, including its not so nice features. The conclusion contains a less hopeful message—that of a potential war of all against all. Political authority would be needed to put order into the chaos and to prevent major violence and conflict from happening. Such a political authority would establish a legal framework under which all citizens would be protected and treated equally and enjoy, at least in principle, universal rights. In contrast to the first view, however, the institutions will not just wither away but remain in place, since theirs is a regulating function. As Habermas states: "A legal order is legitimate when it safeguards the autonomy of all citizens to an equal degree" (in Gutmann 1994, 121).

Both collectivist and atomistic theories rely on the idea of progress in order to justify their own existence. They both conceive of historical time as a continuity without any ruptures and crisis points, in other words, as a constant march forward. Historical events have to find their place on that straight line, some in the distant past, others in the imminent future, moving from past to future. In a way, both ideological projects represent that direct line's continuation to the very summit, the last push and realization of their aims, only held back by traditional "uncivilized" moral communities.

However, at the beginning of the twenty-first century, the failure of both lines of reasoning is evident. It is difficult to support the collectivists' rational project when all of the prophecies made in the name of reason and history have been proved false; when what free and equal people look like becomes harder and harder to define; when the equal society that is allegedly on offer has brought misery and violence in the attempts to realize such utopias. Individualistic and libertarian conceptions are in trouble as well and not easily recommendable. Politics has been offered as a mediating agency that tries to negotiate between communal and social values and individualists' tendencies to be the sole beneficiary of their efforts. However, no such functioning political model has produced satisfactory results; *au contraire*, "neutralism" has, as the latest financial crisis reveals, served as a remarkable excuse for some of the most inappropriate egotistical behavior, summed up in the formulation of "communism for the few and the market for the rest."

All of this calls for a reopening of theoretical and historical debate and asking whether an alternative is available that offers the possibility of overcoming the limitations discussed above. Searching the past for alternatives should then not be understood as a discovery but rather as a recovery operation. The aim should be not to discover any historical "objective laws" or understanding events of in terms of preconstructed discourses. Instead, contextualization is needed on all levels—historically, theoretically, culturally, and politically.

I maintain that the debate surrounding the Cambridge School of Intellectual History and particularly its focus on the humanist republican tradition allows for such contextualization. By drawing on speech act theory and focusing on what texts meant for the writer and the audiences at the time of writing, the Cambridge School approach to intellectual history has distanced itself from "progressive" rhetoric of overarching discourses, but also from the "discoveries" of the individual-collectivist narratives criticized earlier. Through its contextualizing efforts it has established a different paradigm of writing political theory. However, I additionally maintain that the study of the proper historical context may be enriched theoretically by introducing some communitarian aspects to the debate. The reasons seem obvious: communitarianism takes as its starting point the politics of daily life. In fact, communitarian thinkers have been concerned with daily decision-making and practical political concerns. Perhaps this is also one of the reasons why its advocates have been more open to sociological and anthropological discussions and their findings and are less concerned with discovering universal laws of history.

My aim in the remaining part of the text here is to sketch out a contextualizing approach that will allow us to address the question of egalitarianism and equality in traditional Basque society in different ways. In terms of intellectual history and political theory I will draw particularly on Skinner's work. However, I will also argue that Skinner's approach can be enriched and supplemented, particularly when looking at the Basque case, by discussing Michael Walzer's communitarian notions of equality.

Skinner's Approach

As James Tully remarks, by the late 1960s Skinner had already realized that it was necessary to distance himself from ideological discourses and from the apparent extremes of both liberal individualism and Marxist collectivism. In terms of methodology Skinner was on the lookout for something different:

> His initial interest in methodology developed out of a dissatisfaction with the liberal and Marxist forms of analysis, for addressing these issues especially with reference to early modern politics. In a marvellously iconoclastic article in 1969 he argued that the available textualist and contextualist procedures were wholly inadequate and that a new contextual and historically more sensitive practice was required. (Tully 1988, 7)

Skinner, inspired by Wittgenstein's writings, realized that proper contextualization was not just about locating certain historical or political events within an ideological discourse, thus rendering them either more or less meaningful. It was not enough fitting political thought or events into some "priority of paradigms." What was needed instead was a new type of contextualization that offered a real alternative and prevented historians from falling into the trap of either individualist or collectivist points of view. In short, Skinner argues against a "mythology of doctrines", that is "the various ways in which the results may be classified not as histories but more appropriately as mythologies" (Skinner 2002, 59).

The purpose of such a set of doctrines would be to identify and follow the track of some unit idea "through all the provinces of history in which it appears" (Lovejoy, quoted in Skinner 2002, 62), as Skinner says, quoting Arthur Lovejoy in *The Great Chain of Being* (1960). The starting point would be to take a kind of ideal type (for instance, a particular take on equality), look for precedents in history, and then identify the various steps taken toward achieving that ideal form. Against such reprojection, Skinner argues that it is bizarre to maintain that every idea in history has a previous and a subsequent form, and to see ideas developing in sequence or even in some progressive manner. Against such notions Skinner argues that ideas arise and develop always in particular places at particular times and in conditions that cannot be exactly repeated; ideas arise in and pertain to specific contexts with their own needs, values, and virtues.

Skinner's take on the history of ideas does not deny the richness of the past; he merely points out that we must not put ideas through a kind of filter, or assume that all societies must go through the same stages and follow the same logic — the notion of equality being but one such case. Skinner thinks little of historians who look at history with either enthusiasm or anger and then take sides: "My own admiration is emphatically reserved for those historians who consciously hold themselves aloof from enthusiasm and indignation alike when surveying the crimes, follies and misfortunes of mankind. Rather, I am suggesting, intellectual historians can hope to provide their readers with information relevant to the making of judgments about their current values and beliefs and then leave them to ruminate" (Skinner 1998, 118).

It is already a huge undertaking for any historian to show their readers the often forgotten richness of our intellectual heritage. But to identify some supposed universal law and its presumed necessary and universal consequences seems superhuman and ultimately an impossible task. As Skinner writes in Liberty before Liberalism, "It is enough for them [historians] to uncover the often neglected riches of our intellectual heritage and display them once more to view" (Skinner 1998, 118).

Walzer and the Decision-Making Community

Although there are some major differences, there are also some often-overlooked commonalities between republicanism and communitarianism. Among these commonalities are the emphasis on context and the avoidance of individualist or collectivist dogma in order to understand and explain the workings of political communities. Communitarianism sees power as derived from political communities, not from some great principle that works itself through history. The same applies to such concepts and ideas like equality and justice.

In *Spheres of Justice* Michael Walzer places equality at the core of his reflections on justice. Furthermore, for him equality is always linked to some form of community. Walzer consciously avoids any previously defined meaning of equality. Rather than looking at equality in the abstract, he is concerned with different communities and, more specifically, with the ways practices of equality are promoted and how they manifest themselves. For Walzer, any society or community is a model of distribution, one which produces meaningful goods, which are then distributed among those who it considers to be its members. Depending on each community, there will be many different types of mechanisms for distributing those meaningful goods, because the goods will be varied, and because each society will create its own mechanisms for distributing them. As Walzer sees it, communities always establish some form of recognition mechanism (recognition of others and being recognized oneself) and from such recognition systems membership derives. Each individual contributes to the community by taking part in the production of meaningful goods, in the community's decisions, and in the mechanisms and principles for distributing those meaningful goods.

Taking into account such forms of recognition and the mechanisms for distribution, Walzer aims at both justice and equality but avoids the risk of relativism. In order to avoid bias, the first thing to leave out is what he calls "simple equality." Simple approaches to equality tend to make use of single quantitative variables. If we were to argue, as Marx does in his *Critique of the Gotha Programme*, that equality is given to each according to his or her needs, thereby forgetting each person's contribution to the production of wealth, then discontent will necessarily arise. In short, searching for a society in which all have an equal quantity of everything that is available or all become members of a single, universal community does not sound very convincing. After all, we all have different interests, needs, capacities, and wishes. Reducing all of that to a single formula or system would be a truly totalitarian, tyrannical idea.

The task is rather to come up with a more flexible approach that can be applied to different "distributive spheres" that will allow us to reflect on the different principles that operate within those spheres. Walzer suggests leaving aside the quantitative approach and focusing on qualitative components. Equality and inequality will no longer be based on having more, less, or the same. The problem will be using our status (whether in professional, gender, political, or any other terms) to put ourselves above others in other areas of life. For instance, this could involve using a political position to obtain money inappropriately, or a high-level sports status to gain advantages in other parts of life. "There is nothing wrong, for example, with the grip that persuasive and helpful men and women (politicians) establish on political power. But the use of political power to gain access to other goods is a tyrannical use. . . . In political life—but more widely, too–the dominance of goods makes for the dominion of people" (Walzer 1983, 19). Inequality here is to take advantage of certain statuses to prevail upon other groups.

However, Walzer urges us to think about the permeability of communities and spheres. Not all spheres can trade equally and interact freely. In that sense monopolies need to be avoided. According to Walzer, monopolies are formed when a single group dominates the means and goods that are meaningful in a particular sphere or community. A group having a political status only means that the society in question has created a stable group to take charge of political questions, in the same way that the status of an architect means making houses. In terms of an egalitarian point of view, such statuses should be permeable, and, first of all, they should be included in an egalitarian recognition system and without special privileges.

If we wish to examine any community from the point of view of equality, we have to set aside ideological approaches and simple interpretations of equality in order to be able to make situations of tyranny impossible and to be able to see the problems of equality in all their complexity: "The regime of complex equality is the opposite of tyranny. It establishes a set of relationships such that dominion is impossible. In formal terms, complex equality means that no citizen's standing in one sphere or with regard to one social good can be undercut by his standing in some other sphere, with regard to some good" (Walzer 1983, 9).

Some Final Reflections: The Need for Equality and What the Basque Case Might Tell Us

The idea and practical pursuit of equality are not something entirely new in the European context. It formed the basis for most Renaissance humanist republics, including the Basque foru republics. References to equality and recognition can be found in many legal texts and reflections from sixteenth century onward. That it was not some meaningless or forgotten law but actual practice is shown in the proclamation of universal nobility for all Basque-born people. Such a right to nobility has been claimed by Basque people of different statuses and in several situations and eras, both at home and abroad.

I would like to suggest here that resurrecting humanist republicanism and related communitarian theories makes it possible not only to understand equality, freedom, and other basic concepts without referring to ideological agendas, but also introduces new ways of seeing traditional Basque society in different ways. Furthermore, considering traditional Basque society not as an exception but within the wider context of a European republican tradition would constitute a true paradigm change. It would help to overcome the bitter and confusing polemic referred to at the beginning of this chapter, and it would facilitate approaching the Basque tradition in a contextualizing theoretical framework instead of seeing it as an exception to the problematic French "universalist" model.

The link with a humanist republican heritage can be easily established in the sense that the Basque foru system seeks the legitimacy of its political and legal model grounded in the community's precedents, on custom and consuetudinary law. As a specific form of humanist republicanism it fits with the practice of what Fourcade has called "mountain republicanism," with a strong tradition in terms of the decentralization of power. Far from favoring strong, absolutist figures and governments it works on different levels, starting from households up to the Batzar Nagusiak/Juntas Generales (general councils) of each province. Such decentralization has already led some authors to refer to the Basque political landscape as a "Republic of Republics."

References

Aquinas, Thomas. 2002. *St Thomas Aquinas Political Writings*. Edited and translated by R. W. Dyson. Cambridge: Cambridge University Press.

Baron, Hans. 1966. *The Crisis of the Early Italian Renaissance: Civic Humanism and Republican Liberty in an Age of Classicism and Tyranny*. Princeton: Princeton University Press.

Calatrava, Francisco. 1876. *La abolición de los fueros vasco-navarros*. Madrid: Imprenta de T. Fortanet.

Caro Baroja, Julio. 1974. *Vecindad, familia y tecnica*. San Sebastián: Txertoa.

Celaya, Adrian. 2009. *Los Fueros de Bizkaia*. Bilbao: Academia Vasca de Derecho.

Díaz de Durana, José Ramón. 2004. *La otra nobleza: Escuderos e hidalagos sin nombre y sin historia*. Bilbao: Universidad País Vasco-Euskal Herriko Unibertsitatea.

Garate, Justo. 1980. *El carlismo de los vascos*. Donostia-San Sebastián: Auñamendi.

Gutmann, Amy, ed. 1994. *Multiculturalism: Examining the Politics of Recognition*. Princeton: Princeton University Press.

Lafourcade, Maïté. 2011. *La société basque traditionelle*. Donostia: Elkar.

Larramendi, Manuel de. (1754) 1950. *Corografía de la muy noble y muy leal provincia de Guipúzcoa*. Buenos Aires: Ekin.

Otazu, Alfonso de. 1973. *El "igualitarismo vasco": Mito y realidad*. San Sebastián: Txertoa.

Pocock, J. G. A. 1975. *The Machiavellian Moment: Florentine Political Thought and the Atlantic Republican Tradition.* Princeton: Princeton University Press.

Poza, Andrés. (1588?) 1997. *Fuero de hidalguia ad Pragmaticas de Toro & Tordesillas.* Edited by Carmen Muñoz. Bilbao: Universidad País Vasco-Euskal Herriko Unibertsitatea.

Skinner, Quentin. 2002. *Visions of Politics.* Vol. 1, *Regarding Method.* Cambridge: Cambridge University Press.

———. 1998. *Liberty before Liberalism.* Cambridge: Cambridge University Press.

Tully, James. 1988. *Meaning and Context: Quentin Skinner and His Critics.* Princeton: Princeton University Press.

Van Gelderen, Martin, ed. 1993. *The Dutch Revolt.* Cambridge: Cambridge University Press.

Van Gelderen, Martin, and Quentin Skinner, eds. 2005. *Republicanism: A Shared European Heritage.* 2 vols. Cambridge: Cambridge University Press.

Walzer, Michael. 1983. *Spheres of Justice: A Defense of Pluralism and Equality.* New York: Basic Books.

Webster, Wentworth. 1901. *Les Loisirs d'un étranger au Pays Basque.* Chalons sur Saône: Imprimerie française et orientale.

2

Liberties and Equality in a Catholic Republic

José Angel Achón Insausti

Niccolò Machiavelli said: "We see in the world fewer republics than there used to be of old and, consequently, in peoples we do not find the same love of liberty as there then was." When he wondered about the reasons for this decline he referred to the "difference between our education and that of bygone times, which is based on the difference between our religion and the religion of those days." Our religion, he stated, "taught us the truth and the true way of life," which "leads us to ascribe less esteem to worldly honour"; in contrast to the religion of antiquity, "our religion has glorified humble and contemplative men, rather than men of action," and has emphasized "contempt for mundane things"; when our religion demands for us to be strong, "what it asks for is strength to suffer rather than strength to do bold things." The world then, has been made weak, and has been handed over "as a prey to the wicked, who run it successfully and securely, since they are well aware that the generality of men, with paradise for their goal, consider how best to bear, rather than how best to avenge, their injuries." Machiavelli did not blame religion itself for this, but more the interpretation of it: "This undoubtedly is due rather to the pusillanimity of those who have interpreted our religion in terms of *laissez faire*, not in terms of valour. For, had they borne in mind that religion permits us to defend and exalt out fatherland, they would have seen that it also wishes us to love and honour it, and to train ourselves to be such that we may defend it" (Machiavelli [c. 1519] 2013, 363–65). The Florentine's thesis was very clear: given that liberty—both individual and of the group—depends on the involvement of citizens in "mundane things," and that religion always gives an ultimate meaning to our acts, when this leads us only to contemplation to the detriment of an active life, the "love of liberty" is lost (on the concept of freedom in Machiavelli, see Skinner 1984; 1992; 1994).

A few years ago I had the opportunity to delve into the process whereby what are now termed the "Historical Territories" (namely, the individual provinces) were formed in the Basque Country (Achón Insausti 1994; 1998; 2000; 2001a; 2001b; 2001c).[1] I did so by considering particularly the case of Gipuzkoa, which was unusual due to the central role played there by the "urban republics," to the extent of conceiving of the province as a "republic of republics." Very briefly, the "Land" of twelfth-century Gipuzkoa, which was formed by valley communities (Barrena 1989), disintegrated over the following two centuries into various micro-spaces organized around towns. The towns' ownership of their local areas was questioned by the rural nobility—known as *Parientes Mayores* (Elders)—and this led to all the towns coming together to form an *hermandad* (brotherhood). This brotherhood began by taking only such powers as were necessary to prosecute criminals and to maintain peace in the area, but in the fifteenth century an institutional framework and a set of laws and ordinances were developed that could be identified as a community with territorial rights and a personality of its own: the Province of Gipuzkoa (this process is described in Achón Insausti 1995, 102–19).

---

1. We are currently continuing our work in this area of study as part of a research project under the auspices of the Ministry of Economy and Competitiveness of the Government of Spain HAR2103-48901-C6-4-R, entitled "El proceso de la modernidad: Actores, discursos y cambios, de la sociedad tradicional a la revolución liberal" (2014–2017)," led by José María Imízcoz.

I have always thought that the ideas mentioned in Machiavelli's text largely reflected the purpose of the Gipuzkoa case. This process can be defined as the beginning of a struggle for liberties by the republics against some tyrants in the fourteenth and fifteenth centuries (the aforementioned "Elders"), but which resulted in an obsession with finding a place within the Catholic monarchy. To this end, the most extreme values of Catholicism were adopted as their own, and this oriented the idea of liberties and equality that Gipuzkoans had in a very specific direction—which, incidentally, had nothing "Republican" about it. Machiavelli's text provides a background explanation of the phenomenon but, as will be seen at the end of this chapter, with some interesting nuances.

In the years that followed these studies, the debate about "civic republicanism" and its presence or absence in the Iberian Peninsula has been reignited, perhaps fueled by the reflection made by J. G. A. Pocock in the introduction to the Spanish translation of *The Machiavellian Moment* (*El momento maquiavélico*): "I have found little trace of classic republicanism in modern Spanish thought" (Pocock 2002, 75). Studies such as those by Xavier Gil (2001; 2008) and Domingo Centenero de Arce (2012), among others, somewhat qualify this statement, but the issue now is not so much to discuss whether or not there was civic republicanism in the Basque case, but rather to discern how our ancestors understood the concepts of "liberty" and "equality" as they used them, and how they formulated the defense of their "liberties"; what these concepts meant for the main actors involved; and, based on those meanings, what values and commitments were acquired, that is, what political culture gave meaning to the community. In short, it is a question of ascertaining what kind of Basque "free republics" existed between the fourteenth and seventeenth centuries.

Liberties and Equality in the Formation of a Territory

Two of the main characteristics of these republics were developed while they were being formed: (1) the conscience that liberties are acquired after fighting for them; (2) the need to specify the content of those liberties in jurisdictional terms. We are going to explore both aspects in this chapter.

Collective Liberties as Opposed to Tyranny

First, these republics fought for freedoms and retained a memory of this fact. There was nothing special about this phenomenon, and neither Gipuzkoa nor the other Basque territories experienced a particular phenomenon in this regard. As Faustino Martínez Martínez recalls, "the defense of a right, in the sense of concrete and specific liberties, privileges, and the holding of that right, are the same, they are equal and interchangeable and were identified in factual terms. Whoever had rights was able to defend them, and to defend themselves against possible attacks or external interference" (Martínez Martínez in Kern 2013, 42). At the time, the only people who had rights were those who were able to defend them, and the defense of urban "liberties" against the claims of lords who wanted to incorporate those towns into their domains, or even against imperial-like powers that sought to ensure their loyalty, was a leitmotif in the progression that occurred in the late medieval, as is amply emphasized in the literature (for example, Skinner 1978, 23–42; Black 1992, 180–210). In the Basque case, this phenomenon must be viewed within the context of a more general framework that has become known as "the war of the bands" (*lucha de bandos*) (García Fernández 1994; also see the various contributions collected in Díaz de Durana 1998). While there are several features of interest in this conflict, the focus here will only be on one aspect, the confrontation between towns and lineage chiefs (that is, the "Elders") that led to the formation of these bands.

One should stress that, by the fifteenth century, townspeople had a clear idea of who the enemy of their liberties—the tyrant— was. No treaty exists up to the sixteenth century to substantiate the views that were held in towns about the *parientes mayores banderizos* (the Elders of the bands), but, for our purposes, the municipal and provincial documentation is sufficiently illustrative. This clearly shows to what extent the towns saw the Elders and bands as a threat to their liberties and to their very existence as a *universitas*.

Examples such as the towns of Mondragón (Arrasate) or Segura are particularly relevant. In Segura, the town dwellers had to directly confront the Lord of Lazcano and Arana and his followers, who continuously demonstrated their desire to subjugate the town, for example, by breaking its doors, "causing substantial damage to, and showing great contempt for, said town," (Díez de Salazar 1993, 301–6). The case of Mondragón is significant because the struggle against an external lord who wanted to bring the town under his control, the Lord of Oñate, became more complicated due to his alliance with one of the internal "bands" of the town. The town dwellers complained, for example, that some local councilors, "for and on behalf of the band and lineage of bands," had expelled two town representatives who, according to the *banderizos* (band members), "did not administer the local council's business as befits the council"; that is, that the boundaries between the best interests of the band and the common good of the town dwellers had become blurred. Many residents began to realize that loyalty to the band and loyalty to the town were incompatible, despite having long lived together without coming into conflict in this way. So when in 1490 the king decreed the abolition of the town's bands, it was emphasized that no town dweller "should refer to themselves" as belonging to Guraya or Báñez, but that, "all identify themselves as being from Mondragón" (these and other examples can be found in Achón Insausti 1995, 76–77, 133, 167–70, and 194), which demonstrated a clear understanding of what was at stake. In effect, in the case of Mondragón, the final outcome of the internal and external conflicts resulted in the burning of the town in 1448. This was, I believe, a turning point in the conflict and caused the king and the group of Gipuzkoan towns to act decisively against the *banderizos*. Indeed, when the existence of the Elders or the bands threatened the very existence of the urban community, the town dwellers reacted on several fronts. The most important of these were: all urban republics coming together into a "brotherhood" with the capacity to impose peace in the territory; taking direct action against the foundations and symbols of power (that is, through the capacity to bring men together, the patronage of churches, direct confrontations with and direct challenges to the Elders, and so on); and prioritizing the bond to the urban community above loyalty to a particular lineage or band. Certainly the most remarkable of these reactions for the purposes of this paper was the increasingly territorialized nature of the conflict, that is, the coming together of the towns into a brotherhood with its own territorial strategy, in opposition to that conceived of by the

Elders. With the triumph of the former option, the old "territory" of Gipuzkoa became a republic of republics, or the Province of Gipuzkoa, thus laying the foundations for the current Historical Territory of the same name.

The awareness that urban and provincial liberties had been achieved by fighting the Elders became a commonplace theme in Gipuzkoan literature of later centuries. In 1560, Juan Martínez de Zaldibia wrote that the Elders "brought the Oñez and Gamboa bands to these lands and they caused many deaths, fires, and riots" and, above all, that "The towns in the province formed a brotherhood against them and their strongholds were pulled down by the king" (Martínez de Zaldibia [1560] 1944, 82). When in the sixteenth century Esteban de Garibay y Zamalloa, an illustrious figure from Mondragón, referred to the fights in his town during medieval times, he said bluntly that the actions taken by the town dwellers were intended "for the liberty of their country," which he linked, significantly, both to avoiding falling under the influence of a local rural nobleman and to continuing to enjoy the protection provided to the town by its connection with crown. For example: "The town was burned down with great inhumanity, as the town dwellers prefer to suffer more persecution in the service of the crown in these times without justice, than to be subject to tyranny and be disposed of the royal estate, with the zeal with which they always defended their liberty" (Garibay y Zamalloa [1571] 1628, 2: 404; see also Garibay y Zamalloa [c. 1594] 2000, 233).

And two centuries later, Manuel de Larramendi, with his characteristic vehemence, highlighted the fact that the lineage chiefs were deemed to be "the Elders," "not because they were higher in terms of nobility," but because they were "more bellicose, more daring to wreak fatal havoc on the bands"; who "became powerful . . . and agitated and rose up [in arms] in the villages," and that, in order "to forestall the effects, disorders, and deaths every day, they came to name all the places as [being part of] Gipuzkoa and came together in a brotherhood that would shortly remedy so many ills" (Larramendi [c. 1754] 1969, 161–62).

Thus, the Elders ended up being conceptualized as "tyrants," as those that prevented the *universitas* from remaining united, as those that impeded the Christian ideal of peace and harmony (Achón Insausti 1998). The classics had already warned of this.

Thomas Aquinas had advised in the thirteenth century that a "tyranny is wont to occur not less but more frequently on the basis of a polyarchy than on the basis of a monarchy." And polyarchy is even more dangerous, because while the tyranny of a "single ruler" undermines the common good, what inevitably arises from several rulers is also discord, and "this dissension runs counter to the good of peace, which is the principal social good" (Aquinas [1267] 1949, ch. 5: 40).

It is worth emphasizing that the "tyrant," the Elder, was not an external but rather an internal agent, which denoted a progressive fragmentation of the community that materialized only at the end of the process. The studies by José María Imízcoz (1993) and José Antonio Marín Paredes (1998) are excellent illustrations of how the Elders emerged within the process of the internal hierarchy of valley communities. I also believe that the documentation does not make it possible to detect any incompatibility between "bands" and "towns" until the fifteenth century (Achón Insausti 2006). While the valley communities continued to be a reference point (despite the foundational process) and the social positions of the actors involved were not separate, the process lasted almost two centuries, until a true separation was achieved within the old communities between Elders and their bands, on the one hand, and the urban communities associated as a brotherhood, on the other. It must be emphasized that this was the end point, and not the starting point. In this regard, Gipuzkoa seems to offer a model in clear contrast with that provided by neighboring territories, such as those of the Baztán Valley in Navarre (Imízcoz 1993) and Bizkaia, where in the latter the urban communities distributed the territory among themselves and the *hidalgos* (gentry) from the Tierra Llana district, the core area of the province (Dacosta 2003, 223–53). Incidentally, throughout this late medieval process, the king was far from appearing as a "tyrant"; conversely, he was perceived as being the great protector of community liberties and the guarantor of victory over the Elders.

Jurisdictional Definition

As the reader may have concluded, the liberties fought for by the Basque republics were essentially related to the absence of any interference from the nobility. It seems obvious that this "negative" liberty was a sine qua non for the exercise of more "positive" liberties, specifically for the enjoyment of a full self-suf-ficiency and autarky (Skinner 1984, 240–44). It was precisely this self-sufficiency that the urban republics and the provincial republic sought, and it was embodied in the ability to dominate a given land; to have their own authority to impart justice among town dwellers; to be self-sufficient and engage in trade; to de-fend themselves; and to have their own statutes; in short, to look after the common good. There were very clear examples of how a stately presence close and superior to the town curtailed these liberties and prevented full self-sufficiency, as was the case of the Lord of Guevara and the dwellers of the town of Oñate (Oñati). In an exemplary text of 1388, Oñate dwellers complained about the actions of the Lord of Guevara "given his power, more de fac-to than de jure, [imposed] by force." Specifically, they accused him of entering

> into our houses to kill us . . . to take everything from us . . . our belongings and our homes . . . our money, cider, and cereal . . . and expelled us from these places and stripped us of our belongings. And we were disinherited and stripped of our belongings, and they were given to our worst enemies, and they subjected our wives and our children to their power. (Ayerbe 1985, 40)

For his part, the Lord accused the town dwellers of having formed

> forbidden associations and conspiracies against him and his dominion, and organized unlawful brotherhoods and statutes . . . since according to the Law, my vassals cannot develop statutes or ordinances other than with my consent and under my express orders. (Ibid., 50–51)

It followed that the actions taken by the town dwellers were "to the detriment of my estate and my dominion and my land," to which was added that,

> They therefore committed a "Lèse-majesté" crime and a sin of treason, which exceeds all other sins and evils, as Lucifer was overthrown as a result of a comparable sin of treason . . . and also on account of this sin . . . Adam and Eve were expelled from Paradise, because they ate the forbidden fruit, thinking that they would be the same as God. (Ibid., 50–51)

It was situations like this that the urban republics wanted to avoid. The key concept to understanding the ability to live under a fully self-sufficient regime was *iurisdictio,* which literally means "to say justice" but actually implied much more than that; it was the concept that defined the position of its holder on a scale of powers, which epitomized the degree of autonomy of superior powers and manifested their superiority over lower ones. It was also a concept that was naturally associated with all *universitas* (Vallejo 1992, 56–71). It was, in short, the concept that came closest to the modern notion of "political power" (Grossi 1996, 140–41). Therefore, these liberties for which they fought were defended not only militarily, but also primarily by a debate about the jurisdictional rights each side was entitled to. It was the language of the *iurisdictio* that channeled their claims, something that was commonplace in other locations as well, even in those places in which civic rhetoric had a strong presence, as already stated by Skinner (1978, 1:169–77).

It seems worth stressing that, in the case being discussed here, when data started to become available on the process—mainly from the thirteenth century onward—the positions and powers of the subjects in dispute (the towns, the Elders, and also the king himself) were not fixed, and the rest of the process cannot be understood if this point is ignored. My hypothesis is that in 1200 the process of encellment (*incastellamento*), or simply, the full incorporation of Gipuzkoa into a feudal *dominium* structure, was far from consolidated. The king needed to effectively exercise his distant superiority; "Gipuzkoans" still lived in structures closer to "valley communities," whose hierarchies were not clearly translatable in terms of dependence on lords. Among these there were some signs that the "Elders," the visible "heads" of those communities for reasons of kinship, had started this journey. Given the embryonic stage of the process, the qualification of the Elders as "lords" should be taken with caution, but what seems clear is that the appearance of the towns limited their sphere of influence to a part of the space of the former community. There were, therefore, two still slightly undefined focuses of power contesting for the same space. This uncertainty led to an effort to "translate" the influence into jurisdictional terms and, consequently, into a rivalry over the ownership of the *jurisdictio* to that space (an example of this is analyzed in Achón Insausti 1995, 30–85).

It was the ownership of the *jurisdictio* that was at stake when the Lord of Oñate and the town of Mondragón entered into a dispute about who should place the gallows in the Léniz (Leintz) Valley, and whose herds should graze the valley. It was the exercise of *jurisdictio* that was at stake when some residents of the town of Mondragón complained that the heads of the bands had appropriated the keys to the town and the chest in which their documents were kept; the same thing happened when the Lord of Zarauz conveyed a message to the town of the same name (today, Zarautz) through his emblem "Zarauz before Zarauz"; and similarly the Lord of Lazkao made this clear to the inhabitants of Segura when he broke the door latches at the entrance to the town and went inside with his followers; and the Lord of Loyola had a similar intention when he "kidnapped" two locals from Ormaiztegi—a neighborhood of the town of Segura—in order to deliver justice. Examples are numerous (those quoted in Achón Insausti 1995, 75–85, 167–70; Díez de Salazar 1993, 309, 336–37).

It is essential to understand that without jurisdictional capacity there were no real liberties. For town dwellers, then, fighting for their liberties was, as well as a matter of military self-defense, mainly a struggle to assert their jurisdiction. To a large extent, it can be said that the inhabitants of Gipuzkoan towns were "free" in so far as that they did not feel the presence of a nearby lord who interfered with them and prevented them from exercising their almost full self-government. As the king stated, "the town [Segura] has always been, and is, in my service without the interference of a powerful man" (Díez de Salazar 1993, 336).

But there was a second front on which jurisdictional capacity had to be asserted. As noted above, the starting positions were undefined, including that of the king. In order to understand the game of continuous tradeoffs being played between the republics and the royal power, the lack of clear positions at the start and the feudal logic that saw its development need to be the starting point. When centuries later this issue was addressed from the perspective of the existence of the state, which held all sovereignty, the origins of Basque laws and urban *fueros* (charters granted to towns) were heatedly discussed: Were they immemorial? Were they granted by royalty? Such a debate made sense in the eighteenth century, but not in the thirteenth century. It is true that the idea of "time immemorial" jurisdictional capacity was created by modern Basque historiography, but the idea of a king who would hold "central" power and would be provided with a series of quasi-state authorities was also a modern creation. The court's legal experts certainly strived to achieve this central positioning (Hespanha 1993a; 1993b), but whether this was effective at the beginning of the process is a different matter altogether. What existed at that time were two subjects that began a process of continuous interaction and a set of tradeoffs through which, over time, their place in the scale of feudal powers became gradually updated and increasingly more defined (Vallejo 1992, 62–63; Kern 2013, 123–29).

Every time the monarch granted or recognized a jurisdictional capacity or certain liberties, these became a privilege for the beneficiary republic, regardless of whether their origin was attributed to custom or to royal grant. On many occasions a de facto situation was simply coated "with a cloak of legality" (Ullmann 1961, 224), but by standing as someone who was statutorily obliged to recognize or grant liberties, the king achieved a position of superiority that otherwise could have been more theoretical than material. In other words, he effectively ensured the loyalty and *auxilium* of his vassals.

Whenever the towns received or confirmed one of those privileges their self-governing abilities were translated into a feudal language in which they became jurisdictional capabilities or liberties endorsed by the king in writing. That same privileged status conferred on them a status of superiority over the villages and lords of their rural environment. The same game that defined them as loyal but free with respect to the king situated them as a kind of collective lordship in their own environment.

This set of tradeoffs carried over into the fifteenth century and, more clearly still, into the sixteenth century, from the municipal to the provincial level; in this way, the status of "free" and "privileged" that initially only concerned the republics individually became territorialized. In contrast to the Bizkaian case, in Gipuzkoa the remission of the urban fueros to Castilian law brought with it the consequence that the consolidation of a "territorial right" reached Gipuzkoa later and in a somewhat more incomplete fashion than it did in the case of Bizkaia. In contrast to the Fuero granted to the hidalgos that had been recognized in the late fifteenth century, the approval of the first compilation of

Fueros in Gipuzkoa took place in the sixteenth century, and it was not approved and consolidated until the seventeenth century. In any case, this came to substantiate an individual *jurisdictio* and, understood in a very broad sense, a de facto "self-government" (in exchange for loyalty and *auxilium*).

The Catholic Republic

Once republics' liberties are defined we must ask two key questions to read into their meaning. First, we will ask about what kind of equality prevailed in these communities, in which liberties belonged to the collective and not only to some individuals. And second, we will analyze how the meaning of those liberties was marked by the Catholic context in which the republics were framed.

Equals in Privilege

What kind of territorial community did this whole process of anti-Lord and jurisdictional conflict lead to? An obvious feature of the Gipuzkoan community was that at no point (either at the beginning of the conflict, or once it was solved and the province had been established) did it cease to have a self-concept as part of a socially stratified order. In other words, Gipuzkoans fought to be free from feudal lords' interference, and to be part of a privileged order of a society that they always considered to be hierarchical and not as one of "equals" (Rosanvallon 2013; Dumont 1977). It is worth discussing this point in more detail.

The processes described above took place in the evolution phase of feudal societies that has often been referred to as the feudal-corporative phase (Hespanha 1982, 187–215). Among other things, defining one's place within the social stratification hierarchy was essential. In this context, the Elders had tried to monopolize lordly status and to become the noble stratum of the territory. This was a concept of their own whereby they claimed to be "worth more," which contained within the premise the ability to gather men together as well as the rents, honors, and privileges characteristic of the nobility.

The Elders used the "being worth more" leitmotif first for their own internal conflicts (Caro Baroja 1974), but they then ended up wielding it against the rest of the Gipuzkoan community. In that dispute, the town dwellers proposed a notion of "equal worth" (Fernández Albaladejo 1975, 157) that should be understood in relative terms; that is, it was explicitly launched against the claims of the Elders, and not universally valid. The intention was for the Gipuzkoan community not to have a clearly differentiated noble stratum, but rather for the whole community to be made up one single noble state. This was a proposal for a single stratum, as opposed to the multi-strata project championed by the Elders; a reconstruction of the idea of territorial community that prevailed over the concept of its division into social strata. In my view, the origin of "Basque egalitarianism" is to be found mainly in this project based on a single social level, the success of which is not so much the triumph of specific individuals and groups, but of a "way of seeing" (Aguinagalde 1998) the social organization of the community. Moreover, I understand that the fact that, especially since the sixteenth century, it was translated into competitive benefits abroad (Juaristi 1992) that had more to do with its consolidation, and with the zeal that led Gipuzkoans to persist in defending the status of their fellow province dwellers, than with its origins.

It is significant that this "equal worth" was not shaped as an extension of citizenship requirements, but rather as the territorialization of one of the qualities that accompanied the status of noblemen (Fernández Albaladejo and Portillo 1989). The debate on the noble nature of the town dwellers can be traced back to fourteenth-century documentation. I think when the concept of nobility was first used, it did not reflect a perfectly defined status, but rather the quality of being "independent," of being a "nonservant"; a free status resulting from not being subject to a superior other than the king himself; in other words, from being the owner of an *allodium* (an example of this is studied in Achón Insausti 2001b, 161–65). But above all, it seems to be a negative definition, which translated the social leveling of the commoners into terms that would be more understandable within the logic of the noble strata. This relatively undefined concept can explain the speed with which, when a confraternity alliance was formed to bring towns together, they succeeded in obtaining the recognition for the whole that many of its individual parts had enjoyed: commoners on a par with noblemen (on the territorial extension of nobility, see Díaz de Durana 2004; Soria 2006). Its subsequent evolution showed that it became filled with all the "positive" content that came from their identification not only with the quality of "being independent," but also with noble status, even if it was at its lowest level. However, what must be stressed here is that the Republic of Gipuzkoa ultimately perceived itself not as a republic of citizens, but as a republic of noblemen (Portillo 1998). Liberties were inherent to a certain status, and therefore they were a privilege (Dipper 1991, 34).

There are several pieces of evidence to be found of this concept of equality, understood by the Gipuzkoan community as related to social strata. Without going into detail: their own obsession in making themselves appear different and being "worth more" outside of the province (Achón Insausti 2004; Marín Paredes 1998, 309–16); the behavior of the "villas mayores" (main towns) as true "collective lordships" over the villages under their sway, making it clear that those villages were subjugated to them (for an example, see Díaz de Salazar 1993, 209); the difficult balancing act in terms of terminology in Larramendi's writing, when he referred to the impossible notion of a "noble commoner" ([c. 1754] 1969, 156) in order to explain the rather obvious internal social differences, even among those deemed noblemen; the introduction of wealth or the proof of nobility in order to establish internal distinctions (Achón Insausti 1995, 251–301), may suffice as examples. It was Father Larramendi who, in the mid-eighteenth century, clearly showed the consequences of this view. When asked a question by "a few flatterers and projectors who were as serious as they were stupid," he answered:

> Why does Gipuzkoa have to be so free and more so than other provinces in Spain? Quite a discrete question, by the way! For the moment, another question will serve as an answer: Why do noblemen have to be freer than the slaves that serve them? Why do knights and gentlemen have to be nobles, whereas commoners and villeins cannot have such status? God be with you; have good judgement and know that Gipuzkoa is so free because it was born free, grew up free, stayed free until its old age, and remains free in all the strata of its population, which is that of Spain. (Larramendi [1758] 1983, 18–19)

In conclusion, Gipuzkoans were free, but for the same reasons that nobles, kings, or lords were free, that is, because there were others—slaves, commoners, villeins—who were not, because they were privileged compared to others. For the sake of clarity, he later speaks in these terms about those who in his day proclaimed universal equality among men:

> Ah, you ungodly men, so this is why you wear masks! I bet that mask conceals some materialists by using those monstrosities that desecrate reason, blaspheme against the Divine Providence, and laugh at the revealed religion. May they leave, get out of Spain, and from a distance shout that all provinces and all men are equally free of being subjected and dependent. (Larramendi [1758] 1983, 19)

Thinking back to Machiavelli and how he established a significant link between "equality" and "political life," he advised—reflecting on the German republics—that,

> those states where political life survives uncorrupted do not permit any of their citizens to live after the fashion of the gentry. On the contrary, they maintain there perfect equality and to lords and gentry residing in that province are extremely hostile; so that, should any perchance fall into their hands, they treat them as sources of corruption and sources of scandal, and kill them.

He went on to clarify that the gentry are "those who live in idleness on the abundant revenue derived from their estates, without having anything to do either with their cultivation or with other forms of labor essential to life"; such men "are entirely inimical to any form of civic government." He concluded: "Let then, a republic be constituted where there exists, or can be brought into being, a notable equality; a regime of the opposite type, i.e. a principality, where there is notable inequality" (Machiavelli [c. 1519] 2013, 363–65). If we compare the evolution of Gipuzkoa with this idea posed by Machiavelli (namely, that citizens hate the gentry and lords), we could say that they were in agreement in terms of rejecting the powerful, but that they saw themselves more as gentry than as citizens. Therefore, their egalitarianism ended up being based more on social stratification than on the republic. To use a seemingly contradictory expression, it could be said that they felt an "equality in privilege" (to use Marc Bloch's expression [quoted in Gerhard 1982, 45], although they use it in another chronological context).

49

The "Catholic Moment"

The period between the Late Middle Ages and the Early Modern Age in the Basque Country saw the final shaping and creation of what we now call the "Historical Territories." This was a period in which territorial political links took shape in their final form and de jure communities were set up in which typically province-related elements such as the Fueros and governmental bodies like the *Juntas Generales*—general councils, territorial assemblies that gathered together the representatives of the local, urban, or rural organizations—gained great influence in local life. This process also occurred in many parts of Europe (Brunner [1943] 1983, 231–30; Gerhard 1982; Arrieta 2004), although traditional historiography has been mainly focused on the consolidation of monarchies, as precursor entities of modern states.

From a broader perspective, examining the process from the history of the ideas, discourses, and languages that surround these constitutional processes, this province-based time was part of a "Catholic moment" that also involved a good part of Europe and that essentially represented a strong "anti-political" movement (Fernández Albaladejo 1997; Viejo 1997; Iñurritegui 1998; Gil 2000; Viroli 2005).

From the early sixteenth century, the Basque Historical Territories could be considered to have been well established. Once the conflicts with the Elders had been overcome, what was then at stake was the expansion of the province to encompass a greater area and scope, and universal claims, such as the Catholic monarchy (Truchuelo 2004). While there were numerous areas with their own rights that were integrated into it, Castile was not the best example of this, as there was a clear trend toward the loss of territorial entities with "constitutional" value, and a clear subordination of "territorial rights" to "royal rights" (Clavero 1980; Pardos 1988). So the Basque provinces were not the norm, and were almost an anomaly from the Castilian point of view. The discourse that emanated from them had to justify this special treatment, this unique way of being within the monarchy. It was then that the essential components of its discourse ("equal worth," "universal nobility," and so on) were directed more outward than inward, seeking to support this specific way of placing themselves within the monarchy rather than justifying the hidalgos vis-à-vis the Elders.

As is the case in all discourses, the fueros-based discourse that began to appear in Basque territories in the sixteenth century was not merely a reflection of the constitutional development and a form of self-perception of the community; it was also a way to project the community into both the present and the future. Like every discourse, it proposed a framework within which to interpret the concepts, thereby orienting them in a particular moral direction; a "common sense" that was able to mobilize the people around it.

We are concerned here both with the process of the creation of this discourse and with how its success shaped society; not only with the social conditions of the production of that discourse, but also with how a community was conditioned by it; the extent to which society accepted it, that society became constrained to "thinking about it" in terms of the values and references promoted by the discourse, and to project its ideas within its logic, within whatever was reasonable in this context (Fernández Sebastián 1993, 56–57). In particular, as far as this chapter is concerned, it makes a difference whether the struggle for liberty in Basque republics was interpreted in a context of civic and republican reference points, or, as eventually happened, whether the interpretation occurred within a Catholic "language" (Pocock 1987) that was clearly antipolitical, such as that in the sixteenth and seventeenth centuries.

The vehicle chosen to frame territorial liberties in a Catholic culture was the use of the Tubalian myth discourse; or rather, the Basque-ization of it. Its content is well known: after the Flood, as a result of the world being divided among Noah's descendants, Tubal, the patriarch, was placed in Cantabria, where he gave the natives rules to govern, the Basque language, and taught them how to work with iron. The permanence of these elements would be proof of the immemorial relationship between the territory, its rules, and its inhabitants, as well as their not mixing with other people. Beyond the well-known mythical, archaic, and ahistorical components of this discourse, I think it is necessary to emphasize how this matched the defense of a Catholic order in the sense that the discourse had the ability to answer the questions asked by the people in Gipuzkoa, in particular, and by Basques in general; the way it fit within the Catholic monarchy in rather unusual circumstances; the consistency between this and the territorialization of noble status; the justification of these ideas by alleging immemorial custom; and the existence of a territorial right in the form of Fueros. All this was legitimized by the religious matrix of myth, and "forced" the monarch to agree since how could a *Catholic* monarch not wish to defend a heritage of divine origin? It must be also considered that any other attempt to legitimize collective liberties in the midst of religious wars would have sounded suspiciously like "Machiavellianism," that is, heresy. In times of conflict, discourses are radicalized, and, in that discourse under discussion here, the effect was that the defense of the Catholic monarchy and an antipolitical or anti-Machiavellian discourse came to be identified with each other. It was no coincidence that Pedro de Rivadeneira wrote in 1595 the *Tratado de la religión y virtudes que debe tener el príncipe cristiano, contra lo que Nicolás Maquiavelo y políticos de este tiempo enseñan* (Treatise on religion and virtues that a Christian prince must have, contrary to what Machiavelli and politicians of this time teach; a detailed study of which can be found in Iñurritegi 1998). Nor is it a coincidence that Esteban de Garibay, in the preface to his *Compendio Historial*, identified the instruments used for the conquest of the Americas with "Catholic weapons, foreign to tyranny" (Garibay y Zamalloa [1571] 1628, 1:7).

The emergence of these types of arguments and the genealogical understanding of the world that they entailed (Caro Baroja 1972, 174), far from eliminating other battles being waged by the province, instead reinforced them, especially those related to the establishment of their jurisdictional capabilities. Martínez de Zaldibia, the first writer to refer to the Tubalian origins of Basques ([c. 1560] 1944, 9–10), was also the author of an attempt to collect Gipuzkoan ordinances (Martínez de Zaldibia [1562] 1991). Likewise, in Bizkaia Andrés de Poza combined similar references with legal arguments in his defense of universal nobility (Poza [1588] 1997, see ch. 8 and 13). The Fueros-based discourse gradually incorporated all the useful "languages" to defend territorial rights and liberties.

But the process did not end with Tubal. Another set of shared images—still rooted in religion—came to effectively reinforce Catholicism itself. The domestic images, the idea that the whole community was a sort of "home and family," and the territory a single ancestral home, led to the conclusion that the set of "properties"—especially including the fueros-based patrimony, the territorial rights—were an inalienable *mayorazgo* (majorat) to be preserved and defended.

This assumption of a widespread *oeconomical* language at the time (Brunner [1968] 1970; Frigo 1985; Clavero 1991) was perfectly consistent with constitutional development and with the central role that the "house" had acquired within it. Whereas the medieval period was essentially an era of lineages, after the struggles between the bands another one between "houses" began; of the domestication of those lineages around the ancestral homes; and of the renewal, maintenance, and expansion of their strategies for being "worth more." This was a culture of the house that enabled the integration of the descendants of factions and confraternities in the fifteenth century into urban communities and, by extension, into the provincial scope (Achón Insausti 1994, 2001a). And if the Tubalian myth relied on something as tangible as the survival of the Basque language, the *oeconomic* language relied on another equally solid piece of evidence: the extension of the—de jure or de facto—majorats to a broad spectrum of the community (Achón Insausti 1995, 203–50).

In this regard, from the sixteenth to eighteenth centuries, Gipuzkoa perceived itself and presented itself as a "home," and in particular, as a majorat. Different authors reveal a route that moved from the recognition that all lineages were noble (Martínez de Zaldibia [c. 1560] 1944, 81–85), through the concept of territory as "one single lineage of discernible gentry of noble blood" (Echave [1607] 1971, 66; Aramburu [1690] 1976, 2:15.), to, ultimately, Larramendi's conception of the divine right of majorat: "Gipuzkoa is a majorat the principles of which are as specifically directed by God" (Larramendi [1758] 1983, 136). The domestic collective images strengthened, as mentioned, the claims based on social stratification and Catholic images, since the province-based majorat was not just any majorat, but one of divine right. It was therefore immutable and unavailable, it could only be preserved and enlarged, and this obligation applied both to its administrators (the people of Gipuzkoa) and its protector, the Catholic monarch.

And, again, language conditioned expectations, as it did when the province had become a "house," and its models of government could no longer therefore be political but rather *oeconomical*. Clavero indicates the extent to which this *oeconomical* language must be understood in the context of a broader theological source. It contained a catalog of virtues —which could certainly serve as a model for the minor nobles (Clavero 1993–1994, 77)—to be observed for the good governance of a house. The house, as a reflection of the "holy family," was governed by "love," "charity," and "friendship," which were theological rather than political issues. In the same way, its governance was a matter of *patria potestas* rather than of *jurisdictio* (Clavero 1993–1994, esp. ch. 8, 62–79). How could a house be preserved and enlarged? The answer to this question also marked the way forward in the province-based house. So we find in it "domestic" behaviors—such as obtaining favors through networks or clientelist and patronage systems, both at court and in the Americas (Achón Insausti 2001a, 134–37; Imízcoz and Oliveri 2010)—or even an increasingly patrimonial conception of provincial jurisdiction (Portillo 1994). It also turned rights and liberties into something that was de facto unavailable for the population, as a majorat was for its temporary administrators, because it could only be "preserved" or "increased." For the people of Gipuzkoa these liberties were an untouchable divine heritage that they, and also the monarch himself, had to defend. We could say that, in this regard, Gipuzkoans were free "by divine right" or, if you will excuse the paradox, free due to obligation. As Larramendi recalled, "Gipuzkoa can never voluntarily give up its birthright without contravening the primitive institution of majorat and the will of its founder, who is God" (Larramendi [1758] 1983, 136).

And Still, a Republic

The Gipuzkoan people were therefore "more Catholic than citizens" (Fernández Albaladejo 1997) and conceived of their liberties and internal equality from within the context of a more theological and social stratification paradigm than a civic one. Yet, in contrast to Machiavelli's diagnosis, this did not involve a loss of their "love of liberty." Unless one considers that the only authentic liberties are those expressed in civic terms, looking at the path taken by Gipuzkoa in particular and the Basque Country in general in modern times, it can be concluded that the consolidation of the perception of the community as a "house" and their social level consciousness coincided precisely with their insistence on their status as a "free republic" (Portillo 1997).

Examining the phenomenon in a little more detail, it should be noted that the location of the republic "within" a monarchy did not result in a loss of awareness of its own liberties. In this sense, this case appears to resemble models such as that of Bologna, in which the acceptance of another type of *auctoritas* (in this case, that of the pope) reinforced the Bolognese political and legal character (Benedictis 1989, 7–9). This was quite different from the Castilian model, in which recognition of royal superiority led parties to merge around the figure of the royal "head" and a "contemplation" of the monarchy (Pardos 1995). I do not know if it is coincidence that, in other walks of life, the Basque nobility also had less of a sense of an "idle" and "contemplative" life than their Castilian counterpart. A beautiful example of this can be found in the motto of a family's coat of arms in Mondragón: *Solus labor parit virtutem, sola virtus parit honorem,* "virtue is only born of work, honor is only born of virtue" (Achón Insausti 1995, 281). It is worth remembering here that Machiavelli himself emphasized the opposition between republic and idle life, associating the former with an absence of great social distance, which, at least in relative terms, can also be identified in the Basque Country (examples and reasons in Bilbao 1981; Achón Insausti 1995, 280; Fernández Albaladejo 1975, 127; Fernández de Pinedo 1977, 137, 139; and Urrutikoetxea 1992, 17–32).

Indeed, it does not seem that the commitment to the Catholic status of the monarchy resulted in a mere political "contemplation" of it, or a merger of the "body" into its "head." Conversely, the discourses of the provinces strived to specify that their grounding in the monarchy was not against its constitution as a community of territorial law, with its own jurisdiction and institutions. Moreover, the Catholic commitment served precisely to demand that the monarchy fulfill its protective role of territorial liberties. They argued that, despite being within a monarchy, they were republics (Portillo 1997, 760; 1998, 96–110), and they engaged in as many legal and doctrinal debates about this as was necessary to defend it (Arrieta 1996; 2004).

So when it began to be realized that the agents of the monarchy were the new tyrants, the enemies who no longer protected them but violated their provincial liberties, the republican rhetoric intensified. Bizkaia was a republic before it was a Lordship, as Pedro Fontecha y Salazar (Portillo 1997, 749); and even within the most traditional paradigms already described, an author like Larramendi wondered: "And if the King demands that Gipuzkoa remove its Fueros, what is to be done?" He even went on to propose a 'United Provinces of the Pyrenees' as a way of restoring liberty in view of any "unjust abandonment by Castile" (Larramendi [1758] 1983, 58, 159).

The liberties of the Basque republics (which became increasingly more united) were no longer seen only as dating from time immemorial, but also as the result of a historical *continuum* of struggles to maintain them. In ancient times, against rejected invaders; in medieval times, against some internal enemies, the Elders; and in modern times, against the formerly protective figure turned into a new tyrant. In short, a *tradition* began to be created (Hobsbawm and Ranger 2002). The fact that from the outside, and even from enlightened positions, the Basque provinces could be used as an example of "a true and genuine liberty" (Geddes [1792] 1997, 771) comes to show the interest aroused by the Catholic republics.

References

Achón Insausti, José Angel. 1994. "Valer más o Valer igual: Estrategias banderizas y corporativas en la constitución de la Provincia de Guipúzcoa." In *El Pueblo Vasco en el Renacimiento (1491–1521)*, edited by José Luis Orella. Bilbao: Mensajero.

———. 1995. *A voz de concejo: Linaje y corporación urbana en la constitución de la Provincia de Gipuzkoa*. Donostia-San Sebastián: Gipuzkoako Foru Aldundia-Diputación Foral de Gipuzkoa.

———. 1998. "Repúblicas sin tiranos, Provincia libre: Sobre cómo llegó a concebirse al pariente mayor banderizo como enemigo de las libertades de las repúblicas Guipuzcoanas." In *La Lucha de Bandos en el País Vasco: De los Parientes Mayores a la Hidalguía Universal: Guipúzcoa, de los Bandos a la Provincia (siglos XIV a XVI)*, edited by José Ramón Díaz de Durana. Bilbao: Universidad del País Vasco-Euskal Herriko Unibertsitatea.

———. 2000. "Religión y Familia: El mundo de Garibay." In Esteban de Garibay y Zamalloa , *Los siete libros de la progenie y parentela de los hijos de Estevan de Garibay*, edited by José Angel Achón Insausti. Arrasate: Ayuntamiento de Arrasate.

———. 2001a. "La Casa Guipúzcoa: Sobre cómo una comunidad territorial llegó a concebirse en términos domésticos durante el Antiguo Régimen." In *Redes familiares y patronazgo: Aproximación al entramado social del País Vasco y Navarra en el Antiguo Régimen (siglos XV–XIX)*, edited by J. M. Imízcoz, 113–38. Bilbao: Universidad del País Vasco-Euskal Herriko Unibertsitatea.

———. 2001b. "La Provincia Noble: Sobre las raíces históricas de la teoría foral clásica y el discurso político de Esteban de Garibay." In *El historiador Esteban de Garibay*, edited by I. Bazán, 149–76. Donostia-San Sebastián: Eusko Ikaskuntza.

———. 2001c. "Valores identitarios en la historia vasca: Pasado y ¿presente? del concepto clásico de Vida Activa." *Inguruak: Revista Vasca de Sociología y Ciencia Política* 30, (September): 145–53.

———. 2004. "La sociedad vasca en tiempos de Legazpi (1503–1528)." In *España y el Pacífico: Legazpi*, vol. 2, edited by Leoncio Cabrero. Madrid: Sociedad Estatal de Conmemoraciones Culturales.

———. 2006. "Los Parientes Mayores." Iura Vasconiae 3: 221–47.

Aguinagalde, Francisco Borja de. 1998. "La genealogía de los solares y linajes Guipuzcoanos bajomedievales: Reflexiones y ejemplos." In *La Lucha de Bandos en el País Vasco: De los Parientes Mayores a la Hidalguía Universal: Guipúzcoa, de los Bandos a la Provincia (siglos XIV a XVI)*, edited by José Ramón Díaz de Durana. Bilbao: Universidad del País Vasco-Euskal Herriko Unibertsitatea.

Aquinas, Thomas. (1267) 1949. *De regno, ad regem Cypri / On Kingship, to the King of Cyprus*, edited and translated by Gerald B. Phelan, revised with an introduction by Ignatius Thomas O.P. Eschmann. Toronto: The Pontifical Institute of Mediaeval Studies.

Aramburu, Miguel de. (1690) 1976. *Nueva Recopilación de los Fueros, privilegios, buenos usos y costumbres, Leyes y Ordenanzas de la Muy Noble y Muy Leal Provincia de Guipúzcoa, confirmadas por el rey en 1696*. Facsimile edition from the reprint by Andrés de Gorosábel in Tolosa in 1867. Madrid: Lex Nova.

Arrieta, Jon. 1996. "Las autoridades jurisprudenciales de la Corona de Aragón en el "Escudo" de Fontecha and Salazar." *Initium: Revista catalana d'historia del dret* 1: 207–24.

———. 2004. "Las formas de vinculación a la Monarquía y de relación entre sus reinos y coronas en la España de los Austrias. Perspectivas de análisis." In *La Monarquía de las naciones: Patria, nación y naturaleza en la Monarquía de España*, edited by Antonio Álvarez-Ossorio and Bernardo José García. Madrid: Fundación Carlos de Amberes.

Ayerbe, María Rosa. 1985. *Historia del Condado de Oñate y Señorío de los Guevara (s. XI-XVI): Aportación al estudio del régimen señorial de Castilla*, vol. 2, *Documentos*. San Sebastián: Excma. Diputación Foral de Gipuzkoa- Gipuzkoako Foru Aldundia.

Barrena, Elena. 1989. *La formación histórica de Guipúzcoa: Transformaciones en la organización social de un territorio cantábrico durante la época altomedieval*. San Sebastián: Universidad de Deusto.

Benedictis, Angela de. 1989. "'Ius municipale' e costituzione bolognese 'per vim contractus': Argomentazione politica e scienza giuridica in Vincenzo Sacco (1681–1744)." *Ius Commune* 16: 1–25.

Bilbao, Luis María, and Emiliano Fernández de Pinero. 1981. "Factores que condicionaron la evolución del régimen de propiedad de la tierra en el País Vasco peninsular." In *Historia General del País Vasco*, vol. 6, directed by Julio Caro Baroja. San Sebastián: Haranburu.

Black, Antony. 1992. *Political Thought in Europe, 1250–1450*. Cambridge: Cambridge University Press.

Brunner, Otto. 1983. *Terra e Potere. Struttre pre-statuali e pre-moderna nella storia costituzionale dell'Austria medievale*. Translated by Giulana Nobili Schiera and Claudio Tommasi. Introduction by Pierangelo Schiera. Milan: Vita e Pensiero. Originally published in German as *Land und Herrschaft: Grundfragen der territorialen Verfassungsgeschichte Österreichs im Mittelalter*. Brünn: R. M. Rohrer, 1943

———. 1970. "La casa come complesso e l'antica economica europea." In *Per una nuova storia costituzionale e sociale*. Translated and edited by Pierangelo Schiera. Milan: Vita e Pensiero. Originally published in German as *Neue Wege der Verfassungs- und Sozialgeschichte*. Göttingen: Vandenhoeck & Ruprecht, 1968.

Caro Baroja, Julio. 1972. *Los vascos y la historia a través de Garibay (Ensayo de biografía antropológica)*, 2nd ed. San Sebastián: Txertoa.

———. 1974. "Linajes y bandos." In *Vasconiana*. Estudios Vascos 3. San Sebastián: Txertoa.

Centenero de Arce, Domingo. 2012. *De repúblicas urbanas a ciudades nobles: Un análisis de la evolución y desarrollo del republicanismo castellano (1550–1620)*. Madrid: Biblioteca Nueva.

Clavero, Bartolomé. 1980. *Temas de Historia del Derecho: Derecho de los Reinos*. 2nd revised edition. Seville: Secretariado de Publicaciones de la Universidad.

———. 1991. *Antidora: Antropología catolica de la Economia moderna (Per la storia pensiero giuridico moderno)*. Milano: Giuffrè.

———. 1993–1994. "Beati dictum: derecho de linaje, economía de familia y cultura de orden." *Anuario de Historia del Derecho Español* 63–64: 7–148.

Dacosta, Arsenio. 2003. *Los linajes de Bizkaia en la Baja Edad Media: Poder, parentesco y conflicto*. Bilbao: Universidad del País Vasco, Servicio Editorial-Euskal Herriko Unibertsitatea, Argitalpen Zerbitzua.

Díaz de Durana, José Ramón, ed. 1998. *La lucha de Bandos en el País Vasco: De los Parientes Mayores a la Hidalguía Universal*. Bilbao: Universidad del País Vasco-Euskal Herriko Unibertsitatea.

Díaz de Durana, José Ramón. 2004. *La otra nobleza: Escuderos e hidalgos sin nombre y sin historia: Hidalgos e hidalguía universal en el País Vasco al final de la Edad Media (1250–1525)*. Bilbao: Universidad del País Vasco-Euskal Herriko Unibertsitatea.

Díez de Salazar, Luis Miguel. 1993. *Colección diplomática del concejo de Segura (1290–1500)*, vol. 2, *(1401–1450)*. San Sebastián: Eusko Ikaskuntza.

Dipper, Christoph. 1991. "La *libertà* cetuale: 'Jura et Libertates'." In Libertà, edited by Reinhart Koselleck, et al. Venice: Marsilio.

Dumont, Louis. 1977. *Homo aequalis: Genèse et épanouissement de l'idéologie économique*. Paris: Gallimard.

Echave, Baltasar de. (1607) 1971. *Discursos de la antigüedad de la lengua cántabra bascongada*. Facsimile edition. Bilbao: La Gran Enciclopedia Vasca.

Fernández Albaladejo, Pablo. 1975. *La crisis del Antiguo Régimen en Guipúzcoa, 1766–1833: Cambio económico e historia*. Madrid: Akal.

———. 1997. "Católicos antes que ciudadanos: Gestación de una 'Política Española' en los comienzos de la Edad Moderna." In *Imágenes de la diversidad: El Mundo Urbano en la Corona de Castilla (s. XVI–XVIII)*, edited by José Ignacio Fortea. Santander: Universidad de Cantabria.

Fernández Albaladejo, Pablo, and José María Portillo. 1989. "Hidalguía, Fueros y constitución política. El caso de Guipúzcoa." In *Hidalgos e Hidalguía dans l'Europe des XVIe-XVIIIe siècles: Théories, pratiques et représentations*, edited by Martine Lambert-Gorges. Paris: C.N.R.S.

Fernández de Pinedo, Emiliano. 1977. "El campesino parcelario vasco en el feudalismo desarrollado (s. XV–XVIII)." *Saioak: Revista de Estudios Vascos* 1: 136–47.

Fernández Sebastián, Javier. 1993. "Perspectivas actuales en historia de las ideas políticas." In *Historia y pensamiento político: Identidad y perspectivas de la historia de las ideas políticas*, edited by Jorge Riezu and Antonio Robles. Granada: Universidad de Granada.

Frigo, Daniela. 1985. *Il Padre di Famiglia: Governo della Casa e governo della città nella tradizione dell' "Economica" tra cinque e seicento*. Rome: Bulzoni.

García Fernández, Ernesto. 1994. "Guerras y enfrentamientos armados: Las luchas banderizas vascas." In *Los Ejércitos*, directed by Carmen Gómez. Coordinated by Francisco Rodríguez de Coro. Vitoria-Gasteiz: Fundación Sancho el Sabio-Sancho el sabio Fundazioa.

Garibay y Zamalloa, Esteban. de. (1571) 1628. *Los Quarenta Libros del Compendio Historial de las Chrónicas y Universal Historia de todos los Reynos de España*, 4 vols. Barcelona: Ed. de Sebastián de Comellas.

———. (c. 1594) 2000. *Los siete libros de la progenie y parentela de los hijos de Estevan de Garibay*. Edited by José Angel Achón Insausti. Arrasate: Arrasateko Udala.

Geddes, John. (1792) 1997. "Relación sobre la provincia de Vizcaya, en España." In "Locura cantábrica, o la República en la Monarquía: Percepción ilustrada de la constitución vizcaína," by José María Portillo, appendix, 769–75. *Anuario de Historia del Derecho Español*, 67: 749–75.

Gerhard, Dilcher. 1982. *Old Europe: A Study of Continuity, 1000–1800*. New York: Academic Press.

Gil, Xavier. 2000. "La razón de Estado en la España de la Contrarreforma: Usos y razones de la política." In *La razón de Estado en la España Moderna*, by Salvador Rus Rufino, et al. Valencia: Real Sociedad Económica de Amigos del País.

———. 2001. "Ciudadanía, patria y humanismo cívico en el Aragón foral: Juan Costa." *Manuscrits* 19: 81–101.

———. 2008. "Concepto y práctica de república en la España moderna: Las tradiciones castellana y catalano-aragonesa." *Estudis* 34: 111–48.

Grossi, Paolo. 1996. *El orden jurídico medieval*. Translated by Francisco Tomás y Valiente and Clara Álvarez. Prologue by Francisco Tomás y Valiente. Madrid: Marcial Pons. Originally published in Italian as *L'ordine giuridico medieval*. Rome: Laterza, 1995.

Hespanha, António Manuel. 1982. *História das Instituioçoes: Épocas medieval e moderna*. Coimbra: Livraria Almedina.

———. 1993a. "Sabios y rústicos: La dulce violencia de la razón jurídica." In *La gracia del derecho: Economía de la cultura en la Edad Moderna*. Translated by Ana Cañellas Haurie. Madrid: Centro de Estudios Constitucionales.

———.1993b. "Representación dogmática y proyectos de poder." In *La gracia del derecho. Economía de la cultura en la Edad Moderna*. Translated by Ana Cañellas Haurie. Madrid: Centro de Estudios Constitucionales.

Hobsbawm, Eric, and Terence Ranger, eds. 1983. *The Invention of Tradition*. Cambridge: Cambridge University Press.

Iñurritegui, José María. 1998. *La Gracia y la República: El lenguaje político de la teología católica y el "Príncipe Cristiano" de Pedro de Ribadeneyra*. Madrid: Universidad Nacional de Educación a Distancia.

Imízcoz, José María. 1993. "Comunidad de Valle y Feudalismo en el norte de la península: Algunas preguntas desde el Valle del Baztán." In *Señorío y Feudalismo en la Península Ibérica (ss. XII–XIX)*, vol. 3, edited by Esteban Sarasa and Eliseo Serrano. Zaragoza: Institución Fernando el Católico.

Imízcoz, José María, and Oihane Oliveri, eds. 2010. *Economía doméstica y redes sociales en el Antiguo Régimen*. Madrid: Sílex.

Juaristi, Jon. 1992. *Vestigios de Babel: Para una arqueología de los nacionalismos españoles*. Madrid: Siglo XXI.

Kern, Fritz.1956. "Law and Constitution in the Middle Ages." In *Kingship and Law in the Middle Ages: Studies by Fritz Kern*. Translated with an introduction by S. B. Chrimes. New York: Frederick A. Praeger.

——. 2013. *Derecho y constitución en la Edad Media*. Translated, annotated, and introductory study by Faustino Martínez Martínez. Valencia: Kyrios.

Larramendi, Manuel de (c. 1754) 1969. *Corografía o descripción general de la Muy Noble y Muy Leal Provincia de Guipúzcoa*. Edited, introduced, annotated, and indexed by J. Ignacio Tellechea Idígoras. San Sebastián: Sociedad Guipuzcoana de Ediciones y Publicaciones.

——. (1758) 1983. *Sobre los fueros de Guipúzcoa. Conferencias curiosas, políticas, legales y morales sobre los Fueros de la M.N. y M.L. Provincia de Guipúzcoa*. Edited, introduced, and annotated by José Ignacio Tellechea Idígoras. Donostia-San Sebastián: Argitalpen eta Publikapenen Gipuzkoar Erakundea-Sociedad Guipuzcoana de Ediciones y Publicaciones.

Machiavelli, Niccolò. [c. 1519] 2013. *The Discourses*. Edited by L. J. Walker. London: Routledge.

Marín Paredes, José Antonio. 1998. *Semejante Pariente Mayor: Parentesco, solar, comunidad y linaje en la institución de un pariente mayor en Gipuzkoa: Los señores del solar de Oñaz y Loyola (siglos XIV–XVI)*. Donostia-San Sebastián: Gipuzkoako Foru Aldundi-Diputación Foral de Gipuzkoa.

Martínez de Zaldibia, Juan. (c. 1560) 1944. *Suma de las cosas cantábricas y Guipuzcoanas*. Edited by Fausto Arocena. San Sebastián: Excma. Diputación de Guipúzcoa.

——. (1562) 1991. *Libro Viejo de Guipúzcoa*, 2 vols. Edited by José Luis Orella. San Sebastián: Eusko Ikaskuntza.

Otazu, Alfonso de. 1986. *El "igualitarismo" vasco: Mito y realidad*. 2nd ed. San Sebastián: Txertoa.

Pardos, Julio. 1988. "Comunidad, persona invisibilis." In *Arqueología do Estado: Las Jornadas sobre formas de organizaçao e exercício dos poderes na Europa do Sul, Séculos XIII–XVIII*. Lisbon: História & Crítica.

——. "Virtud complicada." *Reppublica e Virtù: Pensiero politico e Monarchia Cattolica fra XVI e XVII secolo*, edited by Chiara Continisio and Cesare Mozarelli. Rome: Bulzoni.

Pocock, J. G. A. 1987. "The Concept of a Language and the Métier d'Historien: Some Considerations on Practice." In *The Languages of Political Theory in Early-Modern Europe*, edited by Anthony Pagden. Cambridge: Cambridge University Press.

————. 2002. *El momento maquiavélico: El pensamiento político florentino y la tradición republicana atlántica.* Translated by Marta Vázquez-Pimentel and Eloy García. With a study and commentary by Eloy García. Madrid: Tecnos. Published in English as *The Machiavellian Moment: Florentine Political Thought and the Atlantic Republican Tradition.* Princeton, NJ: Princeton University Press, 1975.

Portillo, José María. 1994. "Patrimonio, derecho y comunidad política: La constitución territorial de las provincias vascas y la idea de jurisdicción provincial." In *Fallstudien zur spanischen und portugiesischen Justiz 15. bis 20. Jahrundert*, edited by Johannes-Michael Scholz. Frankfurt am Main: Vittorio Klostermann.

————. 1997. "Locura cantábrica, o la República en la Monarquía: Percepción ilustrada de la constitución vizcaína." *Anuario de Historia del Derecho Español* 67, vol. I: 749–75.

————. 1998a. "Historia magistra civis: La interpretación historiográfica de las constituciones provinciales vascas en la Edad Moderna." In *Foralismo, derechos históricos y democracia.* Madrid: Fundación BBV.

————. 1998b. "República de hidalgos: Dimensión política de la hidalguía universal entre Vizcaya y Guipúzcoa." In *La lucha de bandos en el País Vasco: De los Parientes Mayores a la Hidalguía Universal: Guipúzcoa, de los bandos a la Provincia (s. XIV a XVI)*, edited by José Ramón Díaz de Durana, 425–38. Bilbao: Universidad del País Vasco-Euskal Herriko Unibertsitatea.

————. 2001. "El País de los fueros: Política, instituciones y derecho en las provincias vascas durante la Edad Moderna." In *Redes familiares y patronazgo: Aproximación al entramado social del País Vasco y Navarra en el Antiguo Régimen (siglos XV-XIX)*, edited by José María Imízcoz. Bilbao: Universidad del País Vasco-Euskal Herriko Unibertsitatea.

Poza, Andrés de. (1588-1589?) 1997. *Fuero de Hidalguía: Ad Pragmaticas de Toro & Tordesillas.* Edited by Carmen Muñoz de Bustillo. Bilbao: Universidad del País Vasco-Euskal Herriko Uniberstitatea.

Rosanvallon, Pierre. 2013. *The Society of Equals.* Translated by Arthur Goldhammer. Cambridge, MA: Harvard University Press.

Skinner, Quentin. 1978. *The Foundations of Modern Political Thought*, 2 vols. Cambridge: Cambridge University Press.

———. 1984. "The Idea of Negative Liberty: Philosophical and Historical Perspectives." In *Philosophy in History: Essays in the Historiography of Philosophy*, edited by Richard Rorty, Jerom B. Schneewind, and Quentin Skinner. Cambridge: Cambridge University Press.

———. 1992. "On Justice, the Common Good, and the Priority of Liberty." In *Dimensions of Radical Democracy: Pluralism, Citizenship, Community*, edited by Chantal Mouffe. New York: Verso.

———. 1994. "The Italian City-Republics." In *Democracy: The Unfinished Journey, 508 BC to AD 1993*, edited by John Dunn. Oxford: Oxford University Press.

Soria, Lourdes. 2006. "La hidalguía universal." *Iura Vasconiae* 3: 283–316.

Truchuelo, Susana. 2004. *Gipuzkoa y el poder real en la Alta Edad Moderna*. Donostia-San Sebastián: Gipuzkoako Foru Aldundia-Diputación Foral de Gipuzkoa.

Ullmann, Walter. 1961. *Principles of Government and Politics in the Middle Ages*. London: Methuen.

———. 1971. *Principios de gobierno y política en la Edad Media*. Translated by Graciela Soriano. Madrid: Revista de Occidente.

Urrutikoetxea, Josetxo. 1992. *"En una mesa y compañía": Caserío y familia campesina en la crisis de la "sociedad tradicional." Irún, 1766–1845*. San Sebastián: Universidad de Deusto.

Vallejo, Jesús. 1992. *Ruda equidad, ley consumada: Concepción de la potestad normativa (1250–1350)*. Madrid: Centro de Estudios Constitucionales.

Viejo, Julián. 1997. "Ausencia de política: Ordenación interna y proyecto europeo en la Monarquía Católica de mediados del siglo XVII." In *Monarquía, imperio y pueblos en la España moderna*, edited by Pablo Fernández Albaladejo. Alicante: Universidad de Alicante.

Viroli, Maurizio. 2005. *From Politics to Reason of State: The Acquisition and Transformation of the Language of Politics 1250–1600*. Cambridge: Cambridge University Press.

3

Egalitarianism in Traditional Basque Society

Maïté Lafourcade

There are many hypotheses about the origins of the Basques, the most feasible one being that they are of autochthonous descent. What is unquestionable is that they are a very old people, going back to prehistoric times. From their early beginnings, they were self-administered in territorial units and they owned their land collectively under a natural regime of indivisible property.

Later on, with the emergence of an agro-pastoral economy, families established themselves in houses with fixed rules for community life and according to their needs and without any systematic planning. The houses were at the center of their organization. They were and would continue to be the basic cells of Basque political and social order. Families became linked with specific homesteads to such an extent that they took their surnames from them. Thus, houses were maintained over the centuries thanks to a legal system designed to protect them.

These houses, coupled with cultivated land and rights to communal land, were economic units that secured the existence of extended families. Each generation was represented by a core of people who were in charge of everything. In fact, responsibility extended to all family members and members of the community: each house, with its own representative, took part in the administration of communal lands and matters that affected all inhabitants.

The legal system, born out of a strong communal spirit, led to a type of unitary society in which all men were free, all houses were regarded as equal, and in which community interests were put before individual interests.

This original form of organization survived various invasions and other attempts at imposition, such as feudalism, Roman law, and monarchical unification policies. It survived in France, without undergoing any considerable modifications, until the French Revolution in 1789, and in Spain, almost until the present.

The main characteristics of traditional Basque society were its antiquity and longevity, despite various historical challenges. Its solidity was based on the respect for ancestral customs, which were partly formalized between the thirteenth and the seventeenth centuries, varying from province to province.

The first piece of writing we know of in regard to the organization of this traditional society was the Fuero general de Navarra (General fuero of Navarre), an anonymous work, probably dating from 1237 after Theobald I acceded to the throne of Navarre in Iruñea-Pamplona in 1234, succeeding his uncle, King Sancho the Strong (Sancho VII). The people of Navarre distrusted the prince, who was from Champagne beyond the River Loire, a highly feudal land, and drew up their own fueros and urged the new king to honor it. This was a period in which a revival of Roman law and customs was taking place. Therefore, in order to preserve the ancient customs from being subverted by intrusive Roman law they were recorded in the form of the fueros. However, after having been written down, Navarrese law continued to evolve and there were several improvements added to the original text; the latest being the *Novissima Recopilación* (Latest collection), which dates from 1735, and the *Cuadernos de las Cortes* (Parliamentary records) from 1716–1841. The latest amendments were passed on the April 1, 1987. This is the law currently in force in Navarre.

Araba, after Alfonso VIII's reconquest of the province in 1199 from the Moors and its incorporation into Castile in 1332, was governed by Castilian law and the *ordenanzas de hermandad* (Confraternity ordinances) from 1417 to 1463, except in the lordship of Aiaraldea (La Cuadrilla de Ayala), which was part of the federation of Bizkaia at the time and had its own fuero, written in 1373 (rewritten in 1469).

The Fuero Antiguo (Old Law) of Bizkaia was published in 1452 and reformed in 1506. The Fuero Nuevo (New Law) dates from 1526. Thanks to the Spanish constitution of 1978, which created autonomous communities in Spain and allowed each one to have its own law, the fueros were rewritten and updated in the Ley del derecho civil foral del Pais Vasco (Law on foral civil law of the Basque Country) on July 1, 1992. This law also updated the Aiaraldea fuero.

In France, King Charles VII, by the ordinance of Montils-les-Tours in 1454, ordered the kingdom's customs to be officially recorded within the framework of the jurisdictions of bailiffs and seneschals (royal agents in charge of justice), which were the basic administrative units. The *Coutume* (legal customs) of Lapurdi were written up in 1514 and those of Zuberoa in 1520. Lower Navarre, which had been separated from Upper Navarre (that is, Navarre) since the invasion of 1512 by Ferdinand II of Aragon, Isabella I of Castile's husband, was not part of the Kingdom of France at the time; the monarchs of Navarre, Jean d'Albret and Catherine of Navarre, had taken refuge in the north of the country, in the *merindad de ultra puerto* (bailiwick beyond the pass), today Lower Navarre, and set up their kingdom there. At that time the people of Navarre were ruled by local customs and the Fuero general de Navarra. When Henry III of France died without direct issue in 1589, Henry III of Navarre, son of Jeanne d'Albret and Antoine of Navarre, became his legitimate successor. He became king of France and took the name Henry IV, King of France and Navarre. In 1608, he named a commission to record the customs of Lower Navarre. However, at the dawn of absolute monarchy the procedure for recording customs had changed since the sixteenth century; henceforth it was a commission named by the king and dependent on him that did the legal work. In the process, the customs were adulterated, losing their popular character. The *for* (fuero) that was published in 1611 reflected local customs only imperfectly.

A study of these customs, and notarial archives and records of local institutional decisions, allow us to gain a better knowledge of the workings of traditional Basque society. We should point out, however, that these official documents only concern the masters of the houses and their families. Marginal groups of the local population, consisting of those who did not have their own houses—such as the clergy, younger siblings who had not married successors, cagots, gypsies, and simple peasants—were excluded and regarded as not belonging to Basque society.

According to the documents, egalitarianism emerged as one of the main features of traditional Basque society. It is to be found in Basque society's two central hubs, the family and the community.

Equality in the Family

Basque women had the same legal status as men. There was no distinction between the sexes. Likewise, family patrimony was managed by a couple from each generation, and there was total equality between them.

Equality between Sexes

From a legal point of view, nothing distinguished men and women. However, de facto they did have different roles in society; women had their place inside the home, men outside of it, whether working in the fields or participating in public political life.

Equality between sexes was particularly noticeable in laws of succession. Family patrimony, which was indivisible, belonged to all who lived in the house. There could be no more than a single *etxerakoa*[1] or master of the house in each generation. In the Northern Basque Country (Iparralde), this had to be the eldest child, regardless of gender,[2] while in the Southern Basque Country (Hegoalde) parents chose the best-prepared child to manage the estate;[3] they named each other the executors to make this choice, designating their inheritor in a will. Wills signed by both the father and the mother or wills signed by a person designated by them were prohibited under French law at the time. Further-

---

1. A Basque term (*etxerakoa*) meaning "he/she who is for the house"; Spaniards called this person "the one destined for the house."
2. "With regard to property that has been in the family for at least two generations, the first child, whether the son or daughter, inherits from the parents": Article 3 of Title XII of the Lapurdi Coutume.
3. A certain *"zu etxerako"* (you for the house): this was the expression that parents used on farmsteads to choose the child to succeed them.

more, the absolute birthright of the eldest child in Basque law, without distinction of gender, was unknown elsewhere in France.

However, at the time the customs were recorded, Iparralde had already witnessed the arrival of a nobility law, which meant that on noble estates men were privileged over women.[4] Yet the Basque principle of equality between the sexes regained some influence, for example, in second marriages; if there were only daughters from the first marriage, it was the eldest daughter who received the family estate, even if there were sons from subsequent marriages.[5]

In Zuberoa and Lower Navarre, where the nobility had much more influence than in Lapurdi, the male line prevailed in the freehold houses of the foothills. In Zuberoa, the text about customs referred to various parishes, hamlets, and houses that each had their laws,[6] something to which the renowned Basque lawyer, politician, historian, and poet Arnauld de Oïhenart referred to in one of his proverbs: "Each people has its laws, each house its customs." Only the houses in Upper Zuberoa and in the high valleys of Lower Navarre together with houses in the census[7] maintained the ancestral line.

The study of notary practices on the eve of the French Revolution shows that these rules were strictly applied. Exceptions were only allowed if they were in the house's interest, or if the eldest child was "disabled," "a born idiot," "little inclined toward marriage," and so on.

The eldest child could be "disinherited" by his or her parents if he or she married without their consent before reaching marriageable age, as established by the Coutumes.[8] If the parents disagreed about giving their consent, the decision lay with the

---

4. Article 1 of heading XII of the Lapurdi Coutume.
5. "But if there are children from various marriages, and only girls from the first marriage, the eldest daughter from the first marriage succeeds, excluding all children from other marriages, even if there are males": Article 2 of Heading XII of the Lapurdi Coutume and Articles 1 and 2 of Heading XXVII of the Zuberoa Coutume.
6. Articles 3 to 18 of Heading XXVII of the Zuberoa Coutume.
7. Houses of inferior quality that had been granted by a lord.
8. In Lapurdi, this was twenty-eight for men and twenty for women; in Zuberoa, twenty-five for men and eighteen for women; in Lower Navarre, twenty-five for men and twenty for women.

person who managed the estate that would come with the marriage; often the mother's word—if it was she who had received the estate from her parents—was enough.

In the latter case, the eldest of the children would receive the family estate. The unity of the family estate and its preservation through the centuries was a fundamental principle for the Basques. There could only be a single person in charge during each generation.

The family estate was transmitted to the eldest child of the family on the day of his or her wedding. He or she would usually marry the younger daughter or son of another house, which would contribute some money to the matrimonial union. This contribution was termed a "dowry" in the documents, but that term must not have been typical, because in the Coutume a note of clarification was added immediately afterward describing this as a "donation for the union generally known as marriage." Most marriage contracts appear to have been based on this type of legal union.

The dowry could be given to a man or a woman. If it was the husband, he took the name of his wife's house, as did the children from their union.

Husband and wife had equal rights over property that came with marriage, property that had been in the family for at least two generations, known as *avintins* or *papoaux* (family assets).[9] This also included dowry items, which became an integral part of the family estate once a child was born and remained alive. All transfers of assets required the consent of the married couple: "The husband may not sell or remove any assets assigned in marriage without the wife's consent, nor may the wife without the husband's consent."[10] Basque women, in customary law and before the revival of Roman law, were *socia mariti* (companions) before the law. The principle of the legal incapacity of married women that derived from Roman law had not reached the Basque Country.

---

9.   *Avitins* is a Latin term meaning having been in the family for at least two generations and deriving from *avus* (grandfather) while *papoaux* derives from the Gascon for grandfather. These assets, which were the family estate, were irremovable and inalienable.

10.   Article 6 of heading IX of the Lapurdi Coutume. The same was true in Zuberoa: article 5 of heading XXIV of the Zuberoa Coutume.

Women managed the family estate, which belonged to the family as a whole and was indivisible, with the same rights as their husbands; the family was represented by a couple during each generation, by the eldest child and his or her spouse, by his or her parents, his or her grandparents, and so on. They all had equal rights to the family estate, which they managed together. This *coseigneurie* (co-ownership) was a typical Basque institution.

Coseigneurie

The figure of the Roman *patria potestas* (power of a father) had not yet reached the Basque Country. Since his or her marriage and the addition of his or her parent's dowry, the eldest child and his or her spouse were *coseigneurs*, co-owners of the assets received on marriage. Both couples, referred to in the relevant documents as the *maîtres vieux* (old masters) and the *maîtres jeunes* (young masters) lived under the same roof and worked together for the prosperity of the family estate. Administrative acts, especially the transfer of any property, required the consent of all the owners of the indivisible property, that is, both couples as well as the grandparents or any surviving grandparent.

Equality between the old masters and the young masters was such that if there was disagreement, each of the two couples could, at any time, request the family estate to be divided, which, in Lapurdi, meant half and half whereby the old masters chose their lot first. They had three days to make their choice. If they did not choose during that time, the other couple was given the opportunity.

Each couple only had the use and administration of the property that pertained to its lot. The unity of the estate had to be maintained. The two couples lived under the same roof but in two separate parts of the house; and the architecture of Lapurdi bears witness to this practice. Each couple had the right to watch over the other and could demand justice if it thought that the estate was being badly managed. This could include a demand that the whole property be turned over to them, instead of being handed over to bad administrators.[11]

---

11.   Articles 18 to 28 of Heading IX of the Lapurdi Coutume and Articles 22 et seq. of Heading XXIV of the Zuberoa Coutume.

Such arrangements had one important consequence. In order to put back the day when they would have to give up the indivisible half of their rights, the parents, while still young, would not give their eldest child consent to marry under various pretexts such as the dowry being insufficient, that actual the match was unsuitable, and so on. The large number of parents' requests for summons and other documentation related to objections found in notaries' archives demonstrates the difficulty that the eldest children were confronted when it came to receiving their parents' consent to marry.

Young people, who knew nothing of the decrees of the Council of Trent and royal ordinances,[12] went to the priest[13] in order to exchange *arrhes de tendresse* (symbols of affection) that formalized their mutual consent. From that moment onward they considered themselves to be married before God and lived together in the house of whoever turned out to be the eldest child. The parents did not give their official consent to the young married couple until the couple had grown older. Sometimes it did not happen until the couple had children of their own. In fact, in the Basque Country the number of illegitimate children recognized by their parents and conceived before marriage was exceptionally high.[14] Trial marriage (*marriage à l'essai*) was a very widespread practice in the Basque Country that was only "Christianized" at a very late stage. The Fuero de Navarra of 1237 recognized an official status known as *barragana*, which was a kind of openly known cohabitation. According to the fueros of Navarre, Aiaraldea, and Bizkaia, children born in *barragana* were entitled to receive from their deceased parents a part of the matrimonial assets equivalent to that received by the children of *matrimonio canónico* (canonical marriage). These were known as *hijos de pareilla* or *hijos de bendición* (legitimate children). If there were no legitimate heirs, one of them could become the designated ap-

---

12. Ordinance of Blois, 1579, and Declaration, 1639.

13. See *Une paroisse basque et son curé au XVIIIème siècle d'après un Livre de Raison de 1767 à 1804* (1896).

14. During the last fifteen years of the ancien régime, there were 13.56 percent births during the first seven months of marriage and 21.39 percent of recognized illegitimate children, while in the French countryside in general (Chaunu 1982, 121–22), deeply Christian as it was, the average was between 1.5 and 2 percent.

pointee of the family estate. Only children born in adultery or "sacrilegious" children (born from a union with a person in a religious order) had no right to succeed their parents.

Public cohabitation was an official arrangement in the Basque Country until the Council of Trent forbade it in the sixteenth century. However, despite bishops' efforts in their synodal ordinances to punish couples who lived in sin through excommunication, the practice continued for a long time. The seneschal of the lieutenant of Lannes (in the Pays d'Albret, Gascony), based in Baiona (Bayonne), wrote in his *Mémoire sur Bayonne, Labourd et le Bourg Saint-Esprit* (Report on Baiona, Lapurdi and the burg of Saint Esprit) in 1718: "It has long been rumored among the same people that theirs is a great wrongdoing that has, to some extent, been legally recognized; young people who were married after having lived together and after having many children." (Lespès de Hureaux 1718).

Equality in the family, between husband and wife as the managing couples, also existed between the masters and ladies of the house in a community that met regularly to decide on communal issues.

Equality in the Community

Houses were grouped into parishes[15] and parishes into valleys (*pays*). Lapurdi and Zuberoa were provinces, while Lower Navarre was divided into seven valleys and five boroughs.

This organization of the Basque Country dates back to before the eleventh century, to a time when the Church tried to think of and organize Christian society mostly in line with its teachings, along the lines of a strictly compartmentalized order[16] consisting of *oratores*, *belatores*, and *laboratores*, that is, those who prayed (clergy), those who fought (nobility), and those who worked (the rest of the population). In France, this imposed idea of society's workings remained in place until the Revolution in 1789, except in the Basque Country, where it was ignored.

---

15.   This was the name given, under the ancien régime, to communities of the inhabitants in a single place, known as boroughs or villages at present.
16.   It took inspiration from Saint Augustin's *City of God*, in which men had to take their place in society and have a status in society according to their role.

The clergy and the nobility were excluded from having a say in the masters' assembly of houses: only the masters could take decisions. Legal equality between houses was the rule. Each house sent a representative and took part, along with the other masters of the house in the parish and in the community's administration. Each parish sent a representative, who had been given an imperative mandate, to the valley's Biltzar orokorra (general assembly), which in turn took decisions that affected all households.

The Parish Assemblies

In each parish, or district, the masters of the houses met on Sundays in the church porch or in a small room under the porch.[17] In this assembly, called "*capitular*," all the parish's masters of the houses gathered. Women inheritors sent their husbands while widows without male children were allowed to attend. Masters of noble houses were excluded. In Lapurdi, only the Viscount of Urtubie in Urruña (Urrugne) and the Baron of Senpere (Saint-Pée-sur-Nivelle) had the right to attend in their respective parishes. In Zuberoa and Lower Navarre, where the nobility had more influence, attendance of parish assemblies varied from place to place; in Lower Navarre, nobles could take part if they contributed to communal costs, but without having any type of precedence over the masters of the houses. Priests could not participate; they only attended when there were clerical issues involved, but even then they had no influence on the decision-making process and the conclusions reached.

The debates were based on oral performance and exchange and until the sixteenth century nothing was written down.[18] From the seventeenth and eighteenth centuries onward decisions show up in records. The most important subjects dealt with in these meetings were the budget and, in Lapurdi, the administration of communal lands shared by the parish.

---

17. Architecture in Lapurdi churches bears witness to this. In Hegoalde, one term for "village" or "municipal district" specific to the Basque Country actually took its name from these meetings: *anteiglesia* (literally, "in front of the church").
18. See article 4 of heading XX of the Lapurdi Coutume.

The budget often went into the red, especially at the end of the ancien régime, due to the demands from royal tax authorities. Tax income was usually obtained from real estate in the community such as the town hall, the mills, from butchers, the sale and trade of wine and alcohol, and community farming. In Lapurdi, for example, where communal lands were organized on a parish basis, the sale of communally-owned wood was carried out by auction and taxed locally. Communal tax was calculated based on the difference between actual expenses and potential profit. The maintenance of the commons, land, and real estate were taxed, including the church nave, rectory, and *benoîte* or housekeeper (*andere serora* in Basque: a woman in charge of the maintenance of the church and the churchyard)[19]—even the cemetery. Funds were provided for orphaned children in the parish and entrusted to the families who asked for the lowest pension in exchange for looking after them,[20] assistance to the poor, and parish employees' salaries. The highest-ranking employee was the town guard, who had to make sure that regulations passed by the masters of the houses were complied with. They had the right to give fines and identify infringements, and in terms of social ranking they were followed by the schoolteacher,[21] the

19. The woman in question was an unmarried woman "of good customs," chosen by the patron of the parish church or by the parishioners; in the latter case, the *andere serora*'s house was auctioned and whoever offered the highest amount obtained it. Once chosen, she usually lived in a small house next to the church. Sworn to celibacy, she was taken on to serve the church for life and had rights to income from baptisms, marriages, and burials, as well as from the various services that she carried out for parishioners; she was also given a lot of payment in kind. See "Les benoîteries au Pays basque" (1991).
20. See Lafourcade (1989), 299.
21. Only occasionally would priests take part in masters of the houses' assemblies, which named the teacher and fixed his duties and remuneration. Basque peasants were reluctant to pay a schoolmaster, whom they judged to be of no use, and the salaries agreed were often very low, usually no higher than 222 livres or pounds (a royal decree of 1698 having fixed a minimum of 150 livres). According to research carried out by Mgr. de Bellefont, Bishop of Baiona, four of the nineteen parishes in Lapurdi that he had visited did not have schoolmasters. Girls' education was even more neglected; only two parishes, Bidarte (Bidart) and Ziburu (Ciboure), had schoolmistresses; in other parishes it was the *andere serora* who taught the girls how to read and write, including teach-

doctor,[22] and the surgeon,[23] who were all given payment contracts issued by the community of masters of the houses. Between them, and by district, they chose the *cotisateurs*, who were in charge of assigning taxes, depending on the type and level of inheritance. They decided also on the proportionate share that each one had to pay in tax. To this were added the payments of royal taxes. The tax collectors were generally chosen from among the masters of the houses in the district. The community of masters also shared road repair duties, a system that was maintained in Lapurdi until the French Revolution, despite the royal council's wish to entrust the public highways to the Bridges and Roads Administration, which was "not carried out."[24] The council was also responsible for recruiting a sufficient number of volunteers, or in case there were not enough, drew lots to select able-bodied men between eighteen and forty-one to make up the contingent of troops for the valley militia, and, from Louis XIV's reign onward (1643), for the army or the royal marines.

In Lapurdi, the most important decisions to be made were those in relation to the rights and regulations governing the use of communal lands: rights to pasture, pasture for pigs, land cultivation, and forestry. Municipal guards made sure that these statutes were complied with and could give out fines or confiscate (*pignorer*)[25] livestock in case of infringement or trespassing. Some parishes had treaties or *faceries* with neighboring parishes in order to regulate the use of pasture land, both in times of war and peace, and paying no heed to the existence of the official borders between the two kingdoms.

---

ing them the catechism and prayers. In Lower Navarre and Zuberoa, which were further away from urban centers, the situation was even worse.

22. Doctors received annual wages of between 350 and 400 livres from the community, for which they had to cure the inhabitants of the parish at no extra cost, except, on occasion, transport costs. In general, doctors were fairly well-off, being classified as creditors and obtainers of goods.

23. Surgeons, whose profession had been separated from that of barbers since 1717, took care of wounds resulting from fights or accidents and received lower salaries than doctors.

24. Biltzar of July 18, 1783: Pyrénées Atlantiques departmental archives C 1621, 185.

25. From *pignus*: "wage" in Latin. Trespassing livestock could be confiscated until the fine was paid.

After deliberating, the masters of the houses usually preceded to vote, each house having one vote and each vote counting as equal. The decision made was based on a majority vote and afterward became parish law, with the mayor and officials in charge of making sure they were complied with. The council also chose a *maire* (mayor)[26] or *bayle* and a district jury every year, depending on parish customs. In charge of carrying out the decisions taken by the masters of the houses, these two also took care of contingent matters that might arise.

Biltzar Orokorra (General Assembly)

Each province was organized in a particular manner. Lapurdi followed the old customs more than the other provinces. In Zuberoa, the nobility attended, having managed to take part in the *Biltzar orokorra* (general assembly). Lower Navarre, an ancient kingdom, was a *pays d'états* like many others that still existed in France, in which the estates consisted of three orders or ranks: the nobility, clergy, and third estate; however, the case of Lower Navarre has always been very complex due to its administrative separation into seven valleys and five boroughs, the latter still following ancient Basque customs and organization.

The Lapurdi Biltzarra

The Lapurdi Biltzarra resembled the traditional Basque assemblies. "The current regime in Lapurdi is like no other,"[27] the Baiona trade representative wrote to the royal commissioner in 1784.

The etymology of its name comes from the two Basque words: *bildu zahar*, meaning "old assembly." Its origins are lost in the mists of time, but it certainly precedes the separation of society into three orders or ranks, which took place in France in the eleventh century. Thus, the traditional organization of Basque society lasted in Lapurdi until the French Revolution.

---

26. This term, common throughout France, did not appear until the eighteenth century. It replaced that of *Hauz Apeza* (district judge).

27. Taken from a report written by the Baiona trade representative, Boyetet, to the royal commissioner Le Camus de Néville, January 9, 1784: Pyrénées Atlantiques departmental archives C 454.

Based solely on oral communication, there are no medieval documents of these assemblies that could provide historians with more detailed information about the nature of their deliberations and decisions. The oldest known verbal debate dates from October 8, 1567.[28] Apart from a few rare seventeenth-century documents, only two records of eighteenth-century decisions have survived;[29] one of them recording decisions from the period June 23, 1711 to January 28, 1737; the other from November 17, 1758 to November 18, 1789.

The assembly's proceedings were regulated by a judgment of the royal council, established by Louis XIV, on June 3, 1660, in Donibane Lohizune (Saint-Jean-de-Luz), "the king being present," when he married Maria Theresa, the infanta of Spain.

In Lapurdi there were representatives from thirty-five parishes. Clergy and the nobles were excluded. The council met at the bailiff's court in Uztaritze (Ustaritz). The chair was usually the bailiff but, in the eighteenth century, he only turned up once, on May 11, 1779, to reorganize the militia, in his role of noble of the sword, that is, the head of the local militia. His place was usually filled by officials from the bailiff's court, the lieutenant-general, and the royal prosecutor, who were of local origin. These two were accompanied by the syndic general whose responsibility it was to call the meeting and to suggest the agenda for the gathering.

Despite the royal council's judgment of June 3, 1660, no royal commissioners came to the meeting called. In fact, there would have been no point in their going as all the debates were in Basque. The meeting was called by the regional syndic general whenever he felt the need for it, which was at least once a year, sometimes more.

At the opening, the court clerk called all the towns represented, always in the same order, starting with Urruña and finishing with Uztaritze. Any missing parishes, and those that had sent women to represent them, were fined. While the principle of equal legal status independent of gender applied, each person still had his or her place in society—and politics was something that was reserved for men.

---

28. It has been published by Goyheneche and Dassance (1955), 195–200. These authors also published the oral debates of January 24, 1595, 201–6, of August 27, 1641, 322–24, of August 12, 1648, 324–26, of July 30, 1693, 327–29, and of June 8, 1695, 329–30.
29. Pyrénées Atlantiques departmental archives C 1620 and C 1621.

The chair read out the proposals, one by one; they were then discussed and dealt with accordingly. Often the representatives of the parishes, who were bound by imperative mandate, had to go back to their respective parish assemblies the following Sunday to inform the masters of houses of the matters that had arisen and that needed to be dealt with. After debate and deliberation the parish assembly would vote. Decisions were made by majority vote, each house having one vote. The decisions were then communicated back to the *biltzarra*'s second session, which took place eight days after the first.

During this second session, after having consulted the people in each community, the parish replies were given to the court clerk, who read them out one by one. The final decision was then made by majority vote, all votes counting as equal, independent of the prestige or status of some of the individuals involved. The chair announced the results, which were recorded by the court clerk and could be checked by all. The *biltzarrak* or assemblies represented the legal foundation of Lapurdi, which stemmed from the masters of the houses, in a regime of direct democracy.

The people of Lapurdi became attached to these democratic institutions because they guaranteed their secular liberties. They refused any type of government plan that aimed at radically changing or abolishing them,[30] and on occasion caused local disturbances to the effect that the royal commissioner gave up trying to modify this small country's constitution, which he described as "perverted."

Not only was Lapurdi's organization unique in France, it also had considerable powers, which meant it had real administrative autonomy within the kingdom of France. The only change occurred when the *biltzarra*'s judiciary powers, which originated in a medieval conception of people's justice, were abolished when the kingdom of France annexed Lapurdi in 1450 and imposed royal state justice. However, it seems that the *biltzarra* still managed to maintain its power to judge for some time afterward because in the council's judgment of June 3, 1660, the king prohibited the power to "make any statutes or ordinances that led to imprisonment, banishment, penal punishment, or monetary pun-

---

30.   November 24, 1784 plan, published in Dravasa (1950), 299. May 8, 1787 and March 6, 1789 plans, published by Dussarp (1919), 53–58.

ishment." According to the *biltzarra*'s own records, it still received court cases and gave its verdicts on measures to be taken as late as the eighteenth century.

It would appear that when royal decisions did not find support, the people of Lapurdi simply ignored them, following the formula of the people of Hegoalde: "We obey, but do not put it into practice."

As described above, Lapurdi had its own law and the *biltzarra* served as its main institution. This was even true of international treaties, valid in times of war and peace with their "Spanish" neighbors Gipuzkoa and Bizkaia. This applied particularly to the regulation of navigation and the sharing of common fishing waters in the Bay of Biscay. The assembly also reserved the powers to regulate, and to pass legislation, including sanctions in order to keep order, which included anything from the border policing to maintaining control over economic development in the pays or valley.

It also had financial autonomy and oversaw its own budget, including the paying of annual royal taxes. As to the latter, it paid a fixed sum to the royal treasury once a year for each tax category, usually a sum that was agreed for a number of years until its renegotiation or renewal. A *biltzarra* commission divided the agreed sum up between the parishes, depending on the number of houses in each parish. The quota that each house had to pay was determined by a meeting of the masters of the houses and depended on each house's inheritance value.

The masters of the houses were also responsible for public highways—despite the government's attempts to transfer such responsibility to the Bridges and Roads Administration—as was public aid, schooling, and public services.

Lapurdi had its own militia of one thousand men, mostly volunteers, who were recruited and based in every major town. The militia was in charge of policing the valley and guarding the border with Spain. The militia also had the advantage that the people of Lapurdi were exempt from military service in the royal army.

The autonomy of Lapurdi ran counter to the French monarchy's unifying, centralist policy. Proving unable to normalize this province, which was so obstinately attached to its traditions and its freedom, the agents of the crown used all their means to "bite away at" its privileges, committing all sorts of excesses and caus-

ing all sorts of humiliation, something the members of the third
estate complained about in their register of grievances written for
the grand meeting of the estates general in 1789, which ultimately
served as the prelude to the French Revolution, the event that
would put a definitive stop to the autonomy of the Basque Country in France.

The Zuberoan Cour d'Ordre

The Cour d'Ordre in Zuberoa consisted of two assemblies, the
silviet, an assembly similar to the *biltzarra*, which represented the
parishes, and the *grand corps*, in which the clergy and the nobility met. The latter, set up in an unknown period in the past but
certainly in operation prior to 1520, had been conceived as an
institution in juxtaposition to the *silviet*. The two assemblies met
separately, *silviet* in Irabarne (Libarrenx) Wood, near Maule, and
grand corps at Lextarre (Licharre) Court, the Zuberoan court of
justice.

Notification was given by the lieutenant-general of Lextarre Court and sent personally to six members of the clergy[31]
as well as to the nobles. There were many of the latter in Zuberoa,[32] where, influenced by neighboring Béarn, feudalism had
developed during the Middle Ages. The *silviet* meetings were
somewhat more complex to organize because the province was
divided into three local valleys, known as *messageries,* which
were subdivided into seven *dégairies*. The *messageries* were notified and they, in turn, notified the *dégans* (local representatives of
the *dégaires*), who then notified the parishes. While originally all
the masters of the houses attended, after the population growth
of the sixteenth and seventeenth centuries each parish assembly
elected its own representative for the *silviet*. These representatives went there along with the seven *dégans* and those from the
six boroughs.

31. Because they had their own assemblies, the clergy of France had little interest in local problems and did not reply to the notification, as can be seen in
article 48 of their register of grievances sent to the estates general in 1789: "the
clergy, as the first level of the state, never goes to it because there is no rank
there suitable for it."
32. Ten *potestats* (noblemen with legal rights), fifty land-owning gentry, and
the noble masters of houses.

It was a drawn-out process for the *grand corps* at Lextarre Court that was presided over by the lieutenant-general of the court. The nobles debated all the issues before them and then voted, each noble having one vote. Decisions were made by majority vote. The regional syndic general and the seven *dégans* could attend the debates and the get in contact with the *silviet* to inform its delegates about the decisions made.

The *silviet* meeting was usually held after that of the *grand corps*. The chair was usually the same as that who presided over the *grand corps*. After a roll-call of the town delegates present, the debate began. As in Lapurdi, representatives had imperative powers and could not make decisions without consulting their parishes. On their return the following Sunday, the masters of the houses voted (each vote counting as equal). Decisions were made by majority vote and then taken back by the representatives to a second session of the *silviet* in which a final decision was made (again, by majority vote, which was cast by the parish representatives, with each having one vote).

If there was no agreement between *silviet* and *grand corps*, the third estate syndic (who was also the regional syndic general) and the *grand corps* syndic tried to find a compromise between the different points of view. Alternatively, a joint commission was set up within each organization to find a solution. The executive decision-making body was the regional syndic general, chosen by *silviet*.

The main subject of debate at *silviet* was the administration of communal lands, which, in Zuberoa, belonged indivisibly to all the residents of the province.[33] The *silviet* usually agreed on the arrangements about *faceries* (agreements with neighboring towns)[34] for the use of pasture lands. The Cour d'Ordre dealt mostly with finance. Zuberoa, like Lapurdi, paid fixed quotas of taxes to the royal treasury in a single annual payment (this included direct and indirect taxes). Two joint commission were responsible for this: one for the nobles, who paid individually, and one for the parishes.

As noted, Zuberoa had its own jurisdiction, known as the Lextarre Court or the Noyer (walnut tree) Court because of its location. From 1550 onward it was presided over by a court official. It was made up of ten nobles who possessed legal rights and

---

33.   Article 1 of heading 13 of the Zuberoa Coutume.
34.   See *Lies et faceries dans les Pyrénées* (1985).

fifty land-owning gentry, who had rented land out to tenants. It had general civil and penal powers. Appeals were dealt with by the court of the seneschal of Lannes in Gascony (if the decision was appealed again it went to the Bordeaux Parliament and, after 1692, to the Pau Parliament).

The Cour d'Ordre had the regulatory power to impose sanctions in all spheres. It commanded a militia of one thousand men, which could be employed to ensure that decisions were complied with. Zuberoa also had stud farms and the Cour d'Ordre supplied these with fodder for the horses and with salaries for the guards of those horses. It also paid the inspector's salary.

Zuberoa still had considerable autonomy at the start of the eighteenth century despite what appeared to be a rather meddlesome nobility as well as the royal commissioner's and his agents' constant interference in decision-making matters.

In 1727, under pressure by the nobles who had complained about the onerous work involved in calling the regular meetings of the *silviet* and how slow it was in making decisions, the syndic general took on the role of exploring a new way of organizing the *silviet*. He proposed changes to the king and, accordingly, issued a decree on June 28, 1730, that the institutions were to be profoundly reformed.[35] As a consequence of that reform, the *silviet*, the Zuberoan secular democratic assembly, was abolished and the Cour d'Ordre was replaced by the gathering of the provincial estates, made up of the three orders, with each of them having a vote. In the course of events the third estate's number of votes was reduced to thirteen (the local valleys sending seven and the boroughs six representatives), which meant that there was no significant popular consultation anymore. This was a serious assault on ancient Basque democratic custom. The third estate formally complained to the Parliament of Navarre in 1731, accusing the syndic and the governor of corrupt practices and misappropriation. In the first instance this complaint was favorably received; however an appeal against this ruling was presented to the royal council, which resulted in the decision, made on October 13, 1731, to annul the earlier ruling taken by the Pau Parliament and ordering the *dégans* and parliament members to carry out the original orders of June 28, 1730 or otherwise be declared outlaws. Thereafter, the conflict

---

35. See Etcheverry (1937).

between the third estate and the nobles worsened. Fearing public disorder, the royal council prohibited in its order of May 20, 1733, that "local representatives and parliament members and all others from the province of Zuberoa hold meetings, boards, [or] to call such without written permission from the province's lord intendant." This sentence practically ended the Zuberoan estates. They survived until the French Revolution, but with very little power.

Institutions in Lower Navarre

Lower Navarre was governed by estates, as were many parts of France in the eighteenth century.[36] The estates of Navarre were made up of representatives from the three orders of the province, with each representative having a vote. Their main role was to vote on the *don gratuit* (free gift) to the king and, on such occasion, to present also a list of proposals.

However, these men were hardly representative of the people of Lower Navarre. The province was divided into seven valleys and five boroughs, which had kept their ancestral form of organization, similar to that of other parts of the Basque Country: the lordship of Donibane Garazi (Saint-Jean-Pied-de-Port), the valley of Baigorri (Baïgorry), the Garazi Valley (Pays de Cize), the Oztibarre (Ostabarret) Valley, the Arberoa (Arberoue) Valley, the Ortzaize (Ossès) Valley, and Irisarri-Iholdi-Armendaritze (Irrissary-Iholdy-Armendarits).

Each of these territorial units was organized in its own way; they were made up of several parishes and a general court that included delegates from the parishes, each of whom had an imperative mandate. Clerics and nobles were excluded, except when the latter were masters of a house. The general court met twice a year, like most Basque general assemblies. The court was responsible for "all common issues of the district"; that is, its main concern was the administration of communal lands that belonged indivisibly to all the residents of the province. Each valley had its own jurisdiction, presided over by municipal magistrates who were chosen by their respective community representatives and were equipped with complete powers, both civil and penal. Appeals were usually dealt with by the seneschals' jurisdiction in Dona-

---

36. See Destrée (1958).

paleu (Saint-Palais) and, in case of a further appeal, by the Parliament of Navarre, which was transferred to Pau after 1692.

Each valley also had its own militia. There were actually four militias because three valleys had been grouped together in the ancient Kingdom of Navarre before it was annexed by King Louis XIII of France: the Lordship of Donibane Garazi, the Baigorri Valley, the Garazi Valley, and Irisarri-Iholdi-Armendaritze. Its militia, a vestige of the old royal army of Navarre, had been known as the Lordship of Garazi Regiment in the times of Henry IV (1553–1610). Its banner was the old kingdom's flag. At the end of the ancien régime, the Lordship of Donibane Garazi existed in name only and was of no practical importance. Its administrative bodies, however, consisting of well-defined valleys, were very much alive.

There were five boroughs in Lower Navarre as well: Donibane Garazi, the old fortified town, was the administrative capital; Donapaleu, where the chancellery and later the seat of the seneschal of Navarre were based, was the legal capital; Garrüze (Garris), neighboring Donapaleu, had an important market; Bastida (La Bastide), a fortified town founded by Louis the Stubborn (Louis X); and Larzabale (Larceveau), in the Oztibarre Valley. As was the custom in the rest of the Basque Country, the masters of the houses met on Sundays after mass under the church's porches—or, in Bastida, in the cloister around the church—to discuss matters of shared interest and to make decisions that affected everyone. The executive body was the town corps or *jurade*, with four to six members, which in Bastida were called consuls. These were chosen for one year by the masters of the houses. The first appointed member acted as mayor, except in Bastida where that role was reserved for the permanent town bailiff's lieutenant. In 1704, Louis XIV turned municipal posts into remunerated positions that could also be inherited. The boroughs were allowed to buy them back, which they did until 1771, when they no longer had the means to do so. After that, royal authority became responsible for appointing in each borough a mayor, a deputy mayor, two members, two advisors, a royal prosecutor, a court clerk, and a treasurer.

Despite administrative interference and royal preferences for much of the ancien régime, the boroughs and valleys continued to enjoy considerable autonomy, so much so that it came as no surprise when the estates of Navarre demanded the title of Kingdom of Navarre in 1789. Ultimately, it took radical changes on the part of the French revolutionary authorities of 1789 to carry out the French monarchy's dream—the unification of the nation.

The decree of August 11, 1789, abolished all privileges, including the special status of local bodies and institutions. It was the end of the Basque provinces' autonomy. The Basques protested, but the revolutionaries, motivated by the grandiose idea of uniting *la Grande Nation*, paid no attention to this small people at the foot of the Pyrenees, whom they accused of objecting "petrified in sterile obstruction" to their plans. In order to abolish the provinces and "to absorb in the great fatherland what remained of the ancient provinces," the Constituent Assembly divided France into departments, which were and are as anonymous as possible. By a decree of January 12, 1790, France was divided up into eighty-three departments, including that of the Basses Pyrénées (Low Pyrenees), which grouped Béarn and the Basque provinces together. By the end of 1790 the new administrative system was fully in place. From a people that enjoyed privileges and rights, the Basques had become an administered people.

It is indeed a paradox: the Basques, who had always been free, equal, and democratic, lost their real freedom in the name of those very ideals, declared in the Rights of Men and Citizens on August 26, 1789. They became part of a stratified society, with significant inequalities between what would become an empowered bourgeoisie and the rest of the people who fell under the threshold established by the new electoral regime and who were not allowed to vote.

References

Chaunu, Pierre. 1982. *La civilisation de l'Europe des lumières*. Paris: Flammarion.

Destrée, Alain. 1958. *La Basse Navarre et ses institutions de 1620 à la Révolution*. Paris: Montchrestien.

Dravasa, Étienne. 1950. *Les privilèges des Basques du Labourd sous l'Ancien Régime*. San Sebastián: Escelicer.

Dussarp, Maurice. 1919. "Le Labourd à la fin du XVIIIème siècle, d'après les Archives du Contrôle général." *Bulletin de la société des sciences, lettres et arts de Bayonne*, 3rd and 4th trimester: 21–64.

Etcheverry, Michel. 1937. "La réforme des États de Soule au XVIIIème siècle." *Bulletin de la société des sciences, lettres et arts de Bayonne,* 1st trimester.

Goyheneche, Eugène, and Louis Dassance. 1955. "Documents inédits pour l'histoire du Biltzar du Pays de Labourd." *Gure Herria* 4: 195–200.

Lafourcade, Maïté. 1989. *Mariages en Labourd sous l'Ancien Régime. Les contrats de mariage du pays de Labourd sous le règne de Louis XVI: Étude juridique et sociologique.* Leioa: Universidad del País Vasco-Euskal Herriko Unibertsitatea.

"Les benoîteries au Pays basque." 1991. *Ekaina (Revue d'Études Basques)* 37. Special issue.

Lespès de Hureaux, Salvat de. 1718. *Mémoire sur Bayonne le Labourd et le Bourg Saint -Esprit.* Manuscript in Musée Basque de Bayonne-Baionako Euskal Museoa.

Lies et faceries dans les Pyrénées. 1985. Actes de la 3ème journée de recherches de la Société d'Études des Sept Vallées, Luz Saint Sauveur. June 1.

Une paroisse basque et son curé au XVIIIème siècle d'après un Livre de Raison de 1767 à 1804. 1896. Bayonne: Lasserre.

4

Nobles from Known Lineages: Universal Nobility in Gipuzkoa

Oihane Oliveri Korta

Between the sixteenth and eighteenth centuries nobility was universal in Gipuzkoa. This chapter reflects the relationship between nobility and society in the context of what we know as the culture of the Gipuzkoan ancien régime.

Gipuzkoan Universal Nobility

During the late medieval period, Gipuzkoan universal nobility was connected to the process of founding boroughs and changes that Gipuzkoa went through and the conflicts that took place there during the fourteenth and fifteenth centuries (Achón Insausti 1995; Marín Paredes 1998b). Universal nobility became part of the Gipuzkoan "constitution"; it was reflected in the province's fuero framework, the province's political system, its tax regime, and free trade (Truchuelo García 2004). In the process, the Province of Gipuzkoa emerged as a "republic of republics," its boroughs being governed by noble residents.

Universal nobility meant that all residents of the province were recognized as having the same legal status. However, this recognition was, as we will see, also opposed by other powers.

Inside the province it was opposed by the nobility (*parientes mayores*) who tried, unsuccessfully, to become a noble class differentiated from the rest (Marín Paredes 1998a, 230–33). The *parientes mayores* made use of their ability to mobilize men (a capacity they had acquired during the fourteenth- and fifteen-century clan-like factional struggles), their system of patronage, and their links to the king at a time when they tried to establish themselves as lords of their communities. However, the Confraternity of Gipuzkoa, supported by the crown, finally imposed its will and the boroughs became the sole legal authorities in the province. Yet during the sixteenth century, and even during the seventeenth century, there were still lasting conflicts between the *parientes mayores* and other sectors of society—which still managed to maintain some of their social prestige—and only over time would they stop being a political problem.

Outside the province, nobility was defined in contrast to the Crown of Castile, to which Gipuzkoa belonged. Collective nobility depended and relied on relationships, negotiations, and other considerations between Gipuzkoa and the monarchy. The province's position as a border region with a reliable military service loyal to the king was particularly important. The crown's recognition of universal nobility, which was not formalized until 1610, meant that Gipuzkoa was defined as a noble territory within the monarchy and, more important, that the people of Gipuzkoa were recognized as nobles when settling in the rest of the monarch's territories (Castile, Andalusia, the Americas). It is essential to understand this practical usefulness of universal nobility in a territory from which, due to economic conditions and inheritance customs, people commonly emigrated in order to settle in other territories as merchants, bureaucrats, soldiers, and so on (Otazu and Díaz de Durana 2008, 73–117).

During the sixteenth century we can already identify a fairly structured discourse in relation to the Gipuzkoan nobility that continued during the ancien régime. According to this discourse, nobility was based on blood and on the conservation of ancestral seats and lineages, uncontaminated by any other blood or "inferior races." Gipuzkoa had never been conquered and, so the logic went, had been able to maintain the purity of its lineages, descended from mythical Tubal (Martínez de Isasti, 25–26), something that the Basque language served to prove. Therefore, the Gipuzkoan nobility dated from time immemorial; its origins predated the beginning of modern time, and had not been granted by any king. It was consubstantial to Gipuzkoa.

This nobility extended to all Gipuzkoans due to the conversion of Gipuzkoa into a noble ancestral seat that had maintained its unique, pure lineage from time immemorial, and thus recognized all descendants of the province as being of noble origin. This recognition was enjoyed by all, and to the same extent. The only differentiating factor was that of property. However, this did not necessarily alter anybody's degree of nobility: "all the native inhabitants of the province were from known ancestral seats because all the houses in the province were known ancestral seats and no ancestral seats were better known than others except in terms of income and wealth."[1] It had not always been so; there exist records that speak of different statuses among the people of Gipuzkoa during the Middle Ages (Díaz de Durana 2004, 96–102).

In Gipuzkoa, nobility was indissolubly connected to residence. During the late Middle Ages nobility was extended to all residents, and residence became the unifying communitarian link in all boroughs, in contrast to the kinship and factional links of the *parientes mayores*, the latter of which had become an oppositional force, particularly in the context of public affairs (Achón Insausti 1998, 341–64). In the sixteenth century, the defense of the universality and purity of the Gipuzkoan nobility meant that the right to residence had to be strictly controlled. If all the residents of Gipuzkoa were nobles, in order to maintain the purity of that status anyone who wanted to take up residence in the territory had to prove nobility. And in order to make this work, there were a series of provincial bylaws that regulated how this could be proven (Truchuelo García 2004, 558–61).

Compared to Castilian law, the Gipuzkoans enjoyed a series of privileges as nobles: they did not have to pay certain taxes (in fact, the extension of nobility was connected to tax exemption); they could not be imprisoned for debt or be subject to torture. Furthermore, the defense of the territory was the responsibility

---

1. Archivo General de Gipuzkoa—Gipuzkoako Artxibo Orokorra (henceforth AGG-GAO) JD IM 4/9/10, fol. 14r. Testimonio presentado en el pleito de hidalguía de Andrés García de Eguino ante la Chancillería de Granada, hacia 1523.

of the province and its inhabitants, which meant that all residents were involved in military activities, which were considered noble (Otazu and Díaz de Durana 2008, 76–78).

Castilian custom when it came to demonstrating noble status proved to be an obstacle to the idea of Gipuzkoan universal nobility. This was particularly the case in the chanceries and courts of Valladolid and Granada, to which Gipuzkoans turned in order to prove their nobility, especially when taking up residence outside the province. These courts, however, argued that it was impossible to consider a whole territory to be noble and to recognize all Gipuzkoans (and Bizkaians) as nobles, not least because this would reduce the number of taxpayers for the crown. It became even more complicated when individual Gipuzkoans were unable to prove their nobility by recurring to existing legal methods. For example, Gipuzkoan nobles often did not comply with what in Castile was taken to be a noble lifestyle, particularly since they worked in professions that were considered to be common (including trade, craftwork, and so on).

With regard to the chanceries' reasoning, it was recognized in 1608 and confirmed in 1610 that Gipuzkoans did not have to prove their nobility by recurring to hitherto known and accepted legal methods; it was sufficient to demonstrate that they were descendants of ancestral seats in the province. In Castile, nobility was proven, among other things, by relying on the testimony of commoners who declared that the applicants were nobles; however, this was impossible in Gipuzkoa, where there were no commoners. With regards to common work, it was finally agreed that the conditions in Gipuzkoa simply meant that its inhabitants had no choice but to do work in the common professions. Alternatively, the purity of Gipuzkoan lineage could also be recognized on the basic assumption that no type of work it was committed to could be regarded as common labor (Martínez de Isasti 1972, 47). Such acknowledgment was fundamentally important, not inside the province but certainly outside of it.

In short, due to equal noble status, the situation in Gipuzkoa was very different when compared to the kingdom of Castile, where the population was divided into nobles (including the gentry) and plebeians. However, there were actually people who resided in Gipuzkoa who did not have noble status. Various observations can be made in relation to this.

Nobility is usually defined in contrast to other groups, and belonging to the nobility refers to a community of equal status—at least in principle. As mentioned, in Gipuzkoa, as in other Basque territories, the nobles' community was conceived as being congruent with the residents' community. In turn, the idea of residence was linked to that of purity of blood, maintained by pure lineages. In fact, a lack of knowledge about the origins of one's own lineage was taken to be proof of pure blood descent (Hernández Franco 1996, 62). These criteria were established in relation to a Hispanic culture that would make use of purity of blood. Purity of blood, along with nobility, were regarded as prime symbols representing the values of Spanish Christian culture. However, the connection between nobility, residence, and purity of blood automatically excluded a number of people from the community because nobility was not an individual right but a class privilege, even though in this case there was only a single class. One of the consequences of this way of understanding nobility was that provincial regulations demanded the expulsion of Jews and Moors who had converted to Christianity from Gipuzkoan territory. In some cases they had been living there for generations, and now they were expelled from the community (Otazu and Díaz de Durana 2008, 93–95). This measure demanded that any "foreigner" who wanted to reside in the territory during the ancien régime had to prove his nobility. Thus, during this period there were people who lived in the province but who were not regarded as residents, who therefore did not belong to the nobility either and, by implication, did not possess the same legal rights or obligations (Mora Afán and Zapirain Karrika 1996, 157–92).

In the first instance, nobility was closely connected to one's house or seat: one had to belong to a house or descend from one of the province's ancestral seats. Thus, in practice, the noble community's basic social unit was the house. But what happened when links with the house were broken? In the case of exclusion, did one remain a noble and did one continue to belong to the community (Zapirain Karrika 2008, 63–70)?

I will offer a last one critical reflection about the actual reach of that nobility and about belonging to a community that guaranteed noble status to its members. This reflection is about gender, about the relations of power between men and women in Gipuzkoa during the ancien régime. Gipuzkoans considered women to be noble just like men. There is no doubt about this because if someone's nobility was questioned, both paternal and maternal lines were taken into account. Furthermore, Gipuzkoan houses acknowledged the title of "lady of the house," with a recognized status of authority and responsibilities, in particular with respect to looking after the dead and the ritualized relationship between the living and the dead (Oliveri Korta 2010, 89–117). However, this did not mean that women were not subject to their husbands' or fathers' authority. The authority of such ladies was never given the same consideration as that of the masters. Women's lives and the range of activities on offer to them were considerably more limited when compared to that of men. Castilian law, which applied in the province, regarded married women as being underage in legal terms. Last but not least, greater moral demands were made of them when compared to men. All this was clearly reflected in women's status as residents. While houses and farmsteads kept their rights of residence even if a lady was in charge, women's status as residents did not grant them the right to take part in community political structures such as the *concejo abierto* (open council), town councils, elected posts, or other administrative roles (Oliveri Korta 2009, 188–89).

In sum, since time immemorial universal nobility was linked to the house and to the status of residency; additionally, having "old Christian" origins formed part of and gave structure to Gipuzkoan community life.

Community and House

Gipuzkoan culture under the ancien régime was based on community and specifically domestic community. It was not a community of individuals in the modern sense of the word, but rather one of legal subjects, that is, it was not individuals as such who had rights and obligations. It was not a society with individual liberties but a group of humans that thought of themselves as a community made up of units like the house, belonging to professions or a confraternity. It was within those units, with reference to them and to the community as a whole, that people, men and women, gained status as a master, lady, servant, son and heir, marriageable daughter, bachelor, or spinster (Clavero 1986, 78–79). Such status awareness also explained people's expectations about life, social status, and to what extent they could take charge of their own lives.

This was a culture in which the quality, hierarchy, and privileges of individuals were defined through pertaining to one specific community or unit, and by distinguishing who was resident and who was not, whether one was head of the household or belonged to rest of the domestic community.

It was a community with a moral economy that regulated exchanges and relationships between its constituent parts. It was a moral economy in two senses, first in that it referred to a "natural" order, which in Gipuzkoa under the ancien régime was religious, and which made a certain code of conduct obligatory—this happened by way of binding individuals through stronger bonds than those of mere contractual relationships (Thompson 1993); and second, in that it also functioned as a gift economy (Hespanha 1993), that is, it relied on exchanges among people of different statuses. Those in higher positions offered favors, and in exchange received services and loyalties, while those in lower positions could expect to be protected by the former. As a result, a mutual dependency emerged. This moral economy, in contrast to the way in which exchanges work in capitalist societies, established a framework of legitimate behavior that bound both the powerful, obliged by a paternalist idea of power, and the powerless, who received favors. In Gipuzkoa, the framework of such an economy was formalized in the fueros. Those people who took part in several popular uprisings in the eighteenth century believed that the province's patricians had betrayed their part of the obligations of this moral economy and demanded a return to the old praxis (Iñurrategui Rodríguez 1996, 179–84).

The basic community unit was the house. The house was the place in which people were born, raised, learned to behave, and were disciplined. It also framed their expectations about life, depending on their position within the domestic framework. The house was the unit of reproduction and production, a place in which the public and the private became one; the house was a legal entity or subject. The house gave individuals their names and placed them in a community of residents.

The house as a whole, with its estate and rights, its name and status, was passed on as a unit. Only one of the family sons or daughters could inherit, while the other siblings were given dowries or advance gifts. This way of organizing succession guaranteed the continuity of the domestic unit but also made it necessary to find a place for other sons and daughters (Oliveri Korta 2001, 79–154). This created considerable inequality between the heir or heiress and the other siblings. This custom of inheriting has been connected to population pressure and poor soil quality in Gipuzkoa; it also had an impact on emigration and was closely related to the creation of universal nobility (Otazu 1986, 110–12).

There were hierarchical family relationships in the house with the *pater familias* as head. Domestic relationships were governed, to a large extent, by the authority of the master and (to a somewhat lesser degree) the lady of the house. Decisions that affected the house's survival and thus the domestic group's economic, social, and symbolic survival, including each individual's expectations about life, depended on both parents, although the final decisions always rested with the *pater*. Successions, marriages, and types of work were all decisions under his control. In such a system the very idea and the expectations of what individual liberty meant were very different from ours.

In exchange, the house protected its members. The successive masters of the house were obliged to protect, find a place for, and feed its members (this can be seen in the clauses of marriage contracts and wills in which the heir or heiress took responsibility for parents and unmarried brothers and sisters). It was an economy centered on the survival of the group, in which all the group members had to play their part. Far from an idyllic picture, the house was a place with tensions and conflicts over authority, inheritances, and other matters in which relationships were asymmetrical and in which questioning or infringing the norms was punishable (for example, by being disinherited).

This way of interpreting family life is connected to notions of wise domestic management ("oeconomy," from the Greek *oikos*, "house"), which in Europe has a long history (Brunner 1970, 133–64). Its functioning is based on regarding the house as a place of primary importance in political terms.

In this sense, there exists a discourse about the correct maintenance of the house that is closely connected to a specific notion of communitarian management, about the running of public affairs, and about which people should be in charge. The correct management of the house, which guaranteed order and peace, required a competent administrator, in control of public affairs: the *pater familias* (Iñurrategui Rodríguez 1998, 21; Frigo 1985, 165). This arrangement was accepted as representing the "natural" order. As the house was the primary unit for the societal integration process, maintaining order there very much reflected both the social and political order as well as public and private affairs—an arrangement symbolized by the leading role of the *pater familias* (Achón Insausti 2001, 128–29).

Nobility, Patrimony, and Management in Gipuzkoa

Since those houses, represented by the *pater familias* (who in turn were nobles and residents in Gipuzkoa), were regarded as the basic units in the province's community, how did this community of nobles run its public affairs?

As pointed out above, the creation of universal nobility in Gipuzkoa was closely connected to residence as the link through which the community and the creation of boroughs exercised its legal authority over men and land (Marín Paredes 2001, 139–60). As part of this process, the communities of residents had the right to govern the boroughs and the province, which was understood to be a community of communities. But in what way and by which residents?

As we have learned, universal nobility made the status of all residents of Gipuzkoa equal. However, it did not prevent the existence of differences. In the community of nobles there were people of "principle," to use the term used in documents from the period.[2] Those people of "principle" stood out, of course, because of their material wealth, be it houses, land, income, and symbolic wealth, based on social prestige, or linked to a name or some other form of relational capital.

Differences in patrimony related to town taxes that the residents of Gipuzkoa had to pay (traceable through archival documentation of those taxes) and these were considerable (Piquero

---

2. "Said he knows the said Pedro Martinez of Mallea and knows him to be the master of the house of Eyaga in the Durango area and to be a noble and a person of principle of great quality and quantity." Condes de Pañoflorida Archives (henceforth CPA) box 80, file 2017, s/f.

Zarauz and Díaz de Durana 1998, 523–56). The differences were reflected in the councils, and, consequently, in municipal management institutions.

The ability to take part in the real management of the boroughs was soon limited to a smaller number of residents. In the boroughs, the real management of municipal policies was carried out by groups of *regidores* (municipal officials) who presided over the crucial town meetings at which the people elected to public office met annually. This was often at the expense of the *concejo abierto* (open council), which included a wider range of residents and which continued still to meet, despite its decline. Over time, however, and particularly from the sixteenth century onward, the possibility of electing and being elected became increasingly linked to one's estate.

From the end of the fifteenth century onward and in the course of the sixteenth century there was a series of reforms in the electoral systems through which the boroughs of Gipuzkoa chose their *regidores* (García Fernández 1998, 365–98). Although their members and electoral procedures varied from borough to borough, there were some common characteristics. These reforms led to the exclusion of the *parientes mayores* and the factions from politics once and for all. A series of requisites was drawn up: in order to be elected one had to be a noble, know how to speak and write in Spanish (which, by itself, excluded the vast majority), live within the borough walls, and be *abonado* or financially independent (Truchuelo García 1997, 80–83). The latter requisite meant that it was necessary to have a minimum quantity of possessions in order to qualify to vote and a minimum quantity of goods, generally a larger one, in order to be elected. During the sixteenth century this requisite was regulated by the *millares*, which were a type of estate census in which residents' economic resources were recorded and, depending on the data (along with other factors), from which those who qualified were declared eligible to take part in elections and/or become municipal officials (Achón Insausti 1995, 251–302). The electoral system's real representativeness, then, when determined by such qualifications, was not as wide as might seem at first (Porres Marijuán 2001, 169–234). Both voters and, to an even greater extent, those who could be elected to public positions, belonged to the most powerful stratum of society while a significant sector of the residents, whose extent cannot be easily determined, was unable to take part in the borough political system. Gradually, the people in public office started to become the patricians of whom Larramendi spoke in the eighteenth century (1950, 155).

Belonging to the *regimiento* (group of municipal officials) meant being able to control a series of resources in relation to what was regarded as pursuing the common good, bearing in mind the moral economy outlined in the foral system. However, the common good was often confused with the officials' own interests. The *bosques concejiles* (council or municipal forests) can serve as an example. These forests could be communal (open to all and freely used by all the residents) or private (being communal resources managed by the councils, which one could make use of in exchange for a payment). Throughout the ancien régime, from the mid-sixteenth century onward, we can observe a gradual process of acquisition and privatization of these woods by tax paying and voting residents and their families (Aragón Ruano 2001, 48–50, 91–97).

At the same time, it was the boroughs that made up the province, and it was representatives chosen by the groups of municipal officials in the boroughs who took part in general provincial assemblies. Those representatives tended to belong to the same group of residents that managed the groups of municipal officials, and it was also they who were in the regional government, which governed in-between assemblies (Truchuelo García 2004, 35). As a consequence of their privileged access and position, which many of them had in relation to the crown, they were in a position to use their political influence without always holding a higher provincial position. In short, a connection with the monarchy served to obtain favors, influence, and information. In order to further its own power, the province itself made use of the influence of Gipuzkoans at the royal court on several occasions. A typical example in the sixteenth century is that of Juan de Idiáquez, who acted as a protector for Gipuzkoans and Gipuzkoa at the Court (Truchuelo García 2004, 592).

The result was that besides controlling political power in the province, official municipal positions came to be dominated by people from the same lineages. Here, the borough of Bergara is a case in point (Oliveri Korta 2009, 478–95, 508–12).

Such functioning was consistent with the political thinking of the time, which maintained that the *patres familias* were particularly well qualified to manage communities since they had proven themselves running their own houses. One thing seemed to follow another: better marriages led to larger estates, which in turn meant greater service to the king—and to God. In practice an estate (in the material, symbolic, and relational sense) was a stratifying factor in the noble community.

This all begs the question of who were these people of "principle" running the councils and the province's political institutions? The immediate answer must be: residents who possessed the largest estates, who owned large houses or farmsteads with hills and land, and who had income. They were connected, to a considerable extent, to the crown's economic, bureaucratic, and military structures—all connections that constituted or helped to accumulate considerable relational capital. It should be added here that much of their wealth was accumulated outside the province, in territories in which universal nobility proved to be particularly useful (in trade linked to the Americas, for example). The acquisition of wealth allowed them to become *regidores*; marry well, even into families of the *parientes mayores*; and have access to resources that most residents did not have at all or at best only to a lesser extent.

Most wealthy residents were related to each other. Some of the most binding relationships in the Gipuzkoan community came through marriage (marriage meant direct influence and access to property; it created kinship alliances that brought houses together). In praxis this meant that marriages were negotiated by the masters of houses and their relatives. Matrimonial exchanges were made in connection with the scope of the (material and symbolic) estates possessed by the houses. An offer of inheriting a house had to be reciprocated with a dowry, which depended on what was on offer. Usually, the marriage market was governed by norms in which the stratification of estates governed marriage exchanges (Arpal Poblador 1979, 160–61). This meant that residents were often inclined to follow matrimonial strategies that involved marrying among themselves. The praxis of creating and recreating kinship relations was clearly visible from the sixteenth century onward. It increased during the ancien régime, resulting in hereditary estates that became concentrated in fewer and fewer hands as the result of such inheritance practices. The accumulation of wealth achieved through trade and pursuing careers in royal service added to the already accumulated wealth derived from inheritance and marriage strategies (Otazu 1986, 328–29). Such estate accumulation was accompanied by a continuing loss or disappearance of small properties. It also kept small property owners in financial dependency and debt since it was the people of "principle" who lent them the money (Oliveri Korta 2009, 401–4).

This process led to an oligarchization of the councils and an accumulation of estates. Symbolically, this was expressed by signs and symbols of distinction, starting from the use of the formal titles "don" and "doña" to the purchase of luxury items, the use of dresses and jewels, or the wearing of military uniforms (Otazu and Díaz de Durana 2008, 595–605). It was most obvious in the form of Catholic charity and donations to found convents, carry out charitable works, commission works of art, and so on. The people of "principle," as *patres familias*, were obliged to favor Christian charity; in turn, it gave them symbolic power (Oliveri Korta 2009, 495–508).

Such remarkable distinctions were not unknown in Gipuzkoan culture in the ancien régime. In the sixteenth century, the nobles had become the richest people in the province and were able to set up their own primogenitures with their resources. Pedro Martínez de Mallea and Catalina de Araiz (he the son of an iron merchant and she the daughter of a bookkeeper, Martín Sánchez de Araiz) expressed their point of view well when they founded the primogeniture of Mallea in the mid-sixteenth century:

> it is necessary and convenient for kings and princes to have very honorable subjects in their kingdoms and territories and the more subjects and serfs a prince has, the greater he is, his greatness and power shining through them; in addition to this, great advantage is to be had from people and relatives of lineages whose main house is still in existence and in which all other people see themselves in a single person, protected and cared for by him, the opposite of which is to be seen, and is seen every day, in the houses and estates that are split up and divided into many parts . . . the philosopher said that nobody could be wholly virtuous if he did not possess riches, without

which the virtues of liberality and generosity can neither be achieved nor carried out . . . in addition to that, it is well known how many churches, hospitals, and charitable donations, and other pious works have been made and are made in the world by rich, wealthy people and how much worship and Christian religion has been possible thanks to them, and all of this would end if all people were common and if there were no rich and honorable people who wanted and could carry out such good works.[3]

Servicio a la casa, a la república (al rey) y a Dios: Serving the house, the republic (the king), and God—basing themselves on such premises, the Malleas and other families built fortunes that would eventually elevate them socially and politically to a higher elite-of-the-elite status within the community of already noble Gipuzkoans.

Conclusion

During the ancien régime universal nobility gave all the residents of Gipuzkoa the same legal status and defined a community of equals in legal terms. However, the very fact of putting this into practice excluded some people from the community.

Universal nobility emerged in a culture that defined itself largely in terms of community and moral economy. However, not everybody was equal in this. The ideas of nobility were not in opposition to existing inequalities and hierarchies; they just helped to organize the relationships among people in different situations in a particular way. While it defended the nobility of all residents, it permitted for considerable inequalities among individuals, depending on their status and prestige.

In practice, shared nobility did not exclude differences, and those differences made their way into politics. Major differences arose when estates became a stratifying factor in the noble community. The differences in estates and the building of preeminent positions were compatible with universal nobility. Be that as it may, the existence of considerable economic differences (and of expectations and ways of life) during the ancien régime did not cast any doubts over the custom of shared nobility (although it

---

3. CPA box 80 file 1999, folios 20r.–20v. (front and back).

could be asked if it meant the same thing for everyone). In fact, the more "principled" nobles helped to maintain that type of nobility: they were representatives of the institutions that decided how it should be proven, and it was they who promoted the discourse of noble status. It was thus no accident that they also turned out to be the main beneficiaries of the system.

References

Achón Insausti, José Angel. 1995. *"A voz de Concejo": Linaje y corporación urbana en la constitución de la Provincia de Gipuzkoa*. Donostia-San Sebastián: Gipuzkoako Foru Aldundia-Diputación Foral de Gipuzkoa.

———. 1998. "República sin tiranos, Provincia libre: Sobre cómo llegó a concebirse al pariente mayor banderizo como enemigo de las libertades de las repúblicas Guipuzcoanas." In *La lucha de bandos en el País Vasco: De los Parientes Mayores a la Hidalguía Universal: Guipúzcoa, de los bandos a la Provincia (s. XIV a XVI)*, edited by José Ramón Díaz de Durana. Bilbao: Universidad del País Vasco-Euskal Herriko Unibertsitatea.

———. 2001. "La 'Casa Guipúzcoa': Sobre cómo una comunidad territorial llegó a concebirse en términos domésticos durante el Antiguo Régimen." In *Redes familiares y patronazgo: Aproximación al entramado social del País Vasco y Navarra en el Antiguo Régimen (siglos XV–XIX)*, directed by José María Imízcoz Beunza. Bilbao: Universidad del País Vasco-Euskal Herriko Unibertsitatea.

Aragón Ruano, Alvaro. 2001. *El bosque Guipuzcoano en la Edad Moderna: Aprovechamiento, ordenamiento legal y conflictividad*. Donostia-San Sebastián: Sociedad de Ciencias Aranzadi-Aranzadi Zientzi Elkartea.

Arpal Poblador, Jesús. 1979. *La sociedad tradicional en el País Vasco: El estamento hidalgo en Guipúzcoa*. San Sebastián: L. Haranburu.

Brunner, Otto. 1970. "La 'casa come complesso' e l'antica 'economica' europea." In *Per una nuova Storia Costituzionale e Soziale*. Milano: Editrice Vita e Pensiero.

Clavero, Bartolomé. 1986. *Tantas personas como Estados: Por una antropología política de la historia europea*. Madrid: Tecnos.

Díaz de Durana, José Ramón. 2004. *La otra nobleza, escuderos e hidalgos sin nombre y sin historia: Hidalgos e hidalguía universal en el*

País Vasco al final de la Edad Media (1250–1525). Bilbao: Universidad del País Vasco-Euskal Herriko Unibertsitatea.

Frigo, Daniela. 1985. *"Il Padre de Famiglia": Governo della casa e governo civile nella tradizione e dell'economica tra cinque e seicento*. Rome: Bulzoni.

García Fernández, Ernesto. 1998. "La creación de nuevos sistemas de organización política de las villas Guipuzcoanas al final de la Edad Media." In *La lucha de bandos en el País Vasco: De los Parientes Mayores a la Hidalguía Universal: Guipúzcoa, de los bandos a la Provincia (s. XIV a XVI)*, edited by José Ramón Díaz de Durana. Bilbao: Universidad del País Vasco-Euskal Herriko Unibertsitatea.

Hernández Franco, Juan. 1996. *Cultura y limpieza de sangre en la España moderna: Puritate sanguinis*. Murcia: Universidad de Murcia.

Hespanha, António Manuel. 1993. *La gracia del derecho: Economía de la cultura en la Edad Moderna*. Translated by Ana Cañellas Haurie. Madrid: Centro de Estudios Constitucionales.

Iñurrategui Rodríguez, José María. 1996. *Monstruo indómito, rusticidad y fiereza de costumbres: Foralidad y conflicto social al final del Antiguo Régimen en Guipúzcoa*. Bilbao: UPV/EHU.

———. 1998. *La Gracia y la República. El lenguaje político de la teología católica y el Príncipe Cristiano de Pedro de Ribadeneyra*. Madrid: UNED.

Larramendi, Manuel de. 1950. *Corografía de Guipúzcoa*. Buenos Aires: Ekin.

Marín Paredes, José Antonio. 1998a. "¿Qué es un Pariente Mayor? El ejemplo de los señores de Oñaz y Loyola." In *La lucha de bandos en el País Vasco: De los Parientes Mayores a la Hidalguía Universal: Guipúzcoa, de los bandos a la Provincia (s. XIV a XVI)*, edited by José Ramón Díaz de Durana. Bilbao: Universidad del País Vasco-Euskal Herriko Unibertsitatea.

———. 1998b. *"Semejante Pariente Mayor": Parentesco, solar, comunidad y linaje en la institución de un Pariente Mayor en Gipuzkoa: Los señores del solar de Oñaz y Loyola (siglos XIV–XVI)*. Donostia-San Sebastián: Gipuzkoako Foru Aldundia-Diputación Foral de Gipuzkoa.

———. 2001. "'Los servicios y los deservicios de los menores sean derechamente pesados por los mayores. . .': Del uso del parentesco en la Gipuzkoa del siglo XV como criterio de estructuración comunitaria." In *Redes familiares y patronazgo: Aproximación al entramado social del País Vasco y Navarra en el Antiguo Régimen (siglos XV–XIX)*, directed by José María Imízcoz Beunza. Bilbao: Universidad del País Vasco-Euskal Herriko Unibertsitatea.

Martínez de Isasti, Lope. 1972. *Compendio historial de la M.N. y M.L. Provincia de Guipúzcoa*. Bilbao: La Gran Enciclopedia Vasca.

Mora Afán, Juan Carlos, and David Zapirain Karrika. 1996. "Exclusión social en los siglos XVI y XVII: Esclavos, judíos y 'portugueses' en la Gipuzkoa moderna." *Vasconia* 24: 157–92.

Oliveri Korta, Oihane. 2001. *Mujer y herencia en el estamento hidalgo Guipuzcoano durante el Antiguo Régimen (siglos XVI–XVIII)*. Donostia-San Sebastián: Gipuzkoako Foru Aldundia-Diputación Foral de Gipuzkoa.

———. 2009. *Mujer, casa y estamento en la Gipuzkoa del siglo XVI*. Donostia-San Sebastián: Gipuzkoako Foru Aldundia-Diputación Foral de Gipuzkoa.

———. 2010. "El gran gobierno de la dicha señora. Economía doméstica y mujer en el estamento hidalgo Guipuzcoano." In *Economía doméstica y redes sociales en el Antiguo Régimen*, edited by José María Imízcoz Beunza and Oihane Oliveri Korta. Madrid: Silex.

Otazu, Alfonso de. 1986. *El "igualitarismo" vasco: Mito y realidad*. 2nd ed. San Sebastián: Txertoa.

Otazu, Alfonso de, and José Ramón Díaz de Durana. 2008. *El espíritu emprendedor de los vascos*. Madrid: Silex.

Piquero Zarauz, Santiago, and José Ramón Díaz de Durana. 1998. "De la fiscalidad municipal a la sociedad: Notas sobre las desigualdades económicas y cotributivas en Guipúzcoa (siglos XV–XVI)." In *La lucha de bandos en el País Vasco: De los Parientes Mayores a la Hidalguía Universal: Guipúzcoa, de los bandos a la Provincia (s. XIV a XVI)*, edited by José Ramón Díaz de Durana. Bilbao: Universidad del País Vasco-Euskal Herriko Unibertsitatea.

Porres Marijuán, María Rosario. 2001. "Insaculación, régimen municipal urbano y control regio en la Monarquía de los Austrias: Representación efectiva y mitificación del método electivo en los territorios forales." In *El poder en Europa y América: Mitos, tópicos y realidades*, edited by Ernesto García Fernández. Bilbao: Universidad del País Vasco-Euskal Herriko Unibertsitatea.

Thompson, E. P. 1993. *Customs in Common: Studies in Traditional Popular Culture*. New York: New Press.

Truchuelo García, Susana. 1997. *La representación de las corporaciones locales Guipuzcoanas en el entramado político provincial (siglos XVI–XVII)*. Donostia-San Sebastián: Diputación Foral de Gipuzkoa.

———. 2004. *Gipuzkoa y el poder real en la Alta Edad Moderna*. Donostia-San Sebastián: Gipuzkoako Foru Aldundia-Diputación Foral de Gipuzkoa.

Zapirain Karrika, David. 2008. *Gizarte kontrolaren aldaketak: Poliziaren sorrera Gipuzkoan, 1688–1808*. Donsotia: Deustuko Unibertsitatea.

5

The Idea of Basque Egalitarianism in the Nineteenth Century

Coro Rubio Pobes

[The Basques] are faithful and honest, and capable of much disinterested attachment. . . . No people on earth are prouder than the Basques, but theirs is a kind of republican pride. They have no nobility amongst them, and no one will acknowledge a superior. The poorest car man is as proud as the governor of Tolosa. "He is more powerful than I," he will say, "but I am of as good blood; perhaps hereafter I may become a governor myself." They abhor servitude, at least out of their own country; and though circumstances frequently oblige them to seek masters, it is very rare to find them filling the places of common domestics; they are stewards, secretaries, accountants, etc. True it is, that it was my own fortune to obtain a Basque domestic; but then he always treated me more as an equal than a master. (Borrow [1843] 1923, ch. 37, 527–28)

English traveler George Borrow described the Basques in a telling manner in the 1830s. Borrow was an unusual bohemian adventurer and Protestant bible salesman who wrote about his impressions as he traveled around Spain. His book, published in 1843, became

* This study was carried out thanks to the support provided by the University of the Basque Country, UPV/EHU, Research Group GIU 14/30.

a spectacular bestseller. Writing about the Basques, Borrow made use of one of the most successful and lasting stereotypes, namely that the Basques had lived in an egalitarian society since ancient times, and that Basque society had kept intact while the rest of the Spanish monarchy remained marked by a rigid social class and stratification system. The idea of social egalitarianism among the Basques became a consolidated cliché, but it is hard to find a reality that corresponded to it.

From Universal *Hidalguía* to the Idea of Egalitarianism: Myth and Reality

The idea of social egalitarianism was closely linked to the notion of universal *hidalguía* (lower nobility), that is, that the Basques were nobles (*hidalgos*), an essential component of the social ideology on which traditional Basque society relied during the ancien régime. In order to provide an answer to the violent cycle that had marked Basque society in medieval times and particularly during the War of the Bands in the fifteenth century, almost all of the inhabitants of the Atlantic valleys in Álava and Navarre, and all the inhabitants of Guipúzcoa and Biscay became regarded as being of hidalgo status.[1] This extending of hidalgo status relied on the supposed ethnic purity of the familiar lineages of these territories (Martínez Gorriarán 1993, 13–14). With regard to the Spanish Basque provinces—or Provincias Vascongadas, the territory we will examine in this chapter—the status of collective hidalguía was recorded in the *fueros* (provincial consuetudinary laws that regulated the intra-community life and the place of the territory inside the monarchy) of Biscay and Guipúzcoa, but not in Álava, whose *Cuaderno de Leyes y Ordenanzas de la Muy Noble y Muy Leal Provincia de Álava* (Book of laws and regulations of the very noble and very loyal province of Álava, 1463) did not mention it. The *Nueva Recopilación de los Fueros de Guipúzcoa* (New summary of the fueros of Guipúzcoa, 1696) states in section 2, chapter 2:

---

1. I have chosen to use the nineteenth-century historical spellings for the Basque provinces of Gipuzkoa and Araba (that is, Guipúzcoa and Álava), not their current, official spellings. For Bizkaia and Nafarroa, I use the historical English spellings (Biscay and Navarre). In the same way, I use the most usual nineteenth-century term for referring to the whole of Araba, Gipuzkoa, and Bizkaia: Provincias Vascongadas. Basque words and the names of territories and cities in texts cited are written literally as they appear in the documents.

> [Guipuzcoan hidalguía is] based on blood, being a question of lineage and having right to this dignity as inheritors of the human race's first fathers; . . . it is general and uniform for all descendants of ancestral homes, not having been granted by any King of Spain . . . but rather conserved and passed on from father to son without interruption from the first inhabitants of the Province until the present time.

Various Biscayan and Guipuzcoan writers, such as Juan Martínez de Zaldibia, Baltasar de Echave, and Andrés de Poza, justified and defended universal nobility in the sixteenth and seventeenth centuries. The idea of universal hidalguía was also spread further by foreign travelers. For example, French priest Joseph Delaporte, who visited the country in 1755, observed: "There is perfect equality among the citizens and the nobility's only authority is that of persuasion" (Delaporte 1772, 365). The Basques' universal nobility became a mark of distinction that differentiated the province's community from those living outside of it, and therefore it was an element of social cohesion and an identity referent. Eventually, the whole territory became identified with this privilege. Thus, universal hidalguía was used in the eighteenth century by the provinces of Biscay and Guipúzcoa in order to consolidate their own jurisdictional space, since the *Juntas Generales* (traditional provincial assemblies) and *Diputaciones forales* (provincial governments) had to approve the recognition of hidalguía (Portillo 1991, 352–54). In the case of Álava, the discourse that founded provincial jurisdiction referred to the hidalguía of those members of the noble elite who signed the Pact of Arriaga (1332) that incorporated part of the territory of the province into the crown of Castile under Alfonso XI. However, from the start of the nineteenth century, Álava also tried to connect the ideas of universal hidalguía and territory, following the example of Biscay and Guipúzcoa, in order to prevent other jurisdictions from interfering with its laws (Portillo 1991, 362–78). This connection between universal hidalguía and territory had a significant political function: to defend the Provincias Vascongadas from the crown's increasing military and tax demands. The reason for using this argument was simple: if all the people of Guipúzcoa, Biscay, and Álava were of noble status, the provinces would also be exempt from military and tax obligations, just like the nobles of Castile. Consequently, although the abovementioned 1463 *Book of Laws* of Álava did not include the concept of universal nobility, the *Compendio Foral de la Provincia de Álava* (Álava provincial law summary), written by Ramón Ortiz de Zárate and published in 1858, stated on page 86:

> Only the people of the Provincias Vascongadas and, consequently, the people of Álava, have linked nobility to the land, the territory, and have extended it to include everyone born in its valleys and on its hills. Instead of privileges that offend, instead of modern leveling-down equality, we encounter in Álava a type of equality that raised people up and ennobled everybody, without offending or lowering anybody— the equality of original nobility. All people from Álava are equally noble. There are neither patrician nor plebeians here, only a people of brothers. (Portillo 1991, 378)

Notwithstanding the success of the notion of universal hidalguía in the Provincias Vascongadas, which, as Ortiz de Zárate's words reflected, metamorphosed into an idea of social egalitarianism, we should by no means assume the existence of a truly egalitarian society during the ancien régime. Nor did such a truly egalitarian society exist in the nineteenth century, despite the survival of this idea.

In the 1970s, Basque historiography started to address the so-called myth of Basque egalitarianism, which hid the social reality of an actually existing stratified society. Alfonso Otazu (1973) and Jesús Arpal (1979) wrote the classic texts in relation to that myth. Writing about the sixteenth, seventeenth, and eighteenth centuries, Arpal pointed out the existence of a stratified society consisting of four levels: first, the hidalgo class "whose legitimacy was based on neighborhood and ancestral familiar lineage"; second, and above it, there was an oligarchy with economic and social power, the *notables,* and noble lineages, the *lords*; third, below the hidalgos, a small-holding tenant peasant group; and finally, we find some marginalized minority groups (Arpal 1979, 282). One of the most renowned Spanish social history experts of the period, Antonio Domínguez Ortiz, confirmed that: "in the Basque Country there were hidalgos and commoners, lords and vassals" (Domínguez Ortiz 1988, 168). Although the same author recognized that the existence of hidalguía was of an unparalleled importance throughout the whole territory of the Spanish monarchy, he also added that this fact should not be exaggerated. According to the 1787 census, no more than 48 percent of the population of Biscay was hidalgo, and no more than 42 percent of the population of Guipúzcoa (ibid., 162). In Álava, the hidalgo stratum was always smaller than it was in its two sister provinces. Thus, Álava may be regarded as a land of transition, located as it were, between the maritime Provincias Vascongadas and Castile. Wilhelm von Humboldt, who traveled to the Provincias Vascongadas in 1801, even pointed out that "in Álava there is nobility and a *Third Estate*. Nine tenths of the population may belong to the latter" (Humboldt 1925, 652). This confirms that the hidalgos were a minority in Álava, that hidalguía was not universal. In fact, the society of this territory was more rigidly stratified than Guipúzcoa and Biscay.[2] More proof that nobility was not universal in Álava is the fact that in 1817 the Council of Castile rejected a request sent to Fernando VII to acknowledge the status of collective nobility for the third estate in Álava – specifically, for 1,700 peasants. It concluded that, "it is not appropriate to grant the 1,700 peasants in the province of Álava the status they have requested, making them equal to others in order to obtain honorary posts and the right to attend the Juntas Generales."[3]

Although the Guipúzcoa and Biscay fueros mentioned the universal hidalguía of all the natives of their territories as long as they pertained to or were descendants of ancestral homes, such status was of no legal value unless the applicant was able to prove it at court (something that only a few people could afford). Only people who could prove such links could inscribe themselves in the *vecinos concejantes* registration (residents who paid taxes and voted in local elections) and enjoy the prerogatives that the right brought with it, such as, for example, the possibility of obtaining a public office. Those people who were not able to do so—either because they had not been born in the province or because, even though born there, they did not have enough money for the court case—were regarded as belonging to the third estate. As Humboldt explained in his travel notes, there was a list of direct taxes payers in every town: "to be taken off this list, a document, which proved noble status, had to be presented and therefore

---

2. However, there were particular situations and cases, such as in Tierra de Ayala, in which people who could not prove that they were hidalgos were not allowed to have the right of *vecindad* (residency).
3. Archivo del Territorio Histórico de Álava, DH 25-12.

there arose disputes about hidalguía between those who wished to avoid paying taxes" (Humboldt 1925, 191). In other words, only through proven hidalguía could one enjoy nobility's prerogatives. However, most of the natives in these territories still took enormous pride in talking about their blood, a fact well recorded by the travelers who visited the country at the beginning of the nineteenth century:

> To speak, however, with becoming respect to this part of the country, the farm-houses should be called gentlemen's seats, for their owners, although they walk with long staves in their hands, often barefoot, and clad like rustics, . . . assert, notwithstanding, their claim to be called *hidalgos conocidos*, or gentlemen of distinguished families. They are as accurate in their pedigrees as a Welsh genealogist, and sum up, with all imaginable ease, a long line of smoky ancestors as far removed as Pelagius. Some even will venture to strike as high as Tubal, nephew of Noah . . . . The great boast of the Biscayan is, that he has no Moorish nor Jewish blood in his veins, and they proudly style themselves *gente limpísima*. (Quoted by Santoyo 1978, 240)

In order to keep up this pride in their blood origins, it was very important to guarantee that it was not mixed with that of "people of bad races." Jews, Moors, black people, half-castes, Agotes, and Gypsies were prohibited from settling or living in Basque towns, which is not to say that those groups were not present at all. People who were not native to the territories and who wished to live and settle in them had to demonstrate the pureness of their blood, bringing testimony to be approved by the town council at which they were requesting residence.

Access to economic and political privileges was thus reserved for those of proven hidalguía, a status that became the determining factor in terms of social differentiation. This is a very different situation when compared to the cliché about egalitarianism and the picture that travelers' tales often offer. A good place to study the contrast between the country's image and its social reality is its system of access to political power. To go to court in order to prove one's hidalguía and to gain through that very process the right to join the local council was not the only way to get into public office. The source of provincial political power resided in the town councils, characterized by their organizational diversity and by the fact that they remained under direct monarchical control at least until the first half of the nineteenth century. As a matter of fact, during this period a new category of town council, termed *ayuntamiento foral,* was implemented to leave local councils under provincial governments' control (Martínez Rueda 1994). It was the councils that elected the representatives who would be sent to the provincial assemblies, the Juntas Generales, and who, in turn, had the power to select the members of the provincial governments, the Diputaciones forales, and the provincial officers, the only exception being the representative of the crown (*corregidor*) in Biscay and Guipúzcoa, who was appointed directly by the crown. In order to become a representative in the Juntas Generales it was necessary to be a native and to still live in its territory. The person had to be at least twenty-five years old, he had to be literate in Spanish (a requisite that could only be met by people who had received an education), and be sufficiently settled in the sense of being the owner of some real estate and wealth (forty thousand *maravedís* would qualify in Álava while the amount remained unspecified in Biscay and Guipúzcoa). There were similar conditions attached to being a member of the Diputación foral. In order to become a member of the council, one had to be a vecino concejante, that is, a proven hidalgo and, to become a mayor or syndic, it was a requisite to be a *millarista* (a resident who was a local proprietor of real estate). For the latter offices, the size of real estate required varied from town to town (in the small towns of Biscay it was sufficient to own some land). Although each council had its own regulations and the oligarchy did not hold an absolute monopoly over municipal offices,[4] the latter did control the most important posts. To put it more succinctly, municipal power, the base of the pyramid of power, was in the hands of an elite. The data speaks for itself: toward the middle of the eighteenth century the number of potentially electable

4.   In Biscay the post of municipal official (*regidor*), for which one only had to be a resident, was not particularly sought after by the dignitaries, who clearly preferred to be mayors or syndics. In fact, the post was quite often held by tenant peasants: "most of the elected municipal officials were not given the honorary title *don*, which was the symbolic difference between the gentry and the other inhabitants." In order to become mayor or syndic one had to own real estate, know how to read and write, and belong to the "known gentry [*hijosdalgo notorios*]." People who had worked in "mechanical or lowly" jobs could not be elected (Martínez Rueda 1994, 185–86).

millaristas in San Sebastián was 1.8 percent of the population and in Vitoria 1.15 percent. In towns such as Bilbao, the requirement was to receive rent of at least one thousand ducats from real estate in order to become a *millarista*, while in smaller towns such as Portugalete six hundred ducats seemed sufficient (Madariaga 2002, 346). In fact, during the eighteenth century a process of oligarchization occurred. It led to the removal of open councils (*concejos abiertos*, a house-owning residents' assembly existed almost all over the Basque Country until the end of the fifteenth century), especially after 1766, and to an increase in the conditions that a person had to meet for obtaining the right to hold a municipal office (Martínez Rueda 1994, 73–77, 91–103, 235–37).

This is all to show that Basque society under the ancien régime was not an egalitarian society. In contrast, it was a stratified society. There were nobles and commoners, and while differences were less extreme than in other areas of the Spanish monarchy, political power was reserved for the local and provincial elites. In the course of the nineteenth century things did not change much. Thus, it would be a mistake to conceive as egalitarian the Basque society transiting from traditional community to a modern bourgeois society during the nineteenth century.[5] It is perhaps worth noting that until 1864 it was prohibited for people who had worked in mechanical jobs or retail to become representatives in the Juntas Generales of Biscay. In all three provinces the prohibition also applied to the clergy and lawyers, typical representatives of the urban middle class. In fact, the prohibition on lawyers was not removed until the 1850s.

Political Power and Society in the Provincias Vascongadas in Revolutionary Times

The impact of the liberal revolution in the Provincias Vascongadas, unlike in the rest of Spain, did not lead to the end of the landowning nobility's social and political hegemony. The revolution made the nobility disappear as a category in the official census but did not affect its predominance in the country's social struc-

---

5. The modern class-based society only came into being in the last third of the century, due to the consolidation of the emergence of a modern middle class and the creation of a working class as a result of the enforced and accelerated industrialization process in Biscay and Guipúzcoa.

ture. In the Provincias Vascongadas, the *jauntxos* (landowning hidalgos) and *handikis* (titled nobility) still controlled political power and even managed to keep hidalguía as a requisite for joining a local council for a long time, whereas in the rest of Spain old discriminations based on blood had long disappeared. This was an effect of the specific way of the liberal state formation in the Provincias Vascongadas.[6] The Basque elites passionately resisted any imposition from outside, which they feared would lead to the disappearance of the fueros. The elites claimed that the Basque fueros were compatible with the Spanish Constitution and that the Basques as a people were proven to have strong emotional ties with their fueros, as had become evident during the First Carlist War (1833–1839). In addition to other reasons, this kind of argumentation enabled them to keep the fueros alive in the midst of an emerging new liberal state. Although these traditional laws were progressively modified, and although there were also critical moments in which they were almost in danger of disappearing entirely, the parliamentary law of October 25, 1839 recognized their legal status within the new constitutional framework. However, such recognition was enabled "notwithstanding the Monarchy's constitutional unity," and empowered the Spanish Parliament to adapt the fueros to the constitution.[7] This meant that until 1876–1877, when Biscay's, Guipúzcoa's, and Álava's fueros were removed permanently (those of the province of Navarre had already been removed in 1841), there was an unusual coexistence of *foral* and constitutional institutions in those territories. The traditional elites managed to control both. While the upper strata of the trading middle class managed to win some ground in terms of political representation in 1850 and 1868, most of the population remained excluded from the possibility of gaining access to public office. Both filters imposed by the fueros and the liberal restricted franchises proved to be very useful for that purpose.

The municipal areas illustrate this process well. Changes announced at the beginning of the century never took place. When, as a result of Napoleon's invasion of the Iberian Peninsula, the

---

6.   I have researched this in depth in Rubio Pobes (1996).
7.   Later, Sabino Arana (the founder of Basque nationalism) referred to this law as the abolition of the fueros. See Rubio Pobes (2012).

Bayonne Statute was passed to govern Spain (July 1808), the requirement of being a noble to be able to obtain civil and religious public positions and military rank was abolished. Once the Provincias Vascongadas had become permanently occupied, Joseph Bonaparte's government worked hard to implement a loyal bureaucracy. To that effect, in September 1809 the government set up new councils, whose members consisted mainly of property owners, in proportion to the population of each constituency, and "chosen from among those who had expressed their support for the Constitution." The novelty was that the traditional requisite of being from a proven hidalguía no longer existed in order to occupy public office. This opened up new possibilities to other sectors of the population—mostly traders—who demanded greater political representation and power. The emerging urban middle class applauded these new developments and enthusiastically welcomed a new configuration of society based on citizenship and not on old class privileges (Rubio Pobes 1996b, 69–70). The case of Valentín Ma. de Echávarri, from Vitoria, can be taken as a good example: on being named provincial superintendent in 1811, he removed all the nobility's prerogatives and prohibited meetings and acts that distinguished between nobles and commoners: "The distinction between nobles and commoners, which is so inappropriate in the current atmosphere of enlightenment, and the inequality that is so contrary to the general good must be abolished . . . , because nobility consists of the virtue and merit of each citizen" (quote from Orruño 1983, 99).

The Spanish Constitution of 1812, which established the framework for a modern Spanish state, also suppressed nobles' privileges and their special access to power. It recognized equality before the law (articles 247 and 248) and enabled all males over age twenty-five to vote. Some council elections were held in the Provincias Vascongadas in December 1813 under the new constitutional rules and regulations; however, there was insufficient time for the constitutional regime to properly establish itself. The absolutist restoration of 1814 stopped the whole process of renewal of power that could have resulted from this novelty. The old requisites for accessing public offices were removed once more with the reestablishment of the Spanish Constitution of 1812 between 1820 and 1823; although the fueros were not formally abolished, the implementation of the constitution brought about that effect. However, the failure of this second constitutional experience soon allowed old practices to return. The reintroduction of the constitutional regime in Spain from 1836 added some exceptions to traditional electoral practices in the Basque territories: there were council elections in 1836 and 1838 in line with constitutional regulations, but only in some towns (in Bilbao, for example), due to the situation created by the First Carlist War (1833–1839). A decree of November 16, 1839—following the law passed on October 25 that confirmed the fueros—finally sanctioned the reenactment of the traditional electoral system: "town councils will be renewed in the four provinces [Álava, Guipúzcoa, Biscay, and Navarre] according to their fueros and customs." With some minor changes this legislation lasted until a revised council law was passed in 1845. Amid this complex situation in the first half of the century, in which the traditional oligarchy rarely lost its control of council power in the Provincias Vascongadas, the city of San Sebastián constituted a singular case.

During the first half of the nineteenth century, San Sebastián protested against the provincial institutions of Guipúzcoa with regard to the modification of the fueros. Since the eighteenth century, the merchants and traders of that city had been in a difficult economic situation. As a last possible solution to their problems they requested that the customs houses be moved from the inland location (where the fueros had placed them) to the coast. They also demanded that all obstacles to their political representation, as imposed by the traditional electoral system, be removed. The landowning oligarchy, which controlled the foral institutions, was not prepared to give in to such demands. San Sebastián's discontent led to a break with the province in 1834, which lasted thirteen years. The city stopped sending representatives to the provincial assemblies (Juntas Generales) and stopped obeying the provincial government (Diputación foral). During this period it expressed its claims through the *El Liberal Guipuzcoano* newspaper, whose banner was: "Abolition of the Hidalguía Privilege. Customs Houses on the Frontier. Courts of First Instance. Constitutional Unity." San Sebastián celebrated the law of September 19, 1837 because it eliminated the Diputaciones forales, moved customs houses to the coast, and ordered the formation of provincial governments and courts of first instance to be in line with general Spanish legislation. However, satisfaction was short-lived. As a consequence of the law passed on October 25, 1839, which confirmed the fueros, the Spanish government approved the decree of November 16, which nullified the changes introduced two years earlier, thus reestablishing the requirement of hidalguía in order to be an elector or be elected. In a letter to Queen Isabella II, the San Sebastián city council claimed that the decree infringed on the 1837 Constitution, which "stated that all Spaniards can hold public posts and positions depending on their merits and abilities," and that if the decree were enforced, there would be "the anomaly of someone being able to be named a member of the Spanish parliament, a senator, or crown minister without being qualified to be a municipal official [*regidor*] or Secretary in a small village in Guipúzcoa." The day after sending this letter, and as an act of protest, thirty-nine of the forty-nine hidalgos who lived in San Sebastián signed another letter to the Queen in which they gave up their rights as vecinos concejantes and requested that those rights be given to all who should have them according to the constitution. They did not succeed in having the decree repealed; however, at least with this action they contributed to keeping the election of the town council of San Sebastián according to constitutional regulations.[8]

In January 1845, a law was passed concerning the organization of councils (*Ley de Organización y Atribuciones de Ayuntamientos*), a key piece in moderate liberalism's territorial administration. As the fueros were still in force in the Provincias Vascongadas—although by now some of their more substantial features had been modified—the Spanish government had to draw up special instructions in order to adapt the law to these territories' singular characteristics, by ordering that each town's decision should be respected with regard to council election methods, whether traditional or constitutional. This meant that the hidalguía requisite could remain in place, yet not for long. Various royal orders were issued between 1846 (Álava and Biscay) and 1847 (Guipúzcoa), which meant that council elections would be held in the Provincias Vascongadas in line with the general law of 1845, as

---

8. For a more in-depth analysis of this subject, see Rubio Pobes (1996a).

in fact has happened since then. This law was rigidly centralist and led to setting up a highly restricted census-based electoral system. While this increased the number of vecinos concejantes in the Provincias Vascongadas, when compared to the traditional system, the census-based system proved to be very effective in keeping the popular classes out of local power.[9] For example, in 1847 the percentage of electors in Bilbao, the most important town in Biscay, was only 2 percent of the total population and only 1 percent could be elected to public office. The enlargement of the electoral census due to the passing of progressive legislation in July 1856 bore no results because in October of the same year the moderate law of 1845 was reestablished. When the democratic revolution of 1868 broke out, the abovementioned progressive law was reintroduced, albeit only provisionally until a new council law was passed in 1870, which introduced universal male suffrage. Again, this legislation lasted for a short period: in 1877, at the beginning of the Restoration period, a new council law reinstated the census-based suffrage.

Through most of the nineteenth century, access to municipal political representation was limited to only a small part of the population—the elites. The introduction of a constitutional regime did not remove the traditional requisite of hidalguía up to the mid-1840s, despite protests from cities such as San Sebastián. Then the census-based system guaranteed that most people were still excluded from political power. Thus, Basque society in the nineteenth century cannot be described as egalitarian and the corresponding positive image presented in the travel literature of an egalitarian country needs to be corrected.

Basque Egalitarianism: An Operative Stereotype during the Nineteenth Century

Although the idea of Basque egalitarianism did not match social reality, it continued to be a consolidated myth and an influential operative stereotype throughout the nineteenth century. It was

---

9.   For further information about the 1845 councils law, see Orduña (2003, 452). For further information about how this law was applied in the Provincias Vascongadas, see Pérez Nuñez (1996, 356–67).

employed by the foreign travelers to define the literary image of the Basque Country popularized abroad. The English traveler Richard Ford wrote about the Provincias Vascongadas in his travel book, first published in London in 1845:

> Another privilege is universal nobility, secured to all by the mere fact of being born in these provinces. Sons of old and good Christians, free from all Jewish and Moorish taint, they represent the 'Hebrew of the Hebrews' and are the most Gothic gentlemen of Spain, and are consequently all *Caballeros hijos de algo*. It is true that where all are so noble, the distinction is of small importance; nevertheless, like other Highlanders, they are grievously affected with genealogy and goitre . . . . Basque gentility often consists rather in blood than in manners; better born than bred, the Cantabrian is not always courteous nor over quick in rendering honour to whom honour is due; he considers a sort of boorishness to indicate a republican independence, and thinks the deference which one well-conditioned person pays to another, to be a degradation to his noble birth right; their provinces may be the three Graces of Spain, but the natives sacrifice but little to those amiable types. (Ford 1855, 874)

Certainly, the egalitarianism idea continued to be an operative stereotype. But not only among travelers, and not only to define the external image of the Basques. The first Basque liberals made use of it when they tried to legitimize the introduction of the Spanish Constitution of 1812 in the Provincias Vascongadas by referring to the history and tradition of these territories. Thus, the Bilbao liberal newspaper *El Bascongado* explained in December 1813 to its readers that equality before the law and the abolition of privileges did not frighten the Basques as "they have always believed and practiced the principle that merit is the real way to obtain positions, and that these should not be reserved for men of particular classes" (Fernández Sebastián 1991, 168). In the 1837, the liberal Pedro de Lemonauria wrote in his study of the fueros of Biscay, in a chapter entitled "About equality": "All the Biscayans are nobles. All *foral* laws have the stamp of that equality, and there is not even one single law that suggests the slightest taste of privileged classes. Equality before the law is thus a dogma of the public law of Biscay" (Lemonauria [1837] 2013, 49). He had explained previously that: "Since the nobility is, to say thus, linked to the soil of Biscay, the man who is not a native of the country has to prove his hidalguía to enjoy the rights of citizen." Lemonauria linked the idea of universal nobility with egalitarianism, reinterpreting it as a modern liberty, but simultaneously explained that in its application "our ancestors" had developed "secondary legislation" destroying equality "with serious prejudice to the whole society." Among these laws were the rules of residence in Biscay, which he criticized as a "miserable legacy of the Inquisition."

Not only liberals but also *fueristas* (the political conservative hegemonic group in the institutions of the Provincias Vascongadas between 1830s and 1860s) also contributed to keeping alive the idea of Basque egalitarianism. Although they defended an aristocratic conception of power, they also elaborated a political discourse to defend the Basque fueros in which the idea of egalitarianism was implicitly present. It was implicit in their portrait of the Basques as a fraternal people and an idyllic rural society without significant social differences. That rural myth of the Basques as a people of noble mountain dwellers, full of moral virtues who lived in brotherhood making up an egalitarian society and working hard is a myth usually associated with Sabino Arana, the father of Basque nationalism. He developed and popularized it, but he was not the first to formulate it. In fact, the rural myth was already present in the texts of writers in the eighteenth century such as Padre Larramendi;[10] it can also be detected in Juan Antonio Moguel's *Peru Abarka*.[11] During the nineteenth century it was taken up and developed by the fueristas for their political discourse supporting the fueros.

The fueros of Álava, Biscay, Guipúzcoa, and Navarre survived the introduction of the Bourbon monarchy in Spain at the start of the eighteenth century—in contrast to the fueros of Aragón, Valencia, Mallorca, and Catalonia, which were all abolished. They also survived Fernando VII's reformist absolutism, but they seemed to have no place in the nineteenth century when the fueros were criticized as obsolete privileges of the ancien régime, also by some natives of the Provincias Vascongadas.

---

10.   Javier Corcuera Atienza states that "Larramendi preached the nobility of the Basque peasant and the baserri (farmstead) as the source of nobility. After Larramendi, baserri, baserritarra (farmer, peasant) and casa solar (ancestral home) were the paradigm of Basque nobility and even of 'Basquism'" Corcuera Atienza (2006, 228–29).

11.   *Peru Abarka* was written in 1802 by an author who, culturally speaking, was closer to the eighteenth century.

However, it was necessary to find new, strong arguments to defend them. Thus, Basque politicians, mainly fueristas, elaborated a discourse that interpreted the people of Biscay, Álava, and Guipúzcoa—and eventually also the Navarrese—as members of a differentiated people and country, even a differentiated *nationality* within the Spanish nation. They therefore presented the fueros as the *essence* of the Basque people, and argued that their destruction would automatically lead to the disappearance of the Basque people. Consequently, they argued about a close relationship between the fueros and Basque identity. They thus built a new Basque stereotype, which continued through the entire century. They stated that the Basque people were different from the rest of the people and territories of the Spanish monarchy because of their singular political regime, the fueros; because of their singular history, which was shared by the three Provincias Vascongadas (based on myths like their primitive and permanent independence); their very ancient language, Euskara; their long-established Catholic fervor; their incomparable loyalty to the Crown of Castile; and their exemplary social structure, expressed in the myth of a people of noble mountain dwellers full of moral virtues who lived in fraternal harmony in an idyllic society. This discourse especially emphasized the idea of singularity in order to develop the following argument: if the Basques were a singular people, they also deserved singular treatment from the state government, maintaining their particular position at the heart of the new liberal state, which in turn translated into keeping the fueros. The discourse of singularity went even beyond the sphere of politics and impacted on literature and other artistic and cultural—even religious—forms of expression. This discourse was socially diffused by using an array of channels such as the political press, public commemorations, sermons, novels, songs, historical paintings, public statues, and so on.[12]

One of the more prominent arguments was that the fueros served as a guarantee for the conservation and harmonious development of the idyllic people of mountain dwellers as the Basques were seen. The fueros—explained the discourse—in this

---

12. For more in-depth information about the creation and social diffusion of this discourse, see Rubio Pobes (2003). On the images of the Basques in Europe between 1833 and 1876, see Sánchez Prieto (1993).

"sterile land" with its steep mountains, small harvests, weak industry, and outdated trade, still reached levels of well-being unknown elsewhere in the Spanish monarchy. They were a guarantee of survival of a rural Arcadia. The discourse incorporated the rural myth present in the writings of eighteenth century. It stressed the moral virtues of the Basque people as rural virtues, consisting of plainness, frugality, and personal dignity; all virtues shared even by those who were not peasants. As a consequence, this identity discourse portrayed a harmonic world with no contradiction at all between the city and the countryside, in contrast to what, within a few decades, the Basque nationalist discourse of Sabino Arana would affirm. As the Diputaciones forales stated in 1850:

> The Provincias Vascongadas have in the eyes of impartial and fair observers always presented themselves in an enviable image, perhaps unique in the world, of a people without licentiousness, as being religious without being superstitious, favoring order and work, and worshipping the crown, full of personal dignity but, at the same time, respectful toward hierarchies, hospitable like Switzerland in its best times, but without the latter's religious differences and frequent internal fights, encouraged by the principle of free trade, as in the United States, but better able than that country to unite the almost exact state of its social progress with the habits, frugality and virtues of agricultural peoples ... in short, an example for good, honorable, loyal and brave peoples.[13]

The fueros guaranteed the survival of an exemplary peasant universe presented by their defenders as the realization of liberal conservatism's social utopia. That explains also why there were so few explicit references to Basque egalitarianism. Instead, the people's natural subordination to the authorities and respect for their hierarchies was emphasized. The references to egalitarianism were still contained, implicitly—as I have explained before—in the portrait of the Basques as a fraternal people, particularly by emphasizing put on "the fraternal union of all the inhabitants who seem to be motivated by the same sentiment."[14]

---

13. Foral Conference held at Gernika, May 5, 1850. Reproduced in Agirreazkuenaga (1995).
14. These words are taken from Egaña (1870, 3).

Basque writers of the nineteenth century were less cautious than politicians when it came to assuming the idea of egalitarianism. They also incorporated the eighteenth-century rural myth and included it in their literary works in order to make it part of their picture of the Basques. The historical-legendary literature that emerged in the second half of the nineteenth century[15] was romantic and pro-Basque. Whether through the contents of its novels, tales, legends, or poems, it was committed to defining the characteristics of the Basque people's identity and spreading the idea of its singularity. This literature helped powerfully to introduce a specific image of the country and its people among the Basques, full of myths about Basqueness, including the rural myth of the idyllic countryside. As Antonio Elorza points out, the historical-legendary Basque literature in the nineteenth century popularized for the first time the rural myth before Arana's nationalism made use of it.[16]

However, while in political discourse the rural myth remained in the background as an argument to defend the fueros, and hardly ever explicit, in the literary discourse it possessed much more centrality and autonomy, and it is clearly explicit. Basque writers projected in their texts an idyllic image of the Basque farmhouse (*caserío*), its inhabitants, and their collaborative work, "like bees in a hive, helping each other in their domestic chores, following the sacred customs of this exemplary country which was familiar with shared work many centuries before Fourier, Cabet, and other people [discovered it]" the writer Jose Ma. Goizueta explained in one of his most reprinted novels (Goizueta 1857, 116). Another Basque writer, Juan Venancio Araquistain, described the rural myth and the idea of Basque egalitarianism in his novel *El Baso-Jaun de Etumeta*:

> The simple peasant from our mountains, sure of his value and proud of his nobility, feels neither rivalry nor jealousy of the greatness of those higher up, Aide-Naguziac, because he has never seen any difference between them other that the accidental and fleeting difference of the wealth which made his master show off to the world a privilege which he himself had,

---

15. There is an excellent, already classic work about this, Juaristi (1987).
16. See Elorza (1981, 96).

hidden though, but which he could bring into the light with just a change of luck. (Araquistain 1882, 41–42)

Araquistain talked about "the expanse of nobility in the country and virtually everybody being noble in the ancestral farmhouses dwelling their mountains"—note the adverb *virtually*—and added:

> In the Provincias Vascongadas hardly a farmhouse can be found that is not connected to the highest-up families, due to the fact that among these families there is no idea of a different original condition . . . . These simple farmworkers, who only speak Basque and live from the sweat of their brows, will tell you, if you ask them repeatedly, that theirs is the most genuine, purest nobility; it has been preserved without any strange mixtures in the humble farmhouses built by the inhabitants of the country and not the proud fortified mansions on the plains which are no more than offshoots. (ibid.)

Often, these writers idealized and even falsified the relationship between owners and tenant farmers. Antonio Trueba wrote:

> At all times, and similarly today, for the tenant farmer the owner is not just a master as he is in other places; he is, as well as that, the natural counselor for all his doubts, his help in times of need, the custodian of all his savings, the judge in his disputes, his comfort in times of misfortune, in short, his master, father, counselor and friend. (Trueba 1944, 43)

Trueba was one of the most successful writers of his time. He was the official archivist and chronicler of Biscay from 1862 onward and stood out for his idealization of the farmhouse and the rural world. For him, the countryside was the incarnation of the highest human values; the city, on the other hand, was the cradle of deterioration. Such distinctions predated the radical differentiation between the country and the city that became so characteristic of Sabino Arana's thinking.

The myth was handed down to the Basque nationalist doctrine from literature.[17] While the defense of the Basque rural world and its moral values in Arana's thought has repeatedly

---

17. In this as in other aspects the historic-legendary literature served as a connecting space for transferring ideas between *fuerismo* and Basque nationalism. I have explained this connection in Rubio Pobes (2010).

been interpreted as the result and expression of nostalgia and a lack of adaptation to the traumatic changes brought on by industrialization, it was not, in fact, something new or original. However, industrialization and the asserted misfortune of racial contamination, which Basque nationalism took as being part of modern change, helped to deepen his perception of an antithesis between countryside and city that was already present in Basque literature. Within nationalism, the rural myth, systematized by Engracio Aranzadi, became a symbol for the purity of the Basque race and a marker of social stability that stood firm against the conflicts caused by the Spanish "red proletariat" (Elorza 1981, 101). The idea of egalitarianism was used as a means to provide nationalism with arguments about Basque singularity, independence, and sovereignty. Egalitarianism also was useful for denying that Basques had ever lived in a stratified feudal society and for rejecting the validity of modern socialism because it would have nothing to teach a society in which equality was an innate quality.

In conclusion, the Basque egalitarianism idea did remain alive throughout the nineteenth century. It survived the ancien régime, under which it was first conceived, through the accounts of foreign travelers; through the discourses of Basque liberals (who were looking for native liberties that would help the implementation of a liberal regime) and the fueristas' political discourses (associated with the rural myth); and, especially, through the fictional narratives of the historical-legendary literature of the nineteenth century. Egalitarianism, one of the most successful and lasting stereotypes about the Basques, does not stand up to a thorough examination of the social reality of the Basque Country in the nineteenth century. However, it managed to keep itself alive as an operating stereotype and identity marker during that century. At the end of the century, Basque nationalism incorporated the idea into its symbolic identity universe and gave it new life.

References

Agirreazkuenaga, Joseba, ed. 1995. *La articulación político institucional de Vasconia: Actas de las Conferencias firmadas por los representantes de Álava, Vizkaya, Gipúzcoa y eventualmente Navarra*

(1775–1936), 2 vols. Bilbao: Diputaciones forales de Álava, Gipuzkoa y Bizkaia.

Aranzadi, Juan. 2000. *Milenarismo vasco: Edad de oro, etnia y nativismo.* Madrid: Taurus.

Araquistain, Juan Venancio. 1882. *El Baso-Jaun de Etumeta: Novela histórica vascongada.* Tolosa: Imprenta de F. Muguerza.

Arpal, Jesús. 1979. *La sociedad tradicional en el País Vasco.* San Sebastián: Haranburu.

Borrow, George. (1843) 1923. *The Bible in Spain, or the Journeys, Adventures and Imprisonments of an Englishman in an Attempt to Circulate the Scriptures in the Peninsula.* London: John Murray.

Corcuera Atienza, Javier. 2006. *The Origins, Ideology, and Organization of Basque Nationalism, 1876–1903.* Translated by Albert Bork and Cameron J. Watson. Reno: Center for Basque Studies, University of Nevada, Reno. Translation of *Orígenes, ideología y organización del nacionalismo vasco, 1876–1904.* Madrid: Siglo XXI. It was reprinted as *La patria de los vascos.* Madrid: Taurus, 2001.

Delaporte, Joseph. 1772. *Le voyageur françois ou la connoissance de l'ancien et du nouveau monde*, vol. 16. Paris: L. Cellot.

Domínguez Ortiz, Antonio. 1988. *Sociedad y Estado en el siglo XVIII español.* Barcelona: Crítica.

Egaña, Pedro de. 1870. *Breves apuntes en defensa de las libertades vascongadas: Escrito leído a la llamada Comisión de arreglo de Fueros nombrada por el Señor Don Juan Bravo Murillo en 1852, por el Excmo. Señor Don Pedro de Egaña.* Bilbao: Imprenta de J.E. Delmás.

Elorza, Antonio. 1981. *Nacionalismo vasco 1876–1936: Historia General del País Vasco*, vol. 11. San Sebastián: Haranburu.

Ford, Richard. 1855. *A Hand-Book for Travellers in Spain.* 3rd edition. London: John Murray.

Fernández Sebastián, Javier. 1991. *La génesis del fuerismo: Prensa e ideas políticas en la crisis del Antiguo Régimen; País Vasco 1750–1840.* Madrid: Siglo XXI.

Goizueta, José María. 1857. *Aventuras de Damián el Monaguillo.* Madrid: Establecimiento Tipográfico de D. A. Vicente.

Humboldt, Wilhelm von. 1925. "Los Vascos: Apuntaciones sobre un viaje por el país vasco en primavera de 1801." In *Guillermo de Humboldt y el País Vasco*, edited by Arturo Farinelli et al. San Sebastián: Imprenta de la Diputación de Guipúzcoa.

Juaristi, Jon. 1987. *El linaje de Aitor: La invención de la tradición vasca.* Madrid: Taurus.

Lemonauria, Pedro de. (1837) 2013. "Ensayo crítico sobre las leyes constitucionales de Vizcaya." In *Pedro de Lemonauria: Costumbre democrática; Debates liberales sobre fueros vascos, 1837–1868*, edited and introduced by José Ma. Portillo. Bilbao: Universidad del País Vasco-Euskal Herriko Unibertsitatea.

Madariaga, Juan. 2002. "Crisis, cambios y rupturas (1602–1876)." In *De Túbal a Aitor: Historia de Vasconia*, directed by Iñaki Bazán. Madrid: La Esfera de los libros.

Martínez Gorriarán, Carlos. 1993. *Casa, Provincia, Rey: Para una historia de la cultura del poder en el País Vasco*. Irun: Alberdania.

Martínez Rueda, Fernando. 1994. *Los poderes locales en Vizcaya. Del Antiguo Régimen a la Revolución Liberal 1700–1853*. Bilbao: Universidad del País Vasco-Euskal Herriko Unibertsitatea.

Orduña, Enrique. 2003. *Municipios y provincias: Historia de la organización territorial española*. Madrid: Centro de Estudios Políticos y Constitucionales.

Ortiz de Orruño, José Ma. 1983. "La aparición de la burguesía urbana durante la guerra de la Independencia; el caso alavés." *Kultura* 4: 94–102.

Otazu, Alfonso. 1973. *El "igualitarismo" vasco: Mito y realidad*. San Sebastián: Txertoa.

Pérez Nuñez, Javier. 1996. *La diputación foral de Vizcaya: El régimen foral en la construcción del Estado liberal (1808–1868)*. Madrid: Centro de Estudios Constitucionales.

Portillo, José Ma. 1991. *Monarquía y gobierno provincial: Poder y Constitución en las provincias vascas (1760–1808)*. Madrid: Centro de Estudios Constitucionales.

Rubio Pobes, Coro. 1996a. "La burguesía donostiarra y la cuestión aduanera: Un conflicto foral." In *Memoria Justificativa de lo que tiene expuesto y pedido la ciudad de San Sebastián para el fomento de la industria y comercio de Guipúzcoa (1932)*, edited by Coro Rubio Pobes. Bilbao: Universidad del País Vasco-Euskal Herriko Unibertsitatea.

———. 1996b. *Revolución y tradición: El País Vasco ante la Revolución liberal y la construcción del Estado español, 1808–1868*. Madrid: Siglo XXI.

———. 2003. *La identidad vasca en el siglo XIX: Discurso y agentes sociales*. Madrid: Biblioteca Nueva.

————. 2010. "La literatura histórico-legendaria vasca: Puente ideológico entre el discurso identitario del fuerismo y el del nacionalismo aranista." *Ohienart* 25: 281–305.

————. 2012. "25 de Octubre de 1839." In *Diccionario de símbolos del nacionalismo vasco*, edited by Santiago de Pablo, et al. Madrid: Tecnos.

Sánchez Prieto, Juan M. 1993. *El imaginario vasco: Representaciones de una conciencia histórica, nacional y política en el espacio europeo, 1833–1876*. Barcelona: Eiunsa.

Santoyo, Julio C., compiler. 1978. *Viajeros ingleses del siglo XIX*. Introduced, translated, and annotated by Rosa María Sillaurren and José Miguel Santamaría. Vitoria: Caja de Ahorros Municipal de Vitoria.

Trueba, Antonio. 1944. *Obras escogidas*, vol. 1, *Cuentos de color de rosa*. Madrid: Rubiños.

6

Egalitarianism and Gender in the Traditional Basque Country

Anne-Marie Lagarde

Traditional Basque society, including some of its egalitarian aspects, has been the subject of a number of studies. According to a variety of experts, many influenced by the study of patterns derived from the French Revolution, such prerevolutionary or premodern egalitarian dimensions should be considered a myth. Widening Claude Lévi-Strauss's conclusion somewhat, however, my intent here is to demonstrate that in the Basque Country a noncoercive egalitarian sociopolitical base did actually exist. The key to its understanding lies in the study of language usage, which reveals cultural practices, particularly in relation to gender identities and specific matrimonial features that largely prevented the systematic accumulation of landed property. I will deal mostly with conditions in Iparralde,[1] because it is particularly in these territories where original elements of an egalitarian praxis can be detected.

At the core of traditional Basque society is the homestead or *etxe* (Association Lauburu 1980). Thanks to the details

---

1. The Northern Basque Country, i.e., the provinces of Zuberoa, Lower Navarre, and Lapurdi.

and documents given in the *Coutumes* (literally "customs"), we can state that the Basque house (etxe) is not just an economic, political, and social unit but also a symbol of a collective identity. It is at the same time a material entity, a unit within which to manage the available resources, a transcendent "person" that gives its name to and is inscribed in the history of the family, a domestic pantheon through the buried people it shelters, and a juridical and religious concept. It even has a psychological dimension that can be detected by studying certain linguistic expressions and usages.

In order to describe this Basque society we will take a closer look at the meaning and practices surrounding the word *co-seigneurie* (co-seigniory): it is a term used in the Coutumes (Goyhenetche 1985, 203) and in marriage contracts (co-seigneurie of masters young and old). It refers to a sociopolitical framework that can only be found in the Basque-speaking lands and nowhere else in Europe. Both the term and the social practice behind it refer to the status of a house, independent of its size or the number of people living in it, in which the equal status of generations and both sexes, not simply that of individuals, prevails. In what follows I will refer particularly to a group of scholars who have studied practices and patterns based on such status, most prominently among them the work of Maïté Lafourcade (1989).

In contrast to feudal concepts and notions of aristocracy inherited from the Goths and the Franks, in the Basque context the word co-seigneurie refers to both the equal status of a couple and the implicit status of nobility, which the couple(s) was supposed to prolong by giving birth to the future *etxekojaun* or *etxekoandre* (lord or lady of the household).

In modern times, this notion of nobility may seem quite prosaic and reductive; however, establishing and maintaining any form of stable inheritance pattern was not always easy. Basque co-seigneurs were clearly prompted by the same passions as other human beings, and they were certainly not any different in the way they treated non-Basques or the less privileged. Thus, they often forged unnatural political alliances and were not entirely free of misogynous behavior, even though they followed nonmisogynous customs. However, their organization cannot be reduced to the Indo-European pattern described by the historian Georges Dumézil as being either based on orders or on castes (Peillen 1987, 17).

Generally speaking, in traditional Basque society male domination and gerontocracy were not accepted as normal rules of inheritance. In contrast, the Basque legal inheritance system rested on the following two assumptions: (1) The law of full primogeniture applied, which meant that the transmission of landed property was passed on to the first-born child, whether male or female (this is not to be mistaken with the law of male primogeniture enforced in many other places); and (2) the acceptance of the "co-seigneurie of masters young and old" meant that some sense of equality among generations applied when it came to the management of property (Lafourcade 1989).

If those rules were not always enforced it was due to the fact that, under the influence of the church, the privilege of masculinity on occasion managed to prevail in some houses. However, this was far from being the general rule. It should also be mentioned here that inheritance customs were later written down, particularly when Roman law became more influential and when, along with such change, canon law challenged and threatened local customs and traditions (Lafourcade 2007).[2]

Some scholars have argued that such a traditional society could not have been really egalitarian because it implied that the younger children had to leave. Sociologists have termed this "sacrificial eviction," despite the fact that the children's departure was linked to the matrimonial rule of marriage between the first-born and his or her younger siblings. Those who maintain such lines of reasoning seem to overlook Basque legal arrangements, particularly the "co-seigneurie of masters old and young." Referring mostly to examples from outside the Basque Country they think the option of choosing a female heir never really applied (Bourdieu 1972, 1107). An entire generation of social scientists, particularly in France, was influenced by Claude Lévi-Strauss's *Les structures élémentaires de la parenté* (1949), a theory that denies the possibility of traditional societies relying on or demonstrating any signs of gender equality.

Lévi-Strauss claims that equality is not compatible with the rule of prohibiting incest. For him, prohibition allowed for the symbolization of differentiating sexes that are at the heart of society's origins. Logically then, the differentiation of the sexes relies

---

2.   A good analysis of this process is also provided in Galíndez ([1948] 2003).

on the institutional domination of men over women. With regard to lineages and their nominations, he distinguishes two types of systems—patrilineal and matrilineal (the mother giving any off-spring her name). Both systems are androcentric, the father hold-ing authority in the former, and the uncle on the mother's side in the latter case. Thus, Lévi-Strauss classified "domestic" or "house" societies (*sociétés a maison*) as patrilineal systems, asserting that the name was given by the father or the father-in-law, who were the only holders of authority.

Because researchers were not aware of, or simply not famil-iar with, Basque rules of inheritance, proponents of the notion of Basque egalitarianism have had to face objections such as Lévi-Strauss's argument that younger children had to accept their exclusion and the nonapplication of egalitarian principles to in-heritance patterns. However, such objections are contradicted by a documented number of marriage contracts that serve as proof of the existence and application of the law of full primogeniture and co-seigneurie.

In some cases, the rules had to be written down legally (and enforced). A close examination of such concrete formulations sheds light on the specific system of alliance and kinship. Such inspection also highlights their compatibility with laws of prohi-bition (sometimes also referred to as "symbolic law") instead of denying any underlying cause or reason.

Lévi-Strauss's own reasoning leads us to such an examina-tion. On the understanding that, in all societies, gender differ-ence is also symbolized institutionally, we have to ask how the Basques managed in practice to introduce and maintain such co-seigneurial relations and inheritance patterns. In order to find the answer to this question, it is helpful to take a closer look at the Basque language and linguistic patterns. Besides being a means of communication, every language is also a mirror of social practices and institutions, and by definition that also extends to the Basque case. My intent here is to show that the study of certain Basque linguistic patterns hints at other practices and enables us to chal-lenge the Lévi-Straussian assumption of an intrinsic inequality.

My argument is based on four stages. First, I will discuss some of the most relevant theories about Basque society in general. Second, I will take a closer look at the etxe, the matrix and symbol of Basque egalitarian society. This will, third, lead to a discussion about the principle of exogamy and matrimonial rule and its political dimensions. Fourth, I will discuss the compatibility between symbolic law and social equality, something that is expressed and is revealed in certain linguistic particularities.

Theories about Basque Society and Its Peculiarities

In the nineteenth century, two influential theories regarding social systems were proposed: the "matriarchal" theory and the notion of the *famille-souche* (stem family). Johann Jakob Bachofen, a German-speaking Swiss anthropologist, was the first person to promote the matriarchal theory. His work, *Das Mutterrecht* (1861 [1996]), sets out a history of mankind by distinguishing three crucial periods: aphroditic hetaerism (an age of sexual promiscuity), demetrism (a reign of the mother and a time of gender equality, but later incorporating a dionysian age in which patriarchy began to emerge), and, finally, apollonian patriarchy, the triumph of the male sex, which he regards as the symbol of Western consciousness. With regard to demetrism, Bachofen speaks of "maternal law" and "gynecocracy" (the supremacy of women), as practiced in ancient Egypt, Crete, Lycia, and among the Vascones (*Vasconen*) and Cantabri (*Kantabrier*) (the latter two are identified as having been ancestors of the Basques). Apparently, Bachofen was instructed in Basque law by Eugène Cordier (1859, 1869), and wrote an entire chapter about it, which appeared at the end of his monumental work (Bachofen [1861] 1967, 1272–87). He had no doubt that it was a valid example of how "maternal law" functioned.

Bachofen's theory is rejected now because of its strange evolutionism. The idea of a widespread demetrism at the dawn of mankind seems questionable to many, although the prehistorian Marija Gimbutas (1989) and E. O. James (1959), a historian of religion, maintain that the idea still reflects certain practices and periods of early European history. Referring to the existence of prehistoric ivory and stone statues of Venus—discovered near Brassempouy[3]—Gimbutas and James claim that a cult of the

---

3. A village situated in the ancient region of Vasconia, today in Les Landes in the southwest of France, where some statues of Venus and the famous "Dame" (Lady) (a tiny ivory head) have been found.

Goddess-Mother was widespread in prehistoric Europe and that it lasted for some thirty thousand years, and at least as long as the Neolithic period.

In contrast, their detractors claim that the famous statues are no more conclusive of a cult to the Goddess-Mother than are those related to the Holy Virgin today. These critics also point out that the sun has always been a paternal symbol in Europe, which is incorrect, at least in relation to Basque Culture: for the Basques, both the sun and the moon were maternal symbols (Hartsuaga 1987, 37; Caro Baroja 1977, 250). According to ethnologists and historians, Bachofen seems to have mistaken ancient matrilineal societies (well identified nowadays thanks to epigraphy) for matriarchal systems. Since the maternal uncle holds authority (instead of the father) in such matrilineal societies they consider them androcentric and thus the existence of a "Maternal Law" remains unproven. Be that as it may, older Basque customs cannot be included in the categories defined by these critics because they establish neither the father's nor the maternal uncle's preeminence.

The famille-souche or stem family theory can be traced back to Frédéric Le Play, an early sociologist and one of the architects of the social sciences in general. The term famille-souche appeared for the first time in 1857 in Le Play's study ([1856] 1994) of the Melouga family in Cauterets, Hautes-Pyrénées, and became central to his work. The Melouga family had its base in what he termed the *maison euskarienne* (Basque-speaking household) which served as a representation of the *famille-souche* (Le Play 1855). This family was organized within the tradition of full primogeniture: the eldest daughter, Savina, inherited the property, which enjoyed harmony and prosperity until one of her sisters successfully demanded her share of the estate, after which the farm went into steep decline.

In the twentieth century the famille-souche theory became quite popular with sociologists, demographers, ethnologists, and historians.[4] However, the passing on of the house's name was of secondary importance to them, as was female primogeniture, which they did not distinguish from male primogeniture.

---

4. See for example, regarding France, Mendras (1995), Chenu (1994); Augustins (1989); and Bourdieu (2002).

Being unaware of the Basque co-seigneurie practice, these scholars typically viewed the departure of younger children as a form of exclusion or sacrifice; furthermore, they regarded the practice as nonegalitarian. They thought of the famille souche as representing a patriarchal structure in which the name and the property were passed on from the father to the son; or, if there was no son, from father-in-law to son-in-law. This enabled them to classify the inheritance pattern of the Basque and Pyrenean household as being patrilineal on which the entire patriarchal system came to rest.

Etxe: Matrix and Symbol of Egalitarian Practice

Lafourcade (2011) studies the Basque household based on texts that dealt with the Coutume in eighteenth-century marriage contracts. Her research shows that etxe referred to and stood for an inalienable property that included the farmhouse with its outer buildings, movable goods and real estate, farm animals, fertile land, rights to common land, church and grave rights, and the house name. It formed an intangible entity called *troncalidad* (from the "truncal" notion of inheriting through the "trunk" or family) in the southern provinces of the Basque Country (Navarre, Gipuzkoa, Araba, and Bizkaia). No person pertaining to the etxe could just make use of it as he or she pleased. The house had to be passed on to only one of the children, either a son or a daughter. The specific condition of the etxe was that the property was passed on to the young couple when they got married—not on their parents' death. By a tacit rule, the eldest children married junior counterparts to avoid the accumulation of properties. In this system, the passing on of the property to the young couple was of foremost importance since it guaranteed the prolongation and proper functioning of the institution and those who depended on it.

Basque rights enshrined in charters or laws known as the *fueros* (in Spanish), *fors* (in French), or *foruak* (in Basque)[5] and certain customs serve as prime examples of what is specific to the Basque lands. They existed on both sides of the Pyrenees, even

---

5. From the Latin *forum* (market), indicating the place in which justice was initially dispensed, this term took on a meaning referring to the exercise of justice and, finally, to law itself.

in areas in which the Basque language was no longer spoken (Gascony and Béarn in the north and Aragon in the south). Most of the *fueros* appeared in written form between the thirteenth and seventeenth centuries. According to Lafourcade, they constitute a remarkably coherent public and private law, which, in turn, goes back to what Jacques Poumarède terms old Pyrenean law (1974, 34). Customs did change, however, as the centuries went by, mainly due to the introduction of Roman law and its privileged treatment of male descendants. During this time the fueros came to define the status of land that pertained to each house: the land was owned collectively; it belonged to the family, not just to the paterfamilias (Lafourcade 2011). Common lands were the other pillar on which the Basque economy and institutions rested. They were managed and run by all the masters and ladies of all the houses of each district, parish, or county.

The most characteristic feature of the Basque fueros was the system of inheritance they codified.[6] We have already briefly mentioned two very specific customs: the reliance on absolute or full primogeniture and the co-seigneurie of masters, young and old. Primogeniture as practiced in the Basque Country was nonsexist; daughters could inherit in the same way as sons did; and co-seigneurie gave equal power to both the younger and the older couple in the household. There was to be complete equality of rights between them. The symbolic property (*domonyme* or domunym in English, a personal name taken from a dwelling or place of residence) was part of the inheritance and was passed on from the mother or the father, according to the law and tradition of absolute primogeniture. It is still in use nowadays, although patronyms were made compulsory in parish registers by the clergy (and then later by the state). There is no ambiguity in the texts: "The first-born child, either son or daughter indiscriminately, inherits the property" (Grosclaude 1993, 101).

With regard to the cornerstone of the system, the co-seigneurial institution, the terms "co-seigneurie" and "co-seigneurs" are fre-

---

6. "It is rare to find . . . such complete, original, isolated legislation as that of the Basques in the Western world. This legislation basically differs from those of their neighboring countries . . . ; It differs from the Roman law of the South of France, from the Visigothic law of Spain, from the feudal law of the whole Europe" Cordier (1869, 89).

quently mentioned in sixteenth- and seventeenth-century texts. Eighteenth-century contracts also show that these rules had occasionally to be enforced (Lafourcade 1989, 57–60 and 140–43). In one of the Lower Navarrese fors we read: "The sons and daughters, heirs and heiresses . . . will be made co-seigneurs, together with their father and mother [they will become] owners of the property and possessions . . . and they will be able to use half of it as actual owners" (Goyhenetche 1985, 203). Likewise, the Coutumes of Zuberoa (also spelled Xiberoa), Lower Navarre, and Lapurdi all indicate that, in the event of a disagreement between the younger and the older couple, "if the former, either son or daughter, who has given their dowry to their father and mother . . . wants to live separately, they may demand the sharing out of the property. They must then be given half the property and they must pay half the expenses, the other half remaining to their father and mother" (Grosclaude 1993, 90).

As regards the Southern Basque Country, the upper valleys of Navarre followed the same custom as their northern neighbors, and although male privilege was introduced in some families (as it was in Zuberoa occasionally), it seems that in a significant number of cases heiresses were chosen. This was certainly the case in Etxalar, a village in Navarre in which William A. Douglass examined census results from 1842 to 1960 in his *Echalar and Murélaga* (1975) (cited in Chenu 1994; see also Le Play [1856] 1994).

In the Erronkari (Roncal) Valley, in 1684, patronyms were refused and domunyms were maintained.[7] In Gipuzkoa, Bizkaia, and Araba, the parents' choice sometimes outweighed custom. Yet even in Gipuzkoa[8] during the ancien régime, for example, where some *hidalgos* (noblemen) were influenced by Castilian traditions and favored male privilege, nearly 38 percent of daughters still inherited (Oliveri Korta 2001, 174). There is also ample proof of the transmission of names through mothers.

Sometimes, the traditional matrimonial rule was given up in favor of accumulating properties between heirs. However, there was a condominium between the young and old couples that had little to do with patriarchal systems. If the couples did not get on

---

7.   Local assemblies forced people to bear the name of the house they lived in. See Orpustan (1996, 3).
8.   In Gipuzkoa there was no transcription of the custom.

well, the usufruct was divided in two (ibid., 199). A fifteenth-century royal order, for example, stated that neither of the generations living under the same roof could be dispossessed (Azpiazu 1995, 45–46). All legal provisions seemed to have favored and supported co-seigneurie.[9] As Lafourcade observes, co-seigneurie did not exist in any other European legal system (Lafourcade 1980, 55).

The law of absolute primogeniture applied also to the upper valleys of Béarn and the Central Pyrenees, along with matrimonial rules avoiding the accumulation of properties. Although the original system was identical to that which occupied such a prominent place in the Basque Country, co-seigneurie here did not imply power sharing between the two couples but, rather, the reinstitutionalization of patriarchal authority.

A very different terminology appeared in the fors, which conceived younger members of the household as being subservient to the Elders. The unmarried younger child was known colloquially as donado (given away): "They were called *esclaus* [slaves] in Barèges and *sterlès* or *esterlès* [steriles]" (Morère 1967, 86). We do not come across such terms anywhere in Basque texts. Consequently, a transformation occurred in Romance-speaking regions that superseded the Basque practice of co-seigneurie and that transformed the practice of turning away junior children into a sacrificial system. I will come back to this later. Evidence shows, then, that the theory of filiation and *mariage en gendre* (uxorilocal or matrilocal marriage, in which a married couple resides with or near the wife's parents), as defined by Lévi-Strauss, applied to households in Béarn and Hautes-Pyrénées in which authority was no longer shared and very much in contrast to the Basque co-seigneurie, which did not support such a patriarchal logic.

The concern for equality appears at several levels: the management of the household and the passing on of the name, the departing of junior children from home, the marriage of elder children to younger partners, the absence of discrimination in dowries (junior sons and daughters brought their dowry to the house they married into and became "adventitious spouses"), the replacement of dead spouses by their respective brothers or sisters

---

9. The claim of "universal nobility" would, logically, derive from this later. See Achón Inchausti (2001), 149–76.

(a different system from, and not be confused with, the "levirate" and Jacob's marriage that is in use in patriarchal societies), catering for four potential scenarios: (1) a widowed heiress remarries a brother-in-law, who replaces his deceased brother; (2) a widowed heir remarries his sister-in-law, who replaces her deceased sister; (3) an adventitious husband remarries a sister-in-law, who will replace her deceased sister heiress in the house in which they were born; and (4) an adventitious widowed wife remarries a brother-in-law, who will replace the deceased brother heir in the house in which they were born (Lagarde 2006, 55–56).

As we have seen, the house serves as the basic sociopolitical unit (including name and properties). The free-standing farmhouse was linked to its nearest neighbors by mutual aid and solidarity (Ott 1981, 213–14). Together these formed the neighborhood, the *auzoalde* (or *auzoa*). The occupants were bound by a tie of fraternity, mainly through intermarriage between neighboring houses, that is, by junior children (male and female) who married someone from the auzoa or a close-by auzoa.

Such close ties and relationships shaped the Basque social world. They also shaped political life because each household had a say in the people's assemblies.[10] Each household had one vote, independent of size or wealth. The basic criterion was the co-seigneurie of young and old couples with no specific generational preference; in the village assembly there was only one person who could speak in the name of household. There existed a second system of delegation, which, in contrast to the first, was based on the imperative mandate, starting with the village assemblies (*assemblées capitulaires*) to the higher provincial assemblies (*biltzar* in Lapurdi, *silviet* in Zuberoa, *cortes* in Navarre, and *juntas* in Bizkaia and Gipuzkoa).

When compared to past experiences of women in other Western nations, the condition of women in the Basque Country and the Pyrenees seems rather exceptional (Gratacos 1987). This is mainly because of the contrast between Basque and Pyrenean laws and customs and those that prevailed elsewhere.[11] As

---

10.   These were abolished by France after the French Revolution and in Spain after the Carlist Wars.

11.   The oldest customs were those most favorable to women. See Tessier (1918, 11).

authority was shared by the parental couple, there was never any absolute power derived from or exercised by a paterfamilias[12] or any similar institution that kept women under guardianship (or tutelage), as in the Germanic *mundium.*

At home the etxekoandre (the lady of the house) occupied a paramount place, with the daughter-in-law referred to as *erreina* (queen), and an heiress transmitted her name to her husband and her children. Records from almost every village and town in the Basque Country confirm this practice. For example, in Upper Zuberoa people were always greatly attached to heiresses, and breaking with that tradition was regarded as an infringement or transgression.[13]

During the ancien régime, girls were usually treated as adults much earlier than boys; and in terms of legal guardianship and exercising parental authority and tutelage, women were treated as being totally equal. Although women were later gradually deprived of their political rights (Lagarde 2003, 164n263), there is evidence of women's votes in local assemblies. From a penal point of view, acts of violence against women were severely punished. In Lapurdi and Zuberoa a man guilty of a rape was beheaded. In Lower Navarre the law stated that, "all rapists, abductors, and seducers of sons or daughters . . . shall be punished with death" (Goyhenetche 1985, 251). In the field of economics, the historian José Antonio Azpiazu reveals that in the sixteenth century, women, whether married or unmarried, played an important part in the Gipuzkoan economy (1995, 53–138). They occupied important posts in trade, craft and industries, and in transport. There can be no doubt that traditional Basque customs prepared them

---

12.   The number of lawsuits brought by younger children against their parents in Gipuzkoa proves that the father's authority was very relative. On these lawsuits, see Oliveri Korta (2001).

13.   Marie-Josée Capdevielle from Liginaga (Laguinge) in Zuberoa reports that in her father's ancestral home, "Jantzena" in Atharratze (Tardets), Zuberoa, there had been first-born daughters since time immemorial (twelve generations according to the legend!). The last of these, however, Jeanne (born around 1910), married an heir in another village, leaving the farm to her brother (one year younger than her). The grandfather of the Jantzena farm, Edouard Lhande (1848–1943), although having four grandsons, had been very annoyed at this: he considered the custom had been broken and he feared this would bring misfortune to the family. (personal communication).

for such tasks and the responsibilities that came with them. As regards religious practice, the *serorak* (church wardens) were equal to priests (Barandiaran 1960; Azpiazu 1995; Caro Baroja 1974). In funeral rites, womens' roles were more important than those of men. Womens' contribution to passing on important knowledge is testified to by the rich pool of what today is known as oral literature (Orpustan 1996). However, there is historical evidence to show that the situation of women deteriorated somewhat in the course of the seventeenth and eighteenth centuries; and in the nineteenth century their ancestral rights were abolished by the French and Spanish states.

The Political Importance of the Principle of Exogamy and Matrimonial Rule

Since men and women enjoyed the same status as landowners, it is difficult to maintain that men exchanged women as suggested by Lévi-Strauss. In the Basque Country, the principle of exogamy and the persistence of matrimonial rule were not based on the opposition of men and women, but on the opposition of elder and younger children. In other words, they exchanged one another, or rather the household exchanged them for the purpose of creating lineages that would guarantee the existence of the house.

Thus, in traditional Basque society, the key to social and political life lay in the giving away of junior children. There was an asymmetry of treatment between younger and older siblings, the purpose of which was to create two categories of people who could marry; such was the particular mathematics of this remarkable alliance consisting of similarly constructed houses in a neighborhood or village. In the light of such practices reducing junior children's departure to inegalitarianism or injustice seems absurd. Instead, the custom of "exchanging children" (to borrow Lévi-Strauss's metaphor for a moment), was the local version of exogamy: without it, co-seigneurie would have been impossible. Furthermore, the taboo of prohibition, Lévi-Strauss' second point, still applied. The taboo of incest continued to exist in Basque society, as in all other human societies; it was just safeguarded by a different set of rules that relied on a unique kinship system.

Part of the arrangement was that sexual relations within the house were only permitted for the married heir or heiress. Any brothers and/or sisters who stayed at home had to remain single, at least within the confines of the house. They could not marry or, especially, procreate in the same house because that would muddle the lineage and question the authority and decision-making in the house.

The symmetrical dialectics of elder family members "staying" and younger ones "exiting" permitted the establishing of lineages to which the names of the houses were linked. In other words, the parting of brothers and sisters created the dynamics of social life beyond the house and permitted the spreading of names. At the same time, lands, houses, and names were protected from all speculation by the principle of *retrait lignager* (kinship rights).[14] The kind of kinship system established fed directly into egalitarian community politics: since all houses had equal status in local assemblies, all members of a house who procreated were regarded as "brothers" and "sisters."[15]

Some aspects of the Basque kinship system survived until the late twentieth century. These traits diverged somewhat from the traditional Christian kinship system[16] in the sense that kinship was only established through blood relations and in the sense that those related through marriage were not regarded as "real" relatives (Lagarde 2006, 55–56). It seems paradoxical that the traditional Basque world so attached to Catholicism did not adhere to the ideological shaping of the *una caro*[17] religious formula, which considered the husband and wife as being one in flesh and blood, but also forming "a common identity . . . [by being] relatives linked to Ego by consanguinity that, over the centuries, became more separated from Ego" (Godelier 2004, 355).

Kinship terms confirm its egalitarian purpose. Parents and grandparents were taken back to the same degree of kinship,

---

14. If the family house was sold, it could be bought back by the members of the family at the very price it had been sold for; for forty years after the sale in Zuberoa, and ninety-nine years in Lapurdi.

15. By the same logic, selling the house implied political oblivion. That is also the very reason why the *retrait lignager* (see previous note) was instituted.

16. See the analysis of Christian kinship in Godelier (2004, 354).

17. "A single flesh": The principle defining and condemning as incestuous any sexual intercourse, and of course any marriage uniting two identical or too similar beings, because they have the same flesh in common.

since the grandfather was, through his denomination, similar to an uncle to his grandchildren. If we refer to the ancient Basque term *asaba* (grandfather) we realize, as Julio Caro Baroja points out (1997, 201–2), that it is similar to the term *osaba* (an uncle on the father's or the mother's side). Baroja also stresses that the terms *aitajaun* (grandfather) and *amandre* (grandmother) are of much later origin and we would add that the feminine of *osaba* is *izeba* or *izaba* (aunt), a term that perhaps in the past referred to the grandmother. Moreover, the term for both grandchild and nephew/niece is *iloba*: a single word that confirms the traditional Basque way of conceiving kinship.

In a way, such kinship terms demonstrate that biological kinship was "corrected" culturally by giving two generational levels, those of parents and grandparents, the same status as co-seigneurs, which also meant that they received political rights. In contrast, children and unmarried uncles and aunts were excluded from the public arena and did not have the right to voice their views in a political context.

The Compatibility between Symbolic Law and Social Equality, Expressed in Linguistic Terms

By enabling a differentiation of genders, symbolic law became the cornerstone of social life. However, because of its egalitarian dimension, the Basque co-seigneurial institution avoided any distinction of gender differentiation in the usual sociopolitical terms. In order to understand the principle of such a fundamental mechanism, it helps to take a closer look at language patterns. More specifically, the study of the expression of the masculine and feminine in the Basque language shows that the symbolic building of sexual identities is expressed through the use of the second person singular personal pronoun *hi* (a familiar form of address equivalent to the archaic "thou" in English).[18]

In personal communications, in order to express what possesses either masculine or feminine qualities, Euskara (the Basque language) does not behave like Indo-European languages that link gender to the noun system. Instead, it identifies gender through the personal pronoun of the second person singular, *hi*, the English

---

18. On the ancient nature of this pronoun see Azkue ([1905] 1993).

equivalent being the antiquated "thou" or, today, "you" (in French *tu* or in Spanish *tú*; Lagarde 1995). In other words, when one person addresses another, he/she adds to the verb a mark corresponding to the gender of the person he/she is speaking to: -*k*, if he/she is addressing a man, and -*n*, if he/she is addressing a woman.

The two marks -*k* and -*n* appear symmetrically, not only in sentences in which the pronoun *hi* is the active subject (or ergative) of the verb "to have," that is to say in all sentences in the second person, but also in all sentences in the first and third person singular or plural in whatever verb is used. Only in sentences in the second person in which *hi* is the subject of the verb *izan* (to be) are the marks not used, and men and women (or males and females) appear to form a "common essence": *hi hiz* (also spelled *hi haiz*, "thou art," or today "you are").

The Basque language has a "complete hand" of these forms at its disposal, which enable the speaker "to represent the person he/she is speaking to even if the latter is not concerned either as subject, agent, or object of reference"(Lafon 1980, 407). Let us take an example of a sentence in the third person singular: "This is a table." If we address a woman, we say: *Hori mahaina dü*n (which literally translates into "This is a table, o thou woman!"). In other words, the feminine mark -*n* is added to the verbal form *dü*. If we address a man, we say: *Hori mahaina dü*k (meaning "This is a table, o thou man!"). Here, likewise, the masculine mark -*k* is added to the verbal form *dü*. This linguistic form aims at incorporating the person we are speaking to by referring to his or her quality of being male or female.

The conjugation of the auxiliary verbs "to be" and "to have," which helps to express an activity in various tenses, also assigns gender identity by adding -*k* and -*n*. Here is an example for the present tense in the Zuberoan dialect (phonetically, between -*a* and -*i*, -*k* may be dropped and -*n* turned into -*ñ*):

> *izan* (to be)
> *Ni nü*k (I am, o thou man!) / *Ni nü*n (I am, o thou woman!)
> *Hi hiz* (thou art/you are, same form in the masculine and feminine)
> *Hura dü*k (he/ she/ it is, o thou man!) / *Hura dü*n (he/ she/ it is, o thou woman!)
> *Gü gütü*k (we are, o thou man!) / *Gü gütü*n (we are, o thou woman!)

Ziek zide (you are, same form in the masculine and feminine)
Haiek dütük (they are, o thou man!) / *Haiek dütün* (they are, o thou woman!)

The same mechanism exists with the auxiliary "to have" (*uken*). The person-subject *ni* (I), *hi* (thou), *hura* (he/she/it), and so on, carries the ergative mark -*k*, and marks of gender identity are tied to the root of the verb (*di* or *dü*):

uken (to have)
Nik di(k)at (I have, o thou man!) / *Nik diñat* (I have, o thou woman !)
Hik dük (thou has, o thou man!) / *Hik dün* (thou has, o thou woman!)
Hurak dik (he/ she/ it has, o thou man!) / *Hurak din* (he/ she/ it has, o thou woman!)
Gük di(k)agü (we have, o thou man!) / *Gük diñagü* (we have, o thou woman!)
Züek düzüe (you have)
Haiek di(k)e (they have, o thou man!) / *Haiek diñe* (they have, o thou woman!). [19]

The systematization of what are known as *toka* (male interlocutor) and *noka* (female interlocutor) forms possesses compulsory characteristics, thus revealing intent (Austin 1962). It should be noted that in some syntactic cases (interrogative sentences, exclamations, subordinate clauses) and in some modes (subjunctive, imperative) or in hypothetical clauses, whenever the assertion is questioned, the illocutionary forms are blocked as though their significance was submitted to the existing conditions (Rebuschi 1984, 549–66). The purpose of these forms is to confirm gender identities, so anything that weakens that assertion is avoided (Lagarde 2003, 259–78). This a deliberate linguistic choice, which expresses gender equality by mutualizing titles.

The *toka/noka* system allows for a perfectly symmetrical differentiation of genders, thus showing a collective appropriation of the symbolic law. What we see at work here is the building of gender identities through speech acts without any domination of one over the other. There is no equivalent of *toka/noka* in any

---

19. Phonetically, as noted, between -*a* and -*i* the masculine mark -*k* may be dropped and the feminine mark -*n* may turn into -*ñ*, but the opposition between masculine and feminine forms remains the same.

other language in this hemisphere (Alberdi Larizgoitia 1994), just as there is no equivalent of the "co-seigneurie of masters old and young" in other Western legal systems. The fact that they both occur in the Basque Country is highly significant and demonstrates that there existed a systemic coherence that is linguistically corroborated by the existence of titles for each member in the household.

In every household in the Basque Country, Béarn and Hautes-Pyrénées, each member of the household was named by a title linked to his or her status by birth: in Basque, *etxeko prima/etxeko primu* ("first daughter of the house"/"first son of the house"); and *etxeko seme/etxeko alhaba* ("junior son of house"/"junior daughter of house"). However, these titles were revoked after marriage and the people in question become the etxekoandre or etxekojaun, "lady of the house" or "master of the house."

There were, however, some differences between the Basque Country and Béarn and Hautes-Pyrénées. While they shared the same origins, over time a divergence occurred, as can be seen in linguistic expressions such as that maintaining the performative *toka/noka* that refers to the co-seigneurie of men and women in the Basque-speaking areas on one side, and the disappearance of such linguistically associated practices in Béarn and the Central Pyrenees through the substitution of Basque for Roman-based languages on the other.[20]

Another differentiation concerned generations. In these areas outside the Basque Country, the grandfather (or the father) became the guardian of authority and only the birth rank mattered, with all that this implied as regards relapsing into a vertical hierarchy. There was no sexual discrimination as such, but, rather, a sacrificial distribution in which junior children were reduced to the status of "slaves," "sterile," or "non-recognized sons-in-law." Junior males were stigmatized. They were reduced to the status of "lower female," and the law of full primogeniture survived only due to an identification of first-born daughters with male power. Men who married first-born daughters were likened, as Bourdieu observes with reference to the Kabyle society, to the status of *awrith* ("those who have an object function," a euphemistic term by which the man was defined as the husband of his wife) (Bourdieu 1998, 48–49).

---

20. On this transformation see Orpustan (1999) and Luchaire (1877).

With regard to the Basque masculine and feminine forms, which signify a "tracing of the body" as it were, they have been the victims of a real ideological war. For example, they were dismissed by some grammarian clergymen in the course of the eighteenth and nineteenth centuries.[21] If there is a sign of a reverse trend, then it must be the decline in the usage of toka/noka forms (especially the feminine forms). There are indications that, since the Middle Ages, the old pronoun *hi*—earlier common to all the Basque provinces—has been in steady decline. It has almost been entirely supplanted by the unmarked non-familiar second person singular pronoun *zu* (in Zuberoan *zü*), which, derived from a plural form, allegedly expresses courtesy by wiping away the gender mark. Nowadays, the pronoun *hi* is considered vulgar, its decline or nonuse indicating perhaps an erosion of the egalitarian world and the growing power of males in the Basque society.

(For an overview of some of the dynamics described here see table 6.1.)

Conclusion

One cannot judge traditional Basque society and its egalitarian aspects by comparing it with egalitarian notions prevalent in modern Western societies; modern individualism and its call for equal treatment and respect is something altogether different. Contrary to patriarchal societies, the role of the etxekojaun helped to maintain the etxe as a social institution yet without men totally dominating this institution. The gap between Basque egalitarianism and contemporary egalitarianism is due to the fact that Basque society stressed gender differences, whereas modern societies seem to standardize them.

In that traditional society, gender identities were expressed through linguistic patterns that distinguished between females and males while maintaining their equality. Equality was extend-

---

21.   In his *Gramática vascongada* (c. 1820), Fr. Pedro Antonio Añibarro has this very telling argument: "It is not necessary to learn the conjugations of the low, familiar, less polite *hi*. . . . The political, religious, sacred language requires more delicate wording, another culture of style; those basic colloquial moods used by the lower classes must not be used in sermons. . . . They will only be used occasionally, for example when addressing the Devil." Quoted in Alberdi Larizgoitia (1986, 161–62).

Table 6.1. Historic disparities and similarities according to area

AREA	LANGUAGE	BUILDING OF SEXUAL IDENTITIES	MATRIMONIAL RULE = First-born (sons or daughters) with juniors (sons or daughters)	FULL PRIMO GENITURE (IPPARRALDE AND THE UPPER VALLEYS OF NAVARRE)	POWER IN THE HOUSE	SEXES EQUALITY ON DOMONYMS	POLITICAL EQUALITY BETWEEN HOUSES
IPARRALDE, UPPER VALLEYS OF NAVARRA	Euskara	Egalitarian Toka/Noka	Majority	Majority (but cases of masculine primogeniture in Xiberoa and Navarra).	Coseigneurie of generations	In houses of full primogeniture	yes
GIPUZKOA, ARABA, BIZKAIA	Euskara	Egalitarian Toka/Noka	Majority (except in powerful houses)	Majority (but preference to the male after the sixteenth and seventeenth centuries)	Coseigneurie of generations	In houses of full primogeniture but patronymic names after the fifteenth century[1]	yes
UPPER VALLEYS OF BEARN, CENTRAL PYRENEES	Romane based language (Occitan)	Nonegalitarian. First-born daughters = masculine power. Junior boys = objects (lowered feminine)	Majority	Majority (But deprivation of the heiress's quality in the eighteenth century)[2]	Grandfather	Patronyms	yes
BEARN'S PLAINS	Romance language (Occitan)	Patriatical and non-egalitarian	minority	Preference to the male.	Father	Patronyms	yes

[1] OLIVERI KORTA (O), op.cit., p.267

[2] In 1768, the laws in Barèges, Lavedan (Central Pyrénées) were revised: first born daughters were denied their rights to inherit, and they composed a song to lament that. CORDIER, Le Droit... op.cit, 112

ed to generations through the notion of co-seigneurie, with no confusion of genders. The same equality applied to the representation of households in local assemblies. In order to establish a social order one central rule needed to be applied: the departure of younger children. The principle of exogamy was the necessary condition to reach equality. Despite the fact that not all of them would reach the status of co-seigneurs, there was no principle that denied such a role to them. Far from any sort of determinism by birth, the status of the first born child was a title: a younger child or someone who did not belong to the family could still be made heir.[22]

The system was conceived to safeguard lineages. Elder children wove "umbilical cords" while the younger ones had to cut them and weave them elsewhere. As I have tried to show by drawing linguistic examples, mutual donation prevailed as a social practice. In Iparralde and the Upper Pyrenean Valleys with small landed properties, the main concern was to limit the parceling of the land so that a maximum of people could live there. It is still the practice in a number of Basque farms in the region. The Basque language's specific gender features take us back to an age when men and women not only invented an original social contract but also tried to pass on such a custom to succeeding generations.

---

22. In Zuberoa the verb *primütü* (to make someone first) means that someone is given the status of heir.

Appendix:
Social ties and dynamics in traditional Basque society (overview)

<table>
<tr><td colspan="2">SOCIAL GENESIS (SYMBOLIC LAW)
PERFORMATIVE "TOKA/NOKA"</td></tr>
<tr><td>SOCIAL DIALECTIC</td><td>POLITICAL DIALECTIC</td></tr>
<tr><td>I-EXOGAMIA

Opposition "Stay" (heir/heiress)/ "Go" (Junior sons/ daughters).

Sex equality</td><td>I-NOBILITY of SEXES :

Linguistic titles: masc.-k / fem.-n, without domination of gender</td></tr>
<tr><td>2-SYSTEM OF ALLIANCE

-Prima (first daughter)+Etxeko seme (junior son)

-Primu (first son) + Etxeko alhaba (junior daughter)</td><td>2- NOBILITY of GENITORS

-Titles to mothers and fathers

Etxeko andere / Etxeko Jaun
(home's lady/ master)

-"Coseigneurie" to genitors' generations

Etxek(o) andere / Jaun gazte zoin zahar
(home's young and old ladies/ masters</td></tr>
<tr><td>3-SYSTEM OF KINSHIP
-Basic kinship :
Ahizpa (sister of sister) / Arreba (sister of brother) / Neba (brother of sister)/ Anaia (brother of brother)
-Kinship's degrees : two
*parents, grand-parents
*children (young ones and unmarried adults)</td><td>3-NOBILITY of BIRTH
Two categories of titles according to birth rank :
*Prima / Primu (First daughters/ sons)
*Etxeko seme /Etxeko alhaba ("Home's Junior sons / daughters)</td></tr>
<tr><td>4- SOCIAL DEVELOPMENT
-On synchronia : equality between genitors.

-On diachronia : full primogeniture, establishment of lineages</td><td>4- NOBILITY of "ETXEAK"
-On synchronia : <u>one VOICE</u> in popular assemblies ("Coseigneurie" of houses)
-On diachronia : <u>one NAME</u> (transmission of house's nobility</td></tr>
</table>

References

Achón Inchausti, José Angel. 2001. "La Provincia Noble: Sobre las raíces históricas de la 'teoría foral clásica' y el discurso político de Esteban de Garibay." In *El historiador Esteban de Garibay,* edited by Iñaki Bazán. Lankidetza collection. Donostia: Eusko Ikaskuntza.

Alberdi Larizgoitia, Xabier. 1986. "Euskarazko tratamenduen ikuspegia: I. Historia apur bat." *Anuario del Seminario de Filología Vasca Julio de Urquijo* 20, no. 1: 161–62.

———. 1994. "Euskararen tratamenduak: Erabilera." PhD diss., University of the Basque Country, Vitoria-Gasteiz.

Association Lauburu. 1980. *Etxea, ou, la maison basque.* 2nd edition. Saint-Jean-de-Luz: Association Lauburu.

Augustins, Georges. 1989. *Comment se perpétuer? Devenir des lignées et destins des patrimoines dans les paysanneries européennes.* Nanterre: Société d'Ethnologie.

Austin, John Langshaw. 1962. *How to Do Things with Words: The William James Lectures delivered at Harvard University in 1955.* Edited by J. O. Urmson and Marina Sbisà. Oxford: Clarendon Press.

Azkue, Resurrección María de. (1905) 1993. "Article HI." In *Diccionario vasco-español-francés.* Bilbao: Euskaltzaindia.

Azpiazu, José Antonio. 1995. *Mujeres vascas, sumisión y poder. La condición femenina en la Alta Edad Moderna.* Donostia-San Sebastián: R&B.

Bachofen, Johann Jakob. (1861) 1996. *Das Mutterrecht: eine Untersuchung über die Gynaikokratie der alten Welt nach ihrer religiösen und rechtlichen Natur.* Stuttgart: Verlag von Krais und Hoffmann. Published in French as *Le Droit maternel, Recherche sur la gynécocratie de l'Antiquité dans sa nature religieuse et juridique,* translated and with a preface by Etienne Barilier. Lausanne: L'Age d'Homme, 1996.

Barandiaran, José Miguel de. 1960. *Mitología vasca.* Madrid: Minotauro.

———. 1972. *Diccionario ilustrado de mitología vasca y algunas de sus fuentes.* Bilbao: La Gran Enciclopedia Vasca.

Bourdieu, Pierre. 1972. "Les stratégies matrimoniales dans les systèmes de reproduction." *Annales* 27, no. 4: 1105–27.

——. 1998. *La Domination masculine*. Paris: Seuil. Published in English as *Masculine Domination*. Translated by Richard Nice. Stanford: Stanford University Press, 2001.

——. 2002. *Le bal des célibataires. Crise de la société paysanne en Béarn*. Paris: Seuil. Published in English as *The Bachelor's Ball: The Crisis of Peasant Society in Bearn*. Translated by Richard Nice. Cambridge: Polity, 2008.

Caro Baroja, Julio. 1974. *De la vida vasca (Vera de Bidasoa)*. San Sebastián: Txertoa.

——. 1977. *Los Pueblos del Norte*. San Sebastián: Txertoa.

Cordier, Eugène. 1859. *Le Droit de famille aux Pyrénées: Barège, Lavedan, Béarn et pays basque*. Paris: Auguste Durand.

——. 1869. "De l'organisation de la famille chez les Basques." *Bulletin Trimestriel de la Société Ramond*: 89–109.

Chenu, Alain. 1994. "Postface." In Frédéric Le Play, *Les Mélouga: Une famille pyrénéenne au XIXe siècle*. Paris: Nathan.

Douglass, William A. 1975. *Echalar and Murélaga: Opportunity and Rural Exodus in Two Spanish Basque Villages*. New York: St. Martin's Press.

Duvert, Michel. 1993. (Traduit de l'espagnol et annoté par), Barandiaran, J. M. de, *Dictionnaire illustré de mythologie basque*. Translated and introduced by Michel Duvert. Donostia-San Sebastian: Elkar.

Galíndez, Jesús de. (1948) 2003. "Valor de los Fueros Vascos considerados según las circunstancias históricas que les dieron origen." *VIIe Congrès d'Etudes Basques*. Reprint, Donostia: Eusko Ikaskuntza. At http://www.euskomedia.org/PDFAnlt/congresos/07/07623638.pdf.

Gimbutas, Marija. 1989. *The Language of the Goddess: Unearthing the Hidden Symbols of Western Civilization*. London: Thames and Hudson.

Godelier, Maurice. 2004. *Métamorphoses de la parenté*. Paris: Fayard. Published in English as *The Metamorphoses of Kinship*. Translated by Nora Scott. London and New York: Verso Books, 2011.

Goyhenetche, Jean. 1985. *Fors et coutumes de Basse-Navarre*. Donostia and Baiona: Elkar.

Gratacos, Isaure. 1987. *Fées et gestes, Femmes pyrénéennes: Un statut social exceptionnel en Europe*. Toulouse: Éditions Privat.

Grosclaude, Michel. 1993. *La Coutume de La Soule. Texte gascon de l'édition de 1760*. St-Etienne-de-Baïgorry: Éditions Izpegi.

Hartsuaga, Juan Ignazio. 1987. *Euskal mitologia konparatua.* Donostia: Kriselu.

James, E. O. 1959. *The Cult of the Mother-Goddess: An Archeological and Documentary Study.* New York: Frederick A. Praeger.

Lafon, René. 1980. *Le Système du verbe basque au XVIe siècle.* Donostia-San Sebastián: Elkar.

Lafourcade, Maïté. 1980. "Dans l'Ancien-Régime: l'Etxe, axe du système juridique basque d'après la coutume du Pays de Labourd." In Association Lauburu, *Etxea, ou, la maison basque.* 2nd edition. Saint-Jean-de-Luz: Association Lauburu.

———. 1989. *Mariages en Labourd sous l'Ancien Régime. Les contrats de mariage du pays de Labourd sous le règne de Louis XVI: Étude juridique et sociologique.* Leioa: Universidad del País Vasco-Euskal Herriko Unibertsitatea.

———. 2007. "La Résistance des Basques à la pénétration du Droit romain: L'exemple du Pays Basque de France." *Revista Internacióoal de Estudios Vascos* 52, no. 1: 81–94.

———. 2011. *La Société basque traditionnelle.* Donostia-San Sebastián: Elkar.

Lagarde, Anne-Marie. 1995. "Allocutivité et pratiques sociales en Pays Basque." Mémoire de DEA, Faculté pluridisciplinaire de Bayonne, Etudes Basques, University of Pau and Pays de l'Adour.

———. 2000. "L'Univers psychique des Basques. Une instauration de la symétrie des sexes (expression sociale et linguistique)." PhD diss., Faculté pluridisciplinaire de Bayonne, Etudes Basques, University of Pau and Pays de l'Adour.

———. 2003. *Les Basques, société traditionnelle et symétrie des sexes.* Paris: L'Harmattan.

———. 2006. "Loi de prohibition et statut traditionnel de la femme basque." *Bulletin du Musée Basque,* special issue: 55–56.

———. 2016. "La Fabrique du nom dans le monde ancien basque." *Bulletin du Musée Basque* 186: 45–58.

Le Play, Frédéric. 1855. *Les Ouvriers européens,* vol. 4. Tours: Alfred Mame& Fils.

———. (1856) 1994. *Les Mélouga: Une famille pyrénéenne au XIXe siècle.* Paris: Nathan.

Lévi-Strauss, Claude. 1949. *Les Structures élémentaires de la parenté.* Paris: Mouton. Published in English as *The Elementary Structures of Kinship.* Translated from the French by James Harle

Bell, John Richard von Sturmer, and Rodney Needham, editor. Boston: Beacon Press, 1969.

Luchaire, Achille. 1877. *Les Origines linguistiques de l'Aquitaine*. Pau: Véronèse.

Mendras, Henri. 1995. *Les Sociétés paysannes: éléments pour une théorie de la paysannerie*. Paris: Gallimard.

Morère, Maurice. 1967. "Quelques aspects de la condition des femmes dans les fors pyrénéens." *Bulletin de la Société des Sciences, Lettres et Arts de Pau* 2: 77–86.

Oliveri Korta, Oihane. 2001. *Mujer y herencia en el estamento hidalgo Guipuzcoano durante el Antiguo Régimen (siglos XVI-XVIII)*. Donostia-San Sebastián: Gipuzkoako Foru Aldundia- Diputación Foral de Gipuzkoa.

Orpustan, Jean-Baptiste. 1996. *Précis d'histoire littéraire basque, 1545-1950: Cinq siècles de littérature en euskara*. St-Etienne-de-Baïgorry: Izpegi.

———. 1999. *La Langue basque au Moyen-Age (IXe-XVe siècles)*. St-Etienne-de-Baïgorry: Izpegi.

Ott, Sandra. 1981. *The Circle of Mountains*. Reno: University of Nevada Press.

Peillen, Txomin. 1987. "Mythologies pyrénéennes." Paper presented at Le Colloque comparatiste, UPPA (Section d'Etudes Basques), Pau, May 15–16.

Poumarède, Jacques. 1974. "Les coutumes successorales dans les Pyrénées au Moyen-Age." *Revue de Pau et du Béarn* 2: 23–34.

Rebuschi, Georges. 1984. *Structure de l'énoncé en basque*. Paris: Selaf.

Tessier, Albert. 1918. *La situation de la femme dans le Pays Basque et à Bayonne avant la Révolution*. Bayonne: Imp. de Montigleon.

7

Cracks in the Wall: Breaking Down the Myths of Egalitarianism and Matriarchy in the Basque Country

Jone Miren Hernández and Margaret Bullen

The invitation to reflect upon the work of historian Alfonso de Otazu, *El "igualitarismo" vasco: Mito y realidad* (1986), from a gendered perspective is a timely opportunity to revisit another book that also questions a myth pivotal in the construction of "Basqueness": *Mujer vasca: Imagen y realidad* directed in 1985 by anthropologist Teresa del Valle. If Otazu's work questioned the notion of social egalitarianism that from the sixteenth century presents Basque society as classless and free from feudalism (Otazu 1986, 7), del Valle's team exposed the similarly pervasive myth of matriarchy that depicts a gender balance of power in favor of Basque women and presents a society operating outside the dominant gender system in which men generally have the prerogative. There are interesting parallels in these two projects that set out to examine the reality beyond the myth, to go beyond the idealization of Basque society and uncover a different story, one that might challenge the dominant discourse. But what is particularly interesting is the exploration of why such myths prevail even when they have been proven to be erroneous, why—as Otazu asks—"can something false have been able to impose itself as a clarifying explanation of history?" (1986, 8). His answer coincides with del Valle and colleagues because these were of use to the Basque Country in its definition of itself, that is in the interpretation and defense of a separate and exceptional nation.

However, it is significant that in social theories of egalitarianism that evaluate equality in socioeconomic and political terms, there is no contemplation of gender equality. Can a system be egalitarian if, while upholding the same fundamental worth of all human beings and defending the same social status for everyone, it ignores the different positions of women and men? In order to address this question we have decided to focus our discussion on the contribution of the matriarchal myth to the fixing of gender inequality in the Basque Country and the way women have found ways to contest its categories.

For it is not only a question of nation, but also one of power. Neither myth could prevail unless firmly embedded in the sociocultural and political system. Egalitarianism is not matriarchy, which tips power balances toward women, but we would argue— and there agree with Otazu's allegation that egalitarianism was a powerful ideological tool at the service of the powerful—that it works equally effectively as a myth that harps back to an idealized past and projects the image of a paradise lost but that might be recuperated. This is the case of other myths that abound in the construction of "Basqueness." Alongside egalitarianism and matriarchy, we find the idealization of an equal but gender-differentiated sexual division of labor on the farmstead (Bullen 2003, 72–75) or the mythification of the rural way of life in opposition to the industrialization and urbanization that are underplayed— if not vilified—in the construction of an essentialist Basque identity (Douglass and Zulaika 2007, 315–16).

In gender terms, we can surmise that the persistence of a myth that attributes more power to women than they really have is due to its insertion in a gender system in which social and political institutions function together with values, customs, and beliefs to maintain conditions of inequality between women and men. Gender is conceived here as an analytical tool that serves to identify the characteristics and qualities, attitudes and emotions, behavior and activities that a given society at a particular time assigns to women and men as two distinct groups. It not only helps to detect these factors and enables us to describe them, but also leads to examine how they are perpetuated through society's institutions, and how in doing so, a hierarchy is created by which the attributes of men are considered superior and are more highly valued than those of women (Benería 1987, 46; in Maquieira 2001, 159).

It has to be stressed that the very object of gender analysis is to show that the different positions that women and men occupy in the social structure depend on what Gayle Rubin (1975, 159) calls the "the set of arrangements by which a society transforms [supposed] biological sexuality into products of human activity."[1] Raewyn Connell (1987, 92) encourages us to consider gender as a structure of social relations, maintaining that the concept of structure will help explain how relations of production and power work to transform difference into inequality. Structure, as Connell uses it, tends to suggest constraints that the system places on the individual's behavior through the complex network of rules, norms, and values that operate across a series of social institutions both formal and informal (the state and the political arena; the labor market; schooling, education, and socialization; the media; the law and the judiciary; marriage, the family, and interpersonal relations). Connell follows Anthony Giddens (1984) in arguing for a theory of practice that centers its interest in human practice or action as a complement of systems and structures, but that recognizes human agency and looks at the dialectic between practice and system to see how the system produces and reproduces itself and how and why processes of change occur.

It is therefore of the utmost importance to situate the debates around both egalitarianism and matriarchy firmly in historical context, both in relation to the gender system in particular and the social structure as a whole. It is our intention in this chapter to show that these myths have been fundamental characteristics of contemporary thought and used in the construction of political ideologies and identities. They have fulfilled two major functions in Basque society: on the one hand, they have functioned to conceal and even deny internal differences and inequalities; on the other hand, they have served to establish, fix, and institutionalize different social categories.

Our proposal then is a critical look at the myths that have sustained a false sense of female power in the Basque Country and

---

1. We add "supposed" because as Rubin was herself later to admit, sexual differences are not to be assumed as fixed in biological fact, but understood to be culturally constructed.

created a stereotype of the Basque mother and matriarch that has overshadowed other ways of being women. While *Mujer vasca: Imagen y realidad* debunked the myth by exposing the situation of contemporary women, we want to go back to the time of the Basque Revival (Euskal Pizkundea), between the late nineteenth and early twentieth centuries, and see how women then were already breaking the mold and challenging the way women were supposed to be.

Language, Orality, and Cultural Transmission

Before we do this, however, we want to describe a scene in the present that will help envisage how the situation of Basque women has evolved since the turn of the century. The scene takes place in the Bilbao Exhibition Center on December 13, 2009 when Maialen Lujanbio (born in Hernani, Gipuzkoa, 1976) took center stage to receive the winning *txapela* or beret of the Basque Country's *bertsolari* championship.[2] Fourteen thousand people looked on as the first woman to win a national bertsolari competition was proclaimed *txapeldun*,[3] champion. Lujanbio herself called on grandmothers, mothers, and daughters to share with her the historical moment:

> *Gogoratzen naiz, lehengo amonen*
> *zapi gaineko gobaraz*
> *gogoratzen naiz, lehen amonaz*
> *gaurko amaz ta alabaz*
> They come to my mind, the grandmothers of the past
> With wads of cloth on top of their headscarves (for carrying the water jars)
> They come to my mind, those grandmothers
> The mothers and daughters of today

With these verses, the bertsolari presented us with a whole genealogy borne out in the image of the first woman to have ever

---

2. *Bertsolaritza* is oral poetry, characterized by its spontaneity and improvisation; the *bertsolari* is a stand-up poet who performs in competition with others, inventing poems along a given theme and respecting certain rules of verse (Bullen 2003, 191).

3. In Basque the word *txapeldun*, literally "the one with the beret," refers to the practice of awarding the winner with a *txapela* or beret.

won such a championship.[4] It is a powerful image that remains engraved on our memory and fires our imagination, a vision come to life. Joxe Agirre (Azpeitia, Gipuzkoa, 1929), the veteran bertsolari who placed the beret on Lujanbio's head, paid tribute to her with these verses:

> Mila zorion ta goraintzi
> eman gabe nola utzi
> Euskal Herriko txapela horra Maialeni jantzi
> al dezun artean eutsi
> ez dezu meritu gutxi
> emakumerik oraindik ez da hortara iritsi

> Congratulations and greetings
> Cannot be left ungiven
> Maialen has donned the beret of Euskal Herria [Basque Country]
> Keep it for as long as you can
> Your achievement is no small one
> Never before has a women got as far as you.

It is with this picture and these verses in our minds that we want to look back in search of the grandmothers Lujanbio mentions, to try and trace this achievement not only through one bertsolari's story, but through Basque women's history. For Maialen Lujanbio's beret is undoubtedly the fruit of years of arduous personal effort, during which she cultivated her skill and perfected her talent. Yet, if we place it in the context of Basque society as a whole and examine it from a cultural point of view, it is clear that it is also the result of a collective effort: the fight for Basque women's rights. The history of a twenty-first-century female bertsolari champion begins at least a hundred years ago, back at the start of the twentieth century when women decided to confront the prejudices and dissipate the myths that prevailed around them.

One of the areas where we perceive myth to have been particularly powerful is in the area of linguistic and cultural transmission and this has had significant repercussions on present day attitudes toward language use and language planning. The

---

4. Gorka Aulestia (1999) outlines the state of the art of bertsolaritza at the dawning of the new millennium and signals the increasing involvement of women as one of the major areas of change.

myth of the matriarch firmly situates female power within the confines of the domestic space, traditionally the *etxea*—Basque farmhouse—and also infuses the passing on of linguistic competence not only from a mother to her own children but from a schoolteacher to her pupils or a children's writer to her readers. Here we meet one of the first contradictions between the alleged power of Basque matriarchs as pillars holding up the Basque culture and language[5] and the lack of credit given to them in the teaching and promotion of Euskara (the Basque language).

Following the same pattern of feminist scholarship in the social sciences, the first step is to uncover, make visible, and give due importance to what women have done and are doing in terms of cultural transmission (Bullen 2003, 14–15). But the second step is to demystify their contribution. That is, to detach it from any notions of naturalness, of supposed innate female skills or imagined instinctive behavior, and to analyze it critically. In this second step, there will emerge an element of transgression that can still derive mythical force from an alternative interpretation of the Mari myths[6] and be borne out by examples of women who have broken with the archetypal model of the Basque matriarch and made a different mark on the cloth of cultural transmission.

What becomes another interesting dimension to the debunking of the myth is the interpretation of women's actions when seen to go against the grain of matriarchy, when their desire to move beyond the confines of the domestic sphere and aspire to freedoms outside the rural space is seen as betrayal of their native language and traditional culture.[7] It is this transgression that we

---

5. Bullen and Diez (2010, 114) apply Dolores Juliano's image of the caryatids (sculpted female figures used in ancient Greece as a column or pillar) to evoke the notion of women as supporting the social structure though immobilized in doing so.

6. Carmen Diez has re-reexamined the Mari myths and proposed a different interpretation based on Mari's ambivalence and multiplicity, to be read as resistance to the dualism of our gendered cultural system (2010, 117).

7. A prime example of this approach is found in writers like Jose María Sánchez Carrión, *Txepetx*, one of the most prominent Basque sociolinguists in the 1980s and 1990s. In his article "La *Navarra cantábrica* (malda-erreka)" (1981) he defends men's role in language maintenance while criticizing women's attraction to Castilian. In his opinion, women at that time appeared to prefer all things foreign because they were seen as a symbol of social prestige. However,

wish to explore through examples of Basque women in the first third of the twentieth century: women who were both active in the propagation of the Basque language and culture, and innovative in breaking the bounds of their traditional role; women who in the very search for equal opportunities (to study and to work) and for real and not just imaginary power, became transgressors of the model; women who discovered new ways of furthering their language and culture beyond the restrictions of an outdated myth that speaks of power while cultivating inequality.

The Construction and Contextualization of the Basque Matriarchal Myth

First, however, we want to reflect on the power of myth in general and the force of the matriarchal myth in particular. This should also shed some light on Otazu's analysis of the myth of egalitarianism. To begin with, it is worth reminding ourselves that the concept of myth has two broad clusters of meaning: one grouped around a traditional or legendary story, usually involving a deity, hero, or momentous event and serving to explain a natural phenomenon or characteristic of a particular people (origins, practice, ritual); the other, referring to the realm of myth as something imaginary and fictitious that may take the form of a false collective belief used to justify a social institution.

What is particularly fascinating for our reflection is the power of the invented story, even when unproven—or proven to be erroneous. In the Basque case, we find the coexistence of contradicting myths and realities to be part of the tapestry of "Basqueness." Despite the crude realities of women's absence, underrepresentation, or devaluation in many walks of life, we are constantly confronted with the persistence of the myth of the "powerful Basque woman," whether in the classroom or round the dinner table. Year after year students of social anthropology insist on bringing up the issue of the matriarchy in class and initiate a debate. Despite our efforts to convince them to the contrary, there is always someone set on defending the existence of a Basque matriarchy in the past—or even in the present. Moreover, these students frequently extol the merits

---

despite his detailed analysis of women and men's behavior, Sánchez Carrión fails to incorporate a gendered perspective in his reflection.

of the matriarchy as one of the most important founding elements of Basque culture, a practice rooted in the mythological origins of Basque society from the very beginnings of time.

The American mythologist Joseph Campbell (1968) maintains that there are two different orders of mythology: myths that are metaphors of the universal spiritual potential of humankind and myths that are particular to specific societies. He further categorizes myths into four basic functions: cosmological, metaphysical, sociological, and pedagogical. If we examine the Basque myth of the matriarchy, it can be situated in the first order, as an origin myth fulfilling a cosmological function, explaining the shape of the universe and ascribing meaning to the observable physical world. It also performs a metaphysical or mystical function, awakening a sense of awe before the mystery of the universe, mediated through symbols and rituals that compensate for the difficulty of expressing what appears to be beyond reason. As we shall see in more detail below, here we have the interpretations of the Stone Age Basque goddess as a key to understanding the foundation and form of the Basque territory and the mystical link with the land and the culture (Bullen and Diez 2010, 116–17).

In the second order of myths, the sociological function supports and validates a certain social order, often purported to derive from divine intervention. Here we see the idealization of the Basque rural woman, the reproduction of the gender system, and the creation of nationalist discourse. This might be taken along with the pedagogical function, giving guidelines on how to live life and orienting the individual through different stages of development and psychological challenges.

Matriarchy as Foundation Myth

One of the more well-known and widespread versions of myths is the origin or foundation myth that, according to the Romanian historian, Mircea Eliade, takes people back to primordial time and the moment when the sacred revealed itself, when the natural world was created and human society founded. The Basques do not have a foundation myth as such, rather as Joseba Zulaika explains, it is the prehistoric, enigmatic past that is important for Basque identity, shrouded in the mists of a timeless past and swathed in mystery: "no founding myth or political revolution substitutes for such an archaic definition of their group origin" (1988, 7).

The Basque matriarchal thesis, resting on mythology and ethnohistorical data, has to be read as part of the construction of "Basqueness." Based mainly on the work of José Miguel Barandiarán and Julio Caro Baroja, it has been propounded by Andrés Ortiz-Osés and Franz K. Mayr in their work *El matriarcalismo vasco* (1980); and by Txema Hornilla in *La Ginecocracia vasca* (1981). The thesis is pinned on the figure of Mari, a Stone Age goddess, comparable to other goddesses of fertility found across Europe from Siberia to the Pyrenees. Mari is at the same time the Earth Mother—*Ama Lur*—a motif that appears in many mythologies, a goddess embodying the bounty of the earth and representing fertility and motherhood.

Ortiz and Mayr plot the evolution of Basque society from a prehistoric, native matriarchal system to a subsequently imposed patriarchal structure. They establish the existence of a pre-Indo-European, autochthonous, and ancient Basque matriarchal culture, peaking in the Paleolithic period. These authors argue that women exercised power through the control of resources and dominion of the magical-symbolic realm, through their religious role in the worship of the Earth Mother, and their socioeconomic role in hunting and food gathering. They postulate a process of acculturation in the Neolithic period, under the influence of invading groups with patriarchal forms of social organization (such as the Indo-Germanic invasion from the Caucasus). They maintain that this influence continued under the Roman Empire and the introduction of the Christian religion but that the Basque peoples resisted, producing a conflict between the original matriarchy and a superimposed patriarchy.

Their analysis is based on a Jungian interpretation of myth that endeavors to understand the psychology behind world myths, believing that the similarities between myths from different cultures reveal the existence of universal archetypes, held as proof that all humans share certain innate unconscious psychological forces. Ortiz and Mayr hold that the matriarchal base has not disappeared from the Basques' collective subconscious but rather continues to permeate their thinking.

Matriarchy as Social and Political Model

The matriarchal thesis is rooted in the traditional rural world and incarnated in the idealized figure of the rural woman. It is in *Mujer Vasca* that we find the first analysis of the construction of the ideal Basque woman, preferably a mother and presented in the singular, as one woman.[8] The authors examine the image of the ideal Basque woman in the work of different writers, but especially those of Barandiarán and Caro Baroja. Although there is also some reference to the fishwives of the coast, both focus mainly on women's role on the farm—*baserri*—and in relation to the family and beliefs, including religion, mythology, and witchcraft. The *etxekoandre* or "woman of the house" apparently ruled in the home and on the farm, managing the domestic economy and nurturing the household's physical and spiritual well-being. To be in charge of the house and the family was then her duty and obligation but also her source of "power." That seemed sufficient to speak of women's power, in other words of matriarchy.

In another article, del Valle (1989) shows how symbolic and cultural categories of "women" and "men" are constructed through the use of stereotypes, derived from culturally ascribed attributes, and used as if they were diametrically opposed in a simplistic, binary relation when in fact they are complex and varied. The process by which attributes become stereotypes involves the said quality being fixed, distorted, and frequently demeaned, applied to all Basque women (del Valle 1989, 132–33). Stereotypes are part of the ideal traditionally established for Basque women and help understand how elements of that model prevail despite far-reaching changes that have meant a departure, in real terms, from the ideal.

The archetype of the Great Mother has thus been erected as a model for modern women, situating women in the context of the traditional values and social organization of Basque society in which females appear principally as mothers and priestesses. Here we find myth in its more sociological function, as one that

8. The category "woman" emerged in the 1970s as a political subject based on "sameness," common biological and reproductive similarities, and a shared subordination to men. It was later replaced by the plural "women" to indicate women's diversity and show that differences of class, race, and ethnicity intervene and must be contemplated in their social and historical context (Bullen 2003, 19).

idealizes a moral gender order. The Basque myths of the goddess Mari are presented according to an androcentric interpretation of "woman" and an idealized notion of motherhood in which the female body is extolled as the generating principle of life. A moral evaluation is clear in the dichotomy established between Mari-mother and Mari-witch, along the lines of Mother=Good, Woman=Witch=Bad (del Valle et. al. 1985, 48). This suggests a Straussian approach in which myths are held to reflect shared patterns in the human mind that, rather than unconscious feelings or urges, are interpreted as fixed mental structures manifest in pairs of opposites (for example, good/evil, compassionate/callous).

The moral gender order rooted in the matriarchal thesis has also been used as an ideological and political vehicle for nationalism.[9] It feeds into the mystification of Basque culture and its primitive past, stressing its timelessness and antiquity, and emphasizing its difference and superiority over others. In this sense, it fits nationalist ends, for the discourse portrays an official, foreign, and colonizing culture introducing patriarchy in opposition to an autochthonous, natural, and matriarchal culture centered in the community. The thesis suggests that the recuperation of matriarchal society (and autochthonous identity) is a viable way to resist external influences.

As well as taking into account the political, economic, social, and religious context in which the ideal is constructed, del Valle (1989) signals the importance of understanding the socialization processes by which individuals act it out. She mentions women's participation in both nationalism and cultural transmission, a vital function in a minority culture like the Basque one in which, as we shall see in greater detail below, women (particularly in their role as mothers) are a vital link in passing on the Basque language, customs, and traditions. Women have then been held to be responsible for the production and reproduction of the model (del Valle et al. 1985, 22–61; Llona 2002, 168; Bullen 2003, 57–67).

Matriarchy as History

In the 1970s, there was a revival of interest in primitive matriarchies and scholars returned to nineteenth-century works such

---

9.   Del Valle et al. (1985); Juaristi (1987); Bullen and Diez (2010).

as Johann Jakob Bachofen's *Das Mutterecht* to defend an archaic age when women ruled. It is in the wake of this general revival that the Basque matriarchy was unearthed and held up as an example. Matriarchy, according to Bachofen, is the natural, biological right of the mother to hold sway over family and state, exercise authority, make decisions, and wield influence over men. Primitive matriarchies were said to be characterized by a communal spirit of solidarity and sympathy and were essentially nature oriented.

A matriarchal society was purportedly characterized by matrilineage, which refers to the reckoning of descent and the transmission of property through the female line. Matrilineal descent groups also tend to be matrilocal, which means that a couple establishes postmarital residence in the wife's mother's group. These circumstances tend to occur when the women of a community are responsible for agriculture and continue to tend their lands, while men are occupied hunting and fishing. However, a matrilocal-matrilineal arrangement does not necessarily mean that the women in that society exert political and economic control over men, since in most such instances men still control the group's corporate resources. Thus we may have a society in which the mother is the head of the family and descent is reckoned through the female line, and which may be described as matriarchal on this basis, but it does not make it the female equivalent to a patriarchal system in which political power through government is wielded by men.

This leads to attempts to distinguish between a "domestic matriarchy" in which women are the heads of their household and control the domestic space, "political matriarchy" in which women exercise political power in the public arena, and "symbolic matriarchy" in which religious beliefs and practices reflect a matriarchal ideal. The very fragmentation of matriarchal power is in itself indicative of the theory's weakness.

Matriarchy as Invention

The scant evidence for both the historical and the contemporary existence of matriarchies means that the theories incorporate a great deal of conjecture. Here we are less concerned with ascertaining the existence or not of matriarchy than with contemplating the construction of a model and its implications for both Basque culture and Basque women.

The arguments for primitive matriarchies have been contested by scholars such as Juan Aranzadi (1982), whose work was expanded on by the research team of *Mujer vasca* (del Valle et al. 1985, 44–54). The critique of the Basque matriarchal thesis turns on three central issues: the first concerns the use of myths as a basis for building social scientific theories, while the other two take up the androcentric and politically oriented interpretations of the material. The first difficulty is, then, one of unsatisfactory evidence that leaves the matter open to individual interpretation and speculation. Joan Bamberger, in her article "The Myth of Matriarchy: Why Men Rule in Primitive Society," comments skeptically on the popularity of the thesis despite the lack of conclusive evidence:

> Because no matriarchies persist anywhere at the present time, and because primary sources recounting them are totally lacking, both the existence and constitution of female-dominated societies can only be surmised. The absence of this documentation, however, has not been a deterrent to those scholars and popularists who view in the concept of primitive matriarchy a rationale for a new social order, one in which women can and should gain control of important political and economic roles. (1974, 263)

In the Basque case, the use of mythology instead of archaeology as a foundation for explaining early social organization is dubious in accuracy and mixes frames of reference and levels of analysis. It is not that myth should be ignored, but that it should be read differently from history. Where myth is taken as historical fact, the interpretation is doomed to failure, but where it is recognized that myth "recounts a fragment of collective experience that necessarily exists outside time and space" (Bamberger 1974, 267), it may be seen as part of a cultural history that does not coincide with chronological events or historical facts but instead presents a symbolic invention of reality aimed at explaining or legitimating a certain order or state of affairs.

The second problem is the way the proponents of primitive matriarchies project an ideal of woman that is far from the notion of the modern liberated woman. It romanticizes motherhood and places women on a pedestal of moral virtue that inspires men to heroic and chivalrous deeds (ibid. 265). In this reading, it is a male notion of women's purity and perfection that empowers them to rule over the household and beyond. The third is the incorporation of the myth into the political imaginary that Teresa del Valle and her team believe to be the reason why such an academically weak argument is so vehemently defended. It reaffirms the ancestrality and mystique of Basque culture, setting it apart from and claiming superiority over more recent Iberian cultures. At the same time, it presents an ideological opposition between the Spanish central government and Basque nationalist parties; the figure of Mari, the Great Mother, thus becomes a symbol for Basque collective identity.

Furthermore, the idea that women once ruled is attractive to feminists who intuit that they could resume control in the present. The problems of the female matriarchal model are glossed over in projecting a symbol of Basque female power, but there is also the possibility of interpreting the myth differently. Mari could be construed as a model of permanence, the matriarch who fiercely defends tradition and a hierarchical social order; but she could also be depicted as a model of resistance, "Mari the transgressor, ready to overcome imposed limits and increase her power, in order to create a new system where gender and other differences are no longer the basis upon which unequal relationships are sustained" (Bullen and Diez 2010, 123). It is to this tension between tradition and transgression which we will now turn our attention.

Transmission: Building the Matriarchal Wall

According to historic Basque nationalist activist Haydee Agirre,[10] "We [women] were the source of Euskara's life and continuity." So far we have discussed how the myth of the matriarchy emerged as a concept to be reckoned with in the feminist production of the

10.   Haydee Agirre (Santurtzi, Bizkaia, 1907) was a speaker for the Euzko Alderdi Jeltzale (EAJ, the Basque Nationalist Party) and the first woman activist to be imprisoned in 1932. The following year she was once again jailed along with Polixene Trabudua (Sondika, Bizkaia, 1912–Zeberio, Bizkaia, 2003), another famous party speaker in the period up to the outbreak of the Spanish Civil War (1936).Within the EAJ, Agirre and Trabudua were active participants in the Emakume Abertzale Batza (EAB, Women's Nationalist Union).

1970s, how it was taken up by Basque academics and critiqued by feminist anthropologists in the 1980s, and how it seems to have seeped into popular knowledge and the nationalist imagination. What we are interested in probing now is how the myth is actually propounded in society, how it reaches particular social actors, and is taken up or contested by them. To do that, we need to look back to the era when Basque nationalist discourse was in the making, back to the end of the nineteenth and beginning of the twentieth century, and examine cases of "real" women, flesh and blood figures whose (hi)stories can shed some light on the propagation of the myth.

We particularly intend to center on the Basque revival that began in the last quarter of the nineteenth century, in 1876, and ended with the outbreak of the Spanish Civil War in 1936.[11] The turn of the century played its part in those sixty years of creation and revival, of external influences and internal dynamics, of the energy of many actors and the voices of many speakers. And it is voice, speech, and orality that we have made the focus of our analysis because not only is language "a fundamental factor through which Basques look at their prehistoric past in search of their identity" (Zulaika 1988, 6), it is considered a crucial cultural element to be protected, preserved, and transmitted by the pillars of tradition: the Basque matriarchs.

It is, then, against the backdrop of the Revival that we must situate the modern formulation of the matrarchical ideology. The in-depth studies at the end of the nineteenth and beginning of the twentieth century give us several pointers as to how the concept of matriarchy was invented and established a parallel with the dawning of contemporary nationalism and its projection in the Revival. Instigated by Sabino Arana (the founder of Basque nationalism) and other intellectuals and politicians, a new ideological discourse was elaborated in which certain concepts emerged in connection with Basque identity: people, community, ethnicity, egalitarianism, matriarchy, and so on. It is not just that these ideas filtered into political discourse but that they became part of

---

11. We have based our analysis particularly on the work of the following historians who have covered this period: Amezaga (1980); Aresti (2007); Nuñez-Betelu (2005); Llona (2000, 2002, 2008); Otaegi (2000); and Ugalde (1993).

the social structure and gender system; in short, they were institutionalized. For the purposes of our argument it is important to
stress two major functions or results of this process. On the one
hand, internal diversity was obscured, glossed over, and even denied altogether. On the other, differences determined by one's origins were institutionalized. These ideas are expressed in relation
to egalitarianism by the historian Miren Llona:[12] "The supposed
ancestral egalitarianism among the Basques made it possible to
cover up social differences among the locals, at the same time as it
institutionalized the difference of origins as a real and legitimate
social divider" (2002, 168).

The concept of the matriarchy can be seen to work on the
same principle of origins as egalitarianism or any of the other
aforementioned concepts (people, community, ethnicity). Your
lot in life is determined by your original status, whether in terms
of ethnicity or gender: women are born women and must therefore perform certain duties and meet certain conditions; there are
no exceptions, no deviation from the norm, no possibility of diversity. In the Basque case, this essentialist logic was applied both
to gender and ethnicity. In Llona's words (2002, 170) women were
to be women, and in the case of Basque women they were to be
Basque—*euskaldun*—not only in their customs and behavior, but
in their very way of thinking.

With the emergence of Basque nationalism, the figure
of the "the mother of the nation" was added to the role of the
etxekoandre, duplicating the demand to be mother: in the home
and in the nation. In keeping with the slogan *"Jaungoikoa eta Lagi
Zarra"*—God and the Old Laws—"good" Basque women had to
perform certain duties: on the one hand, they had to be ready
to help out and give to the needy (whether at school or church,
collaborating with charity or in catechesis); on the other, they
were to be the guardians of tradition and especially of the Basque
language: "The figure of the mother of the nation is born. To her
were entrusted the responsibility of the nation's well-being and
the duty of watching over tradition, of which language was considered to be the quintessence" (Llona 2002, 171).

In recent years, various authors have written on the need to

12.   In the interests of brevity, we have translated all literary citations from the
Spanish and omitted the original quotation.

incorporate a gendered perspective when analyzing the elaboration of nationalist discourses and the process of nation-building. Mercedes Ugalde shows that this dual symbolism of woman as both homeland and mother has been taken up throughout history and is used to legitimate the prevalence of "nation" over the will of individual people by appealing to symbolic referents of Nature, God, and History itself (1994, 40). Basque nationalism uses the archetype of the Basque woman to represent all Basque women, drawing from a well of symbols that project an image of the ideal woman as mediator and transmitter of Basque culture. It takes up the stereotype of the Basque matriarch described above and presents the etxekoandre as the cohesive element that keeps the baserri running not only on a daily basis but down through the ages. She is the mediator between the past and the present, which meet at the crossroads represented by the baserri, and she enacts the meeting of these paths through various ritual practices, principally those related with death or those destined to keeping alive the memory of the departed. Together, woman and baserri represent the essence of Basqueness (del Valle et al. 1985).

Drawing from the nature-culture debate, the linking of woman and nation strengthens itself through the association of homeland with mother-goddess in both a divine and a natural way. Nira Yuval-Davis (1996) argues that the conceptualization of "woman" as "reproducer of the nation" is made possible by the naturalization of cultural transmission that impedes the proper evaluation of what women do beyond the domestic space. The discourse of honoring one's ancestors and handing down traditions from one generation to the next is part of an imaginary through which people put together a genealogy—Benedict Anderson's "imagined community"—in which neither are the members necessarily related nor even belong to the same town or village (Bullen and Diez 2008).

> We understand that Basque nationalism as a political ideology has fabricated a unilateral concept of the Basque woman, based on attributes of the rural woman in which elements of the woman as mother with a role in teaching and passing on the Basque language and culture stand out. Therefore, we consider that the fundamental objective of this image of the Basque woman is to preserve the structure of the family as a strongly stabilizing factor resisting any possible changes that might jeopardize her traditional role. (del Valle et al. 1985, 61)

In the Basque case, initially a distinction was made between political work, reserved for men, and patriotic action, allotted to women. Social work (via charity) and patriotic action (creating and recreating the nation) were seen to be women's spheres of activity at that time and both were joined by a spatial representation: the house. The house, household tasks (education, care, cleaning, feeding, and so on) and extensions of these in the care of the nation, in cultivating society's well-being, are at the root of the matriarchical order. The matriarchal thesis laid down that contemporary women had power, but it is clear where the limits of that power lay. Rather it was a question of responsibility to do one's duties and these obligations were assigned an additional emotional charge. In other words, the sexual distribution of labor was reinforced by the distinction not only between women and men but between reason and emotion. Patriotic action was linked to the heart, feelings, and emotion, key aspects of the traditional model of femininity; political activity, on the contrary, was linked to reason and intelligence, and as such was seen—at that time at least—to impose a bar on women's participation: "Politics, identified with intelligence and the brain, was to be a masculine prerogative, and political activity was to be directly associated with intervention in the public sphere, thus ruling out any role being assigned to women in this area" (Llona 2002, 171).

Nevertheless, while in theory hard-and-fast lines were drawn between the political and the patriotic spheres of activity, in practice what (at least some) women did was another matter. Over the years, feminist critique has maintained that the differentiation of reason and emotion is the result of the gender system that has produced two clearly defined and gender differentiated categories. Reason is seen to be masculine, men are hailed as its legitimate spokesmen and invested with its authority; they both meet the social standard to exercise reason and to guard its use. Emotion, on the other hand is feminine, it lacks legitimacy and represents spontaneity, impulse, and irrationality, calling for control and self-control.

However, although women's practice in patriotic activity was linked to the emotive side of nationalism, their very incursion in the public sphere made it increasingly difficult to deny the political nature of their work. In this sense, the creation of the

Emakume Abertzale Batza (EAB)[13] in 1922 signified a step forward in Basque women's sociopolitical participation. Elías Gallastegui was one of the founders of the women's branch and according to Llona he was one of the first to call for women's presence in politics. As well as forming several commissions, he set up a propaganda working group within EAB: "the propaganda commission was set up and this contributed to the implication of women in the task of spreading patriotic ideas and emotions" (Llona 2002, 172).

This sphere of activity achieved more than just the dissemination of political propaganda: it marked a turning point in the nature of women's participation. Although propaganda was viewed as patriotic action and therefore in the field of women's activity, in practice it appropriated certain characteristics of the political sphere that manifested themselves through the women propagandists: they claimed for themselves the right to speak and to be heard; they took up position center stage, sometimes alongside the men, but at other times on their own; and they became agents and authors with the opportunity to write or improvise their speeches.

Transgression: Shaking the Foundations, Making Cracks in the Wall

Recalling her public speaking role on behalf of the EAJ, Miren Nekane Legorburu comments that, "I put my heart where my mouth was."[14] The Basque Revival brought Basque society and

---

13. Emakume Abertzale Batza or the Women's Nationalist Union was fashioned on the Irish nationalist version, Cumann na mBan. It was outlawed during the dictatorship of Primo de Rivera in the 1920s and disappeared until 1931, when it reemerged and expanded throughout the Spanish Basque Country. Its goals, like the Basque Nationalist party in general, were "God and the Old Laws" (the latter a reference to the *fueros*) and Euskara, and its main areas of activity the teaching of the language and education in Basque (especially at nursery and primary levels), propaganda, and social issues. However, the Spanish Civil War broke out when it was at its peak and its members were forced into exile.

14. Legorburu was a propagandist for the Basque Nationalist Party, joining the Women's Nationalist Union at the age of sixteen. She made her debut in public speaking the following year at the opening of a Batzoki (EAJ party club house) in Ermua (Bizkaia) and her success was such that Sunday after Sunday she repeated her rousing rhetoric in different EAJ club houses. During the

culture to a crossroads at which the spirit of renewal and renovation met with the promotion of women's participation in society. At this juncture, two contradictory forces collided: on one side, the call to transgression from without; on the other, the cry to resistance from within. In the face of new, revolutionary ideologies for women blowing in from Europe came the need to do something about them and the development of a discourse aimed at keeping women "in their place" at home.

While it is clear, even if only implicitly so, that Basque women at the turn of the century had interiorized this discourse, it would appear that by acting out and defining the role of "propagandist" or "public speaker" women were beginning to transgress the traditional mold or, metaphorically speaking, they were opening up a crack in the wall of traditional Basque nationalism. That was not of course the objective of the movement, which, by using female propagandists, had intended to exploit their emotional leverage. Women were believed to best represent "the heart" and so deemed the most suitable figures to convey the essence of the Basque soul and pass on the cult of the motherland. However, the very building of the Basque matriarchal thesis into a political discourse to use in nationalist propaganda was at the same time its downfall. The possibility afforded women of entering the world of public speaking—taking part in political gatherings, giving talks, or both—was a training ground for women to gain confidence in the public sphere and in their own abilities. As Policarpo Larrañaga recommended: "[The woman] should practice and prepare herself for this, overcoming her natural shyness" (Llona 2002, 173).[15] They had the advantage of a structured environment in which everything was prearranged and the women received guidance in their participation and assistance in the preparation of their speeches.

The contradictions of the situation soon became apparent. At that time, women and their speeches were seen as crucial to introducing, consolidating, and spreading the concept of nation,

---

civil war she went into exile in France and England, returning after forty years of the dictatorship (www.euskomedia.org/aunamendi/80041 last visit Dec. 7, 2012).

15.   Quote taken from Policarpo Larrañaga, *Emakume Abertzale Batza: Las mujeres en el nacionalismo vasco* (Donostia-San Sebastián: Auñamendi, 1978), 52, cited in Llona (2002, 173).

emotionally, sentimentally, from the heart. Women's contribution to nation-building was seen as a labor of love, and in that framework, the political character of what they were doing was dissipated. In addition, women were assigned the role of reining in the trends brought in from Europe and threatening traditional Basque femininity. Fashions from abroad (from dress to dance) were perceived as ridiculous and, from a Basque nationalist point of view, dangerous. Thus women became the targets of the harshest criticisms that contemporary intellectuals, such as Xabier Lizardi in the early twentieth century (see Otaegi 2000) and José María Sánchez Carrión (1981) toward the end of that same century, made at those betraying the model of the ideal Basque woman. Here emerges the figure of woman as traitor: one who rejects the feminine role socially ascribed to her, who abandons her traditional environment in search of a better life, or who decides to explore the wide world beyond the farm and expose herself to alien influences. As Lourdes Otaegi (2000) points out, Lizardi blamed the pitiful situation of the Basque language on two factors: the Church and women. Most schools were run by the Church and taught in Spanish. Women, on the other hand were guilty of being besotted with fashion and taking up customs and behavior that had nothing to do with nationalism: "Lizardi holds it totally unthinkable for the majority of women to be interested in anything but being up to the minute with the fashion for makeup, clothes, hairstyles, and dancing. He also suggests that it is useless to try and reason with women" (Otaegi 2000, 293).

Throughout the combatant countries—which excluded Spain—World War I (1914–1918) brought about various changes in the situation of women. The wartime roles and responsibilities that women had to take on helped in the projection of a new image for women, and when the war was over, it was impossible to imagine that women could just drop their newly acquired economic, social, and cultural activities. The changes in women's position throughout the world, but especially in Europe, started to be heard in Euskal Herria from the beginning of the twentieth century. The press of the day (*Argia, El Día, Euzkadi*) is full of news items about women both at home and abroad: the call for the vote for women in some other countries of Europe; the new figure of the working woman; fashions from abroad, and the influence of all this on Basque women. In the 1920s and 1930s, we find questions expressing a palpable concern in the face of change, an identity crisis even: "Women, where are we heading?" ("*norantz goaz emakumeak?*"). And there is the recurrent theme of language; in magazines like *Euskal Esnalea* (The Basque Rouser)—published by a Basque cultural association of the same name from 1908 on—we find several articles with titles like "Women and Euskara" ("*Emakumiak eta Euskera*").[16]

These contemporary texts (whether in the press or those signed by writers like Lizardi) tell of a new kind of woman in the making, even while criticizing her. In Llona's opinion (2002) even though significant changes were occurring among the Basque middle classes, they were not as sweeping nor as profound as in other parts of Europe and that is why we cannot talk of a modern Basque woman. The model of woman that was emerging in other European countries—free, independent, sexually active, and in charge of her own life—was still virtually unthinkable in the Basque Country. Nevertheless, the social participation of women did have important implications for Basque women, who, according to Llona, were active, conscious, and committed. In fact, it was their participation in collective projects that would be influential in feeding the consciousness of these "new women."

After the war the discourse on women that had prevailed previously became untenable. Women increasingly challenged the theory that they were the weaker sex and frequently showed that in practice they were far from incapable of certain intellectual and physical activities as had previously been thought. By forcing women to take up men's jobs, the war annulled many prejudices. In the 1920s a new model based on practice rather than theory emerged in Europe. If we consult the studies documenting that period we find a new model of woman, described by the historian Nerea Aresti as rebellious, revolutionary, and transgressive:

> The modern woman rebelled against the imposed order and pushed back the frontiers of gender: her appearance, her intrusion in forbidden places, her male company, her personal

---

16. As well as in the written press, the subject of women and Euskara was often a topic for conferences and receptions. For example, María Etxabe took part in the fifth Congress of Basque Studies (Nov. 6, 1930) with a speech entitled "Women's tribute to Euskara" that she had given a few months before in Basque (July 30, 1930).

projects, her sympathies and explicit public opinions, her daring in standing up to conventionalities, all this made her a rebel figure who deserved the most vehement condemnation. (2007, 176)

Up until till then it seems hard to say that such a model of woman emerged in Euskal Herria (at least not at the start of the twentieth century) but changes in women's situation and representation were apparent. In any case, it is our impression that until the 1920s, the transformation took place in practice rather than in discourse, or at least change was more perceptible in what people did. Between 1920 and 1930, however, the discourse on women began to be adapted to the new situation and it became increasingly difficult to consider women as a lower-class being. Llona describes these changes as reflected in the discourse of the contemporary intellectual Gregorio Marañón: "Doctor Marañón affirmed in 1926: now the formula of women's inferiority has been replaced by this other one: the two sexes are neither inferior nor superior to each other; they are simply different" (Llona 2002, 79).

From then on, the gender discourse was not one of inequality, but rather of difference. In theory, the "differences" between men and women were no obstacle to achieving and strengthening equality, but in practice, the models of masculinity and femininity would be notably reinforced, men's and women's roles remaining rooted in essentialisms. As we said earlier, women's role in society was linked to a specific set of tasks related to care, motherhood, and education; always looking to others, always looking out for the wellbeing of others. This was the philosophy of the matriarchal thesis. The work women performed as mothers (even though practically devoid of prestige or recognition) was (discursively) to be praised and extolled. Nonetheless, it was virtually impossible to break the boundaries and enter other areas of society considered inappropriate for women. She who fulfilled the social role of woman was accepted and "valued"; she who rebelled against the strictures of her sex would find herself criticized for being too manly and consequently marginalized, cast out as a woman against "nature." This is the way the gender system works.

As we have said, socialization and cultural transmission are important mechanisms in the naturalization of femininity. Because language transmission is presented as something natural when related to women, it is discursively applauded as a natural asset of motherhood but practically devoid of social value. Teresa del Valle (1997) takes us back to the nature-culture debate to show how the passing on of a language from mother to child is closely associated with women's "natural" role of reproduction: giving birth, child-rearing, and passing on a language are all seen as "natural" female roles: "In this way, the woman as transmitter keeps the language intimately related to the house, the domestic universe, and the traditional world. The concept of procreation, of giving life, is inextricably linked to the vitality of the language. To transmit a language is to keep it alive" (1997, 15).

Linda White analyzes the reception of women's incursion into Basque literature and shows that by magnifying motherhood and placing women firmly in the domestic space, their literary activity beyond the home is silenced, ignored, or undervalued.

> The perpetuation of this link between women and the home invades their creative space as well, the world of the mind and the imagination. Even there, though they produce volumes, they cannot be viewed separately from their primary functions of wife and mother. (1999, 135)

Both authors demonstrate that prestige is only acquired in this area when language learning leaves the "natural" domestic domain and enters the public arena, in which case it is assigned to men. Where women have made an incursion into literature, says White, they write within the "limitations of Basque society's domestic expectations by creating child-related and education-related materials" (ibid., 136). It is in the public world, in which Euskara is institutionalized—in which it enters the world of language planning and politics, pedagogical techniques, and media and literature—that it generates the most interest and social significance and this world has been, on the whole, dominated by men.

Another area of linguistic activity and cultural transmission where women have been particularly active is in the primary education of the *ikastolas*, Basque language schools, in which women are to be found both in teaching posts and as parents, in which mothers may be visible militating in public meetings or protests. Del Valle suggests that, since ikastolas sprang from initially home-based, family-oriented organizations that have always favored a high level of parent-teacher coordination and emphasized the crucial part the mother has to play in children's linguistic acquisition, the scale of values that marks women's role as natural language transmitters is carried over and wrests prestige from their activity (1997, 15).

There is a contradiction, then, inherent in the way women's importance has been recognized in the continuity of the language and at the same time ignored in areas in which decisions are made about language planning and usage and undervalued in the construction of the Basque literary canon. In the same process, we can situate the women active in the Basque revival: not just teachers and writers, but also public speakers. It is the public and political nature of their work that we now wish to address.

Mercedes Ugalde documents the cases of ninety-two women who acted as public speakers in Euskal Herria during the 1930s (1993). Although there are not data for all of them, if we compare their profiles we find certain common characteristics: they were young (some were only fifteen or sixteen but most were in their twenties); they were single (only a few were married) and had no children; and teaching was their most common occupation. The case stories of women such as those we have mentioned—Haydee Agirre, Polixene Trabadua, and Nekane Legorburu—have been documented in interviews and biographical work (Amezaga 1980; Llona 2000) and reveal fascinating information about women's incipient public participation, actions of course considered completely transgressive. These testimonies speak of women who took the floor and, often improvising their speech, expressed their feelings and emotions in public. As Miren Nekane Legorburu confesses in an interview with Arantzazu Amezaga (1980), she put her heart where her mouth was and, speaking from the heart, publicly performed the role of the emotional woman.

Emotion: Bringing Down the Wall

Legorburu goes on to say that, in doing so, "I discovered myself." As we have said, women were traditionally assigned the emotional universe but while some emotions were accepted—especially those attached to motherhood—others, related to the body or sexuality for example, were chastised. Catherine A. Lutz explains that, on the one hand, the expression of emotion is seen as the source of great strength, energy, and vigor; yet on the other, it is perceived to be irrational and dangerous (2008, 77). That is why the relation between women and emotion has often been subjected to scrutiny. The way emotion is viewed is riddled with contradiction: sometimes its expression evokes praise; sometimes it provokes a call for repression and self-control. These two interpretations of emotion unite in one female prototype: the emotional woman. Emotional women are seen to be dangerous: they display the strength needed to face life and all its challenges, but at the same time, they can be impossible to control. As a result, these emotional women (or more usually, emotional situations in which women are protagonists) become a mirror that reflects the gender system.

It is the gender system that considers the emotional woman model dangerous, and that is why it operates certain mechanisms of control. Men, broadly speaking, are not supposed to be emotional: the model of the white Western adult middle-class male is a rational not an emotional one and therefore does not require the same attention. In order to rein in women's emotions, they are assigned to the individual level and are denied a collective entity: they are not shared but particular to each woman and as such they are conceived to be chaotic and antisocial. These individual emotions should be restricted to the private, intimate sphere (within the family, among friends); they should not be made public (they do not have that status), they do not exist at a formal level and have no economic value. This is in keeping with the cultural tradition that lays down the following qualities for the Basque woman: "resolve, strength, serenity, and self-restraint" (Llona 2005, 153, recalling the words of del Valle). As a result, the gender system calls on women to control their emotions: they must learn to manage their emotional selves: in short, they must exercise self-control.

A recent feminist approach to the analysis of emotion can enhance our comprehension of the way myth works in people's practice. It departs from the premise that emotions are not synonymous with chaos, but rather symptoms of underlying structural problems pertaining to women's lives. If we follow Kate Millet's affirmation that the personal is also political, these social problems can be perceived as political problems. Hence, the demand for women to control their emotions is a way to avoid, cover up, and even deny the existence of a problem at all. Feminism proposes a new reading of emotional women, apparently perched on the edge of reason, and advocates that the emotionalness that expresses a problem should be transformed into social criticism.

The public speakers interviewed attribute great importance to their emotions, claiming that in the expression of their emotions they discovered themselves. Some mention how proud they were of what they did, of their public presence and political role. Their projection of the Basque woman is one of strength, action, and energy:

> [The Basque woman] is a strong woman, a woman who participates with the men, if necessary, even in the fight. She is not a woman who sits crying in the kitchen, nor stays reciting the rosary, but an active woman, who ups and goes. We propagandists went out with the men for first time, after the rallies. Perhaps there were problems, fighting, chasing, and we never ran away from those difficulties, but us women, we took part as well. (Llona 2000, 471)

Emotion becomes a medium for breaking the norm of self-control, for overcoming fear of reproach, and for galvanizing the speaker into action, as Polixene Trabudua explained to Llona:

> How scared I was! I'm aware of that, of the fear, the anguish of putting my foot in it. But the court was full to overflowing, people were outside too and I started to recite my speech and I saw they were clapping me and the more they clapped, the better I spoke, and the better I spoke, the more they clapped. (2000, 468)

This brings us to the point at which speaking becomes action: not what is said, but the fact—and act—of saying it. Speech, act, and performance unite here and reveal that women's practice, getting up on stage and speaking in public, becomes a vehicle through which they try out a new way of behaving, a new way of defying the discourse that portrays them in another fashion. And here we can see the significance of performance in a gendered sense as Judith Butler conceptualizes it: gender as a process by which a cultural reality laden with rules, taboos, and sanctions is acted out.

The choice to assume a certain kind of body, to live or wear one's body a certain way, implies a world of already established corporal styles. To choose a gender is to interpret received gender norms in a way that reproduces and organizes them anew. Less a radical act of creation, gender is a tacit project to renew a cultural history in one's own corporal terms. (Butler 2004, 26)

In order to understand better the changes that would come about in women's lives throughout the twentieth century, we should look at the micropolitics inaugurated by women like the public speakers of the Basque Revival (Reverter 2007). When we talk of micropolitics, we are talking of the development of agency, the capacity to confront the established system: "What is interesting to see are the changes in the gender models that are generated by individual actions but that leave their mark on institutions and discourse" (Reverter 2007, 223).

The women of the Basque Revival departed from conventional practice and their actions helped them to find new ways of doing things. Rather than what was said, it was the act of saying—through public speaking—that became the vehicle through which the model of a new Basque woman emerged. It is often said that the Basque Revival was important in making people conscious of being Basque, that is, in forming and shaping Basque identity; but parallel with that process, we would say that the consciousness of a gender identity was also born. Women felt a certain uneasiness, a kind of frustration that would recur through the next decades: some saw themselves as nationalists and hence they felt themselves crushed through the Franco years; but sometimes together with that feeling of defeat came another tied to their being women: they felt marginalized in their own culture. Maite Nuñez-Betelu calls this "internal exile" ("*barne erbestealdia*") and in reference to female writers, describes the feeling thus:

If in the case of exile forced by Franco, the official organs controlled publications, in the Basque case it was the old ways that exerted this role against women's writing. The deeply seated belief that women did not know how to write in Euskara considerably reduced the attempts to publish. (2005, 65)

It is our belief that the same tension and uneasiness persists today in one way or another. But those women speakers created new revolutionary models of an active, politically conscious, Basque woman who participates in the public just as in the domestic sphere.

A couple of years ago, we came across an interview with Maialen Lujanbio (published in English in 2001) in which she reflects upon her life and the changes she has been through. At one point, she talks of a certain transformation, using the notion of "*bertsolari* persona" (Eizagirre 2001, 192). Lujanbio seems to have heard the echo of the grandmothers of the Basque Revival and decided to fuse her identity as a person and as a bertsolari and make them one. And in that union, the action, the doing is paramount, for it is in so doing that she recognizes what it means to herself as a woman. She sets aside the essentialist nature of performance and poses the question: What is it to be a woman? What is it to be a Basque woman?

Conclusion

Our exploration of the working of the matriarchal thesis through the Basque Revival should give some pointers as to the way myths are integrated into social discourse, institutionalized in the social structure, and interiorized in individuals' performance of ethnic and gender identities. The power of myth lies largely in its symbolism and in its sacred dimension, which sets it apart from everyday experience and projects upon it an aura of unquestionable and untouchable truth. Yet, mythologies—like traditions—cannot address the realities of contemporary life unless they evolve with the changing cosmological beliefs and sociological circumstances of each new era. As with all cultural inventions, it is vital to comprehend that myths are far more than a collection of stories attached to a particular time and place in history: they are an ongoing social practice that is created and re-created by social actors, in tune with varying social trends and traditions, and in accordance with different needs or demands

Modern Basque nationalism developed a particular ideology of women and assigned them a role as mothers. The maternal role was both physical and symbolic: on the one hand, destining women to the biological and relational model of mother, wife, sister, and daughter; on the other, requiring of them an emotive—and emotional—representation of the nation. At a time when social control was strong, mostly men, but some women, spoke publicly of what Basque women were supposed to do. The print media and academic articles clearly expressed the discourse of the time and reflected the gender ideology of emergent Basque nationalism that defined equality in terms of naturalized differences. It conceived of biologically determined differences between men and women, but claimed that all contributions (including those of women) were crucial to the constitution of the nation. While that was the discourse, in practice, women were kept apart from the "real" power of politics, economics, and culture, and maintained no more than a symbolic power at home.

However, at the same time, far from the Basque context, in other parts of Europe and in the United States, a new ideology was taking the social stage in the form of feminism and the "modern woman" made an appearance. As some Basque historians such as Miren Llona and Nerea Aresti have shown, an inkling of this new woman reached the Basque Country, though it is difficult to measure the impact of this emergent figure in contemporary discourse. However, an analysis of the practices of Basque women at the beginning of the twentieth century reveals something of their transgressive nature. Women giving public talks. Women exhorting thousands of people in political meetings. Women improvising, talking from the heart. As public speakers and political propagandists maybe they did not break the traditional mold, and they even asked other women to keep up their traditional roles as mothers, wives, sisters, and daughters, but from today's viewpoint, their performances were certainly significant.

The incipient changes in the situation of Basque women came to a halt with Franco's dictatorship (1939–1975), but the first women's meetings in Bilbao after Franco's death signaled the end of forty years of silence when the feminist movement came to the fore in 1976. A few years later matriarchy become one of the main topics in the Basque social sciences. We are dealing here with an academic and scientific discourse, but one that has a lot to do with the kind of nationalism produced. Introducing new elements (such as Mari) and making connections between natural phenomena (motherhood and land), the discourse on matriarchy in the 1980s signified a revival of modern Basque nationalism's strategy to place women in the symbolic center but away from real power.

Anthropology, like history, has been used to construct arguments that defend the reality of matriarchy or egalitarianism. But both have been argued to be myths that veil different kinds of realities. Historians like Otazu and anthropologists like del Valle have uncovered other aspects of Basque men and women's lives, showing how the bricks have been put together, revealing the cracks in the wall.

References

Amezaga, Arantzazu. 1980. *La mujer vasca: Euzkadi y su historia*. Bilbao: Geu.

Aranzadi, Juan. 1982. *Milenarismo vasco. Edad de Oro, etnia y nativismo*. Madrid: Taurus.

Aresti, Nerea. 2007. "La mujer moderna, el tercer sexo y la bohemia en los años veinte." *Dossiers Feministes* 10: 173–85.

Aulestia, Gorka. 1999. "The Basque Bertsolari in the New Millennium." In *Basque Cultural Studies*, edited by William A. Douglass, Carmelo Urza, Linda White, and Joseba Zulaika. Reno: Basque Studies Program, University of Nevada, Reno.

Bamberger, Joan. 1974. "The Myth of Matriarchy: Why Men Rule in Primitive Society." In *Women, Culture, and Society*, edited by Michelle Zimbalist Rosaldo and Louise Lamphere. Palo Alto, CA: Stanford University Press.

Beneria, Lourdes. 1987. "¿Patriarcado o sistema económico? Una discusión sobre dualismos metodológicos." In *Mujeres, ciencia y práctica política*, edited by Celia Amorós et al. Madrid: Debate.

Bullen, Margaret. 2003. *Basque Gender Studies*. Reno: Center for Basque Studies, University of Nevada, Reno.

Bullen, Margaret, and Carmen Diez. 2008. "Fisiones/fusiones: Mujeres, feminismos y orden social." In *Feminismos en la Antropología: Nuevas propuestas críticas*, edited by Liliana Suárez, Rosalva Aída Hernández, and Emma Martín. Donostia-San Sebastián: ANKULEGI antropologia elkartea.

———. 2010. "Matriarchy versus Equality: From Mari to Feminist Demands." In *Feminist Challenges in the Social Sciences: Gender Studies in the Basque Country*, edited by Mari Luz Esteban and Mila Amurrio. Reno: Center for Basque Studies, University of Nevada, Reno.

Butler, Judith. 2004. "Variations on Sex and Gender: Beauvoir, Wittig y Foucault." In *The Judith Butler Reader*, edited by Sara Sahli and Judith Butler. London: Blackwell.

Campbell, Joseph. 1968. *The Masks of God*, vol. 4, *Creative Mythology*. London: Secker and Warburg.

Connell, Raewyn. 1987. *Gender and Power: Society, the Person and Sexual Politics*. Stanford: Stanford University Press.

Del Valle, Teresa. 1989. "The Current Status of the Anthropology of Women: Models and Paradigms." In *Essays in Basque Social Anthropology and History*, edited by William A. Douglass. Reno: Basque Studies Program, University of Nevada, Reno.

———. 1997. "El género en la construcción de la identidad nacionalista." *Ankulegi* 1 (November): 9–22. Also in *Foro Hispánico: Revista Hispánica de los Países Bajos* (1999) 18: 37–44.

Del Valle, Teresa, et al. 1985. *Mujer vasca. Imagen y realidad*. Barcelona: Anthropos.

Douglass, William, and Joseba Zulaika. 2007. *Basque Culture: Anthropological Perspectives*. Reno: Center for Basque Studies, University of Nevada, Reno.

Eizagirre, Estitxu. 2007. "Interview with Maialen Lujanbio Zugasti." *Oral Tradition* 22, no. 2: 187–97.

Giddens, Anthony. 1984. *The Constitution of Society: Outline of the Theory of Structuration*. Cambridge: Polity Press.

Hornilla, Txema. 1981. *La Ginecocracia vasca. Contribución a los estudios sobre el eusko-matriarcado*. Bilbao: Geu.

Juaristi, Jon. 1987. *El linaje de Aitor: La invención de la tradición vasca*. Madrid: Taurus Ediciones.

Maquieira D'Angelo, Virginia. 2001. "Género, diferencia y desigualdad." In *Feminismos: Debates teóricos contempóraneos*, edited by Elena Beltrán and Virginia Maquieira. Madrid: Alizana Editorial.

Nuñez-Betelu, Maite. 2005. "El exilio interior femenino vasco: La negación de las mujeres en el Bersolarismo." In *Non zeuden emakumeak? La Mujer Vasca en el exilio de 1936*, coordinated by José Ramón Zabala. Donostia-San Sebastián: Saturrarán Argitaletxea.

Llona, Miren. 2000. "Polixene Trabudua, historia de vida de una dirigente del nacionalismo vasco en la Vizcaya de los años treinta." *Historia Contemporánea* 21: 459–84.

———. 2002. *Entre señorita y garçonne: Historia oral de las mujeres bilbaínas de clase media (1919–1939)*. Málaga: Universidad de Málaga.

Lutz, Catherine A. 2008. "Engendered Emotion: Gender, Power, and the Rhetoric of Emotional Control in American Discourse." In *Language and the Politics of Emotion*, edited by Catherine A. Lutz and Lila Abu-Lughod. Cambridge: Cambridge University Press.

Ortiz-Osés, Andrés, and Franz K. Mayr. 1980. *El matriarcalismo vasco. Reinterpretación de la cultura vasca*. Bilbao: Servicio de Publicaciones de la Universidad de Deusto.

Otaegi, Lourdes. 2000. "Lizardi y las mujeres. Desde la conjura femenina a la gran guerra pacífica." In *Breve historia feminista de la literatura española*, vol. 6, edited by Iris M. Zavala. Barcelona: Anthropos.

Otazu, Alfonso de. 1986. *El "igualitarismo" vasco: Mito y realidad*. 2nd ed. San Sebastián: Txertoa.

Reverter, Sonia. 2007. "Performatividad en la Bohemia: Aspectos teóricos en las transgresiones de género." *Arenal* 14, no. 2 (July–December): 213–34.

Rubin, Gayle. 1975. "The Traffic in Women: Notes on the 'Political Economy' of Sex." In *Toward an Anthropology of Women*, edited by Rayna R. Reiter. New York: Monthly Review Press.

Sánchez Carrión, Jose María. 1981. "La Navarra cantábrica (malda-erreka): Estudio antropolingüístico de una comunidad euskaldun." *Fontes linguae vasconum* 13, no. 37 (January–June): 19–97.

Ugalde, Mercedes. 1993. *Mujeres y nacionalismo vasco: Génesis y desarrollo de Emakume Abertzale Batza, 1906–1936*. Bilbao: Universidad del País Vasco-Euskal Herriko Unibertsitatea.

———. 1994. "La historia de las mujeres y la historia del nacionalismo: Una convergencia necesaria." *Revista de Extremadura* 13: 33–42.

White, Linda. 1999. "Mission for the Millennium: Gendering and Engendering Basque Literature for the Next Thousand Years." In *Basque Cultural Studies*, edited by William A. Douglass, Carmelo Urza, Linda White, and Joseba Zulaika. Reno: Basque Studies Program, University of Nevada, Reno.

Yuval-Davis, Nira. 1996. "Género y nación: Articulaciones del origen la cultura y la ciudadanía." *Arenal: Revista de Historia de las mujeres* 3, no. 2: 163–75.

Zulaika, Joseba. 1988. *Basque Violence: Metaphor and Sacrament*. Reno: University of Nevada Press

8

Notions of, and Attitudes toward, Property in the Basque Country: Testing Some Practices and Interpretations

Francisco Garmendia and Patxi Juaristi

Different Notions of and Attitudes toward Property

Research into society's practice in relation to passing on durable property in the Basque Country reveals different points of view, some of them contradicting each other. When categorizing those different interpretations, three main paradigms can be distinguished: (1) those who say that the particular and original Basque type of attitude and practice in which durable property belongs to the people has prevailed; (2) those who say that that type of traditional attitude and private property have existed alongside; and (3) those who say that private property has prevailed and existed in the same way as in other countries.

Peculiar Notions of and Attitudes toward Property in the Basque Country

According to those authors we put in our first group, private property as the Roman legal tradition understood it has not usually been known in the Basque Country: "The Basques were not aware of the Roman concept of the right to absolute and indivisible property. In Lapurdi, as in the other Basque provinces, land had always belonged to all of the inhabitants. Uncultivated lands were divided up among the parishes or valleys and cultivated lands among the families" (Lafourcade 1986, 172).

In the lands under Roman rule, the attitude to durable property was based on private property (hence the terms *butendi, fruendi,* and *abutendi,* referring to the rights to use property as people wished, even the right to destroy the property). Various items and rights were passed on from one generation to another as defined by a number of different property rights and categories. In the Basque Country, on the other hand, it was solely the responsibility for the house and for the land and nothing else that was passed from one generation to another. It was confidently assumed that property would be properly administered.[1] The heir, whether the son or daughter of the house chosen, inherited the house and lands from his/her parents after showing him/herself capable and willing to do so (Lafourcade 1986, 176). When the son or daughter was chosen, anyone who might take the house to ruin was excluded from the potential successors in order to assure the house's well-being and continuity (Caro Baroja 1976, 128).

The chosen successor, rather than being all-powerful in terms of durable property and the house, inherited responsibility, liability, and duties from their parents (Lafourcade 1986, 164). The principal task of the inheritor was to maintain the property for the next generation. Thus, a heavy responsibility lay on the successor: "giving each brother and sister their rightful share, providing for the unmarried family members and others who stayed on in the house, keeping respect for those who had gone before, taking care of the whole house, doing everything possible to improve the house, etc. In fact, inheritance from parents seemed to be more a question of taking on duties than of receiving property" (Manterola 1978, 582). In fact, taking on all those responsibilities left to them by those who had died, but barely benefitting from the inheritance since the rights related to the house and lands were limited, many were reluctant to take on the burden. As Francisco Salinas Quijada points out in relation to Navarrese inheri-

---

1.   As Antonio de Irala puts it: "Land was not held in property, and the right to use it was simply based on the confidence that the community had in the successors. . . . Merit was not inherited: it had to be achieved" (Irala, N.D.).

tance practice, "rural or core families are permanent organizations that survive changes in leadership; the leader, while the owner of the goods, in fact operates socially and economically like an administrator or factor and, in some cases, is legally connected to the house in such a way that his/her powers are very similar to theirs" (Salinas Quijada 1983, 127; see also Celaya 1971, 199).

As the basis of such a society, responsibility was toward others: durable property was not passed on from one generation to another; rather, it was responsibility for that property that was passed on. That responsibility, however, was not passed on to all sons or daughters equally: the parents chose for the house from among them (Galíndez 1985, 87). As Julio Caro Baroja describes it: "a son or a daughter was chosen for each house from among the numerous offspring; the male did not have to be the eldest, nor did the female" (1985, 24). The remaining sons and daughters married into other houses, went off to the Americas, or opted to join the church or one of its religious orders (Caro Baroja 1978, 580).

The head of the house chose a single successor because the extended family could only have a single head or person in charge: "Those who are in charge today have to choose and name those who will be in charge tomorrow. But if the parents were not to take that decision, and there were nobody else in charge, then all the sons and daughters would have to choose the person to be in charge of the house" (Manterola 1978, 580). Thus, while there existed laws and regulations in other societies to prevent land being divided into ever smaller sizes, durable property being left to a single person is a basic principle of Basque society and has deep roots in Basque families. All the members of each house accept the choosing of a single person to be in charge because they do not wish the house to be split up (Angulo Laguna 1903, 41; Garmendia and Iriarte 1978, 718).

However, while a single person was chosen to be in charge, the other brothers and sisters were not left without an inheritance. There were thus no successors in the Basque world in the sense that there were for the Romans. As Antonio de Irala (N.D.) underlines the praxis that prevailed in Bizkaia and Navarre: The head of the house designates their successor to administer the branch of the family that is represented by the farmstead. Only one administrator can be designated: an entity can only have a single head. The other brothers and sisters are not disinherited, given that inheritance in the Roman sense does not exist: the question is that not everybody can be chosen to be the head of the property.

With regard to this particular set of regulations about property, the authors whom we have placed in our first group find that, in their attitudes to property, the Basques differed considerably from their neighbors:

> The territories in the West were profoundly influenced by the civilization of the Lower Roman Empire with regard to its concept of the sovereign state: a supreme power; absolute, indivisible, and independent; with hierarchical structures that were centralized and uniform. Individuals were protected, it is true, but they were also isolated, protected, and subject to the influence of power, and subject to the authority of the *pater familias*; men were superior to women and the latter were classified as *imbecilitas sexus*. Property was individual and absolute. . . . The Basques, on the other hand, held onto their secular legal system, which was egalitarian and democratic" (Lafourcade 1986, 165).

Private Property and Common Land and the Basque Attitude toward Property

The second group of authors we categorized above who have investigated attitudes and practices to durable property maintain that the Basques showed particular attitudes to durable property, but that from ancient times onward private property, too, has existed in the Basque Country. In contrast to the argument of the first group or paradigm, this second group of scholars believes that there are two types of attitude to property in the Basque tradition: property that belongs to all the people and citizens' private property. More specifically, the houses and land used for cultivation were regarded as private property while woods and pasture land belonged to the commons. As Florencio Idoate points out in relation to practices observed in the Erronkari (Roncal) Valley of Navarre: "In Erronkari, as in many other communities and valleys, there exist various types of land ownership, from common land and collective ownership (which fits in the general formula of 'everything for everyone') to private property, though always with certain limitations" (Idoate 1977, 113).

The examples from the Erronkari Valley seem to confirm that all members of the community had the right to use common land and to make use of its produce: "local people could not 'claim any property right' but only use it and profit from it 'to the extent that while all members of the community have inherited property or neighboring lands there, only the valley grants them the right to make use of them by cultivating them, harvesting their crops and other produce through their own work and diligence'" (Allí Aranguren 1989, 252).

However, there were many restrictions to the way in which members of the community could make use of common land and woods. For instance, they could not fence land off when they were not using it. Likewise, while there was free use of common grazing land and woods, buying and selling these were strictly prohibited (Floristán Samanes 1978, 114; Idoate 1977, 119). In many places, the neighborhood's livestock was cared of in form of a single herd when it was taken to mountain pasture lands in spring and summer. One could not use such pastures for individual purposes (Arizcún Cela 1988, 53).

Along with common land, there is proof that there were some houses, kitchen gardens, mountain huts, and cultivated land held as private property from the twelfth century onward (Allí Aranguren 1989, 247). While there are different interpretations about the origins of this private property, scholars agree that such forms of private property have a long and undisputed history.[2] Donations and inheritances left to the monasteries in the Middle Ages involved private property changing hands—irrefutable evidence it seems. As Florencio Idoate points out, the gentry, soldiers, and *meliores homines* ("best men," that is the most upright men in a legal sense) were able to make donations without any difficulties or limitations. And referring to an example of the donation of a

---

2. "The use of rotation farming, along with inscribing the properties in family registers, meant that there was ownership of property. However, in most cases the passage of time and successive entries in registers determined a transformative process with regard to ownership of property and the possibility of acquiring property, something that was never opposed by the valley, which recognised the existence of private property since time immemorial. The concept of private property expanded to include not only houses and kitchen gardens but also individual fields and cultivated areas within common land" (Allí Aranguren 1989, 221).

mansion in Bidankoze (Vidángoz) he notes: "The same church records include another donation that was a mansion in the Bidankoze area; it, too, was undated, but all the evidence points to it being from the eleventh century. Both cases seem to be real estate donations, with no apparent limitation to the property transmission. . . . So it is clear that what might, potentially, be common property could be transmitted to another owner by donation or inheritance" (Idoate 1977, 114).

In contrast to those of the first aforementioned group, the scholars of the second group and paradigm contend that the Roman understanding of private property (*ius utendi, abutendi et fruendi*, the right to use, enjoy the fruits of, and dispose of a property) and the right to leave property as inheritance or to donate it existed in the Basque Country since ancient times: "Our conclusion is that in the Middle Ages landed property already existed, arable land was split up into small fields, and property was passed on as inheritance or by donation" (Idoate 1977, 116). However, Florencio Idoate's caveat about such forms of private property should equally be taken into account: "Certain reservations must be made because of the norms and customs about land. . . . Within municipal limits, everyone had the right to cultivate freely and pass on the fields to their descendants after inscribing them in the family registers, which still exist" (Idoate 1977, 114). Other scholars have pointed out that citizens were obliged to pass property on to each other through donations or inheritance (Allí Aranguren 1989, 248).

While some scholars underline that private property and the right to transmit it through inheritance or donation was an ancient right and practice, there is also considerable evidence, sometimes quoted by the same scholars, which contradicts such assumptions. Florencio Idoate, for instance, says that there was private property in the Erronkari Valley, only to point out that,

> in this case the same things were used against a person from Uskartze [Uscarrés] who claimed to own a private property in the Pampillone area of Burgi [Burgui]. This seemed to be an attack on the community, which had to defend its territory in its entirety. Any member of the Erronkari community had the right to cultivate land in the valley, and the valley's legal advisor points out that "this is as long as this cultivation lasts for one or two years; after that, any other member of the valley's

community can freely enter the land, cultivate it, and sow seeds without the previous user preventing this. This is how the valley has always lived and been organized." Of course, the sale of common land to outsiders was never permitted, whether for cultivation or not, among other things because this would lead to excessive cultivation that would damage wild plants and the water supply. (Idoate 1977, 118)

While Idoate is discussing private property, he does not do so in *absolute* terms; rather, he points out that there were always some restrictions. For example, after underlining that there was incontestable private property in the Erronkari Valley in the Middle Ages, he stresses that such private property was neither complete nor absolute. He quotes the valley's legal advisor from a manuscript dating from 1775: "In the first place, and since time immemorial, the inhabitants of the seven valleys that make up this area, which is where I come from, have always been able to take any piece of land they want to in the common land to cultivate it and take the produce that it gives, but with the certain, unquestioned knowledge that they have never owned and will never be able to own it or any other piece of land: they can only make use of it, and only while they continue to cultivate it" (Idoate 1977, 117).

So here we have an interpretation that private property existed but also that this private property was severely limited. Similarly, Alejandro Arizcún Cela points out in his study into norms about durable property in the Baztan Valley that, "in order to cultivate an unused piece of land, all you had to do was mark it out with four cornerstones; the member of the community who did so acquired the right to use it for an undefined period of time. This right of use was limited by two things. It had to be regularly cultivated and, if more than a year went by without this happening, any other member of the community could take it over" (Arizcún Cela 1988, 52). The same applied to huts in the mountains that had been erected for the purpose of keeping tools or livestock. While they were private property, they could be locked while they were in active use (Arizcún Cela 1988, 343). As soon as they stopped being used, anybody had the right of access, as Juan Cruz Allí Aranguren points out, "the animal pens and shelters in the mountains were also private property, although subject to certain limitations about their use . . . they could only be locked if they contained grain, grass, or suchlike. Otherwise, they had to be kept open and anybody could keep a flock there in the established order of preference" (Allí Aranguren 1989, 250).

Farmers also had to cultivate and use vegetable gardens year by year. Furthermore, once what had been sown was harvested, livestock farmers had the right to the pasture land; so arable farmers were obliged not to fence off their land after the harvest (Allí Aranguren 1989, 250; Arizcún Cela 1988, 52). Thus, arable farmers were not entirely free to do with the land what they wanted. As far as buying and selling, donating, or leaving properties was concerned, this could only be done between the people of the valley.[3] If and when there were sales, donations, or bequests, it was only the right to use the land that was passed on, never the land itself (Arizcún Cela 1988, 52). Idoate summarizes such limits to private property very well by pointing out that

> the members of the community could not "grant any property rights," only their shared use and exploitation "in so far as, although all the members of the community had inheritances or neighboring fields, the valley only grants them the right to use them so that they can cultivate them, collect and make use of their produce through their work and diligence." While it is true that sales and donations were allowed, it is no less true, according to the regulations, that "those purchases and sales cannot be made nor are permitted other than between inhabitants of the same valley, and are specifically forbidden to people from outside the valley. And if some community members mortgaged or included them in the census, it has never been understood that said mortgage includes or could include the direct property right, which is the valley's, but rather only the right to use and make use of it, which is the only right granted." This is what the valley maintained in 1775 and again in 1856. This was certainly the orthodox doctrine, which was not formally contradicted for centuries, although there might have been lapses in some practical cases. (Idoate 1977, 117)

---

3.   "In the Statutes of the Union of the Valley of 1534 the sale of houses and places is forbidden: '...if any inhabitant of the Erronkari Valley... wishes to sell his/her house or place... he/she will not be able to sell it, nor to remove it from the valley's rights...'. Transmission by donation or will is forbidden: '...if any inhabitant of the valley... were to remove a property by donation or will from the valley, may that person be removed from the valley" (Allí Aranguren 1989, 248).

It should be added here that further evidence of this particular type of property use is that taxes were not paid depending on the land but on the produce obtained from it or the livestock kept on it. In other words, as nobody owned the land, it was impossible to tax it.[4]

To conclude this section, while it is right to say, like the scholars and sources we have referred to do, that private property was ancient and remained undisputed, it is also worth pointing out that it was a very particular type of private property.

Regulating the Predominance of Private Property

A third group of scholars has argued that in the Basque Country, as in the surrounding territories, society's attitude to property has been mainly based on private property and servitude. In other words, there has never been any differential attitude to durable property in the Basque Country. As in many other places, in the Basque Country, too, there have always been servitude and different social classes; and from generation to generation, powerful people owned land and woods and those ownership rights have been passed on in the form of legal inheritance. It is their belief that there have never been any distinguishing attitudes to property in the Basque Country (Aranzadi 1982; Fernández de Pinedo 1974; José Ángel García de Cortázar 1989; José Ángel García de Cortázar and Arizaga 1991; José Ángel García de Cortázar et al. 1979; Fernando García de Cortázar and Montero 1980; Fernando García de Cortázar and Lorenzo Espinosa 1988; Otazu 1986). Like Fernando García de Cortázar and José María Lorenzo Espinosa, they have succinctly maintained that "although it may be a simplification to talk about the way of life of medieval Basque peasants, there is no doubt that it was similar to that of other European peasants: they were serfs. This term describes their relationship of servitude with the owners of the land. Their main characteristic was that they made use of a piece of land that belonged to a no-

---

4. "In fact, the people of Erronkari did not pay taxes on these rural properties but rates which were based on the records, which must have existed since ancient times. However, it should be taken into account that the usual doctrine, repeated in many oral testimonies, with regards to inheritances and pieces of land was that there were rates charged on produce and livestock rather than on the land itself, which seems to restrict private property to an extent" (Idoate 1977, 116).

ble for which they paid rent in return" (García de Cortázar and Lorenzo Espinosa 1988, 57).

In the Middle Ages, the differences between social classes were mainly linked to different people's attitudes to durable property. Each member of society's place or situation was related to their attitude to property. In the Middle Ages in Bizkaia "each individual and group's situation within the hierarchy was connected with their land ownership: there was 'class' division in a wholly rural society" (García de Cortázar and Montero 1980, 51). In the Erronkari Valley, for instance, there were two types of inhabitants: on the one hand, people who owned livestock and, on the other, those who only had the right to a small kitchen garden next to their houses, a few chickens, and a pig. The latter were obliged to work for the former. The use of common land and woods was not everybody's right, only that of livestock owners:

> Until very recently in Erronkari, there was a traditional distinction between "livestock houses" and "herders' houses." The former were the only ones who could own livestock, while the latter, apart from the house in itself, were only allowed to own a small kitchen garden, next to the house, a few chickens, and a pig or two (a type of self-sufficiency). The owners of those houses had to work as herders for the owners of the "livestock houses," who were the only people with rights to use the common land on which their flock and herds grazed, looked after by the owners of the "herders' houses." Within such a rigid structure, a class system, what type of services did the "herders" have to carry out for the "livestock owners"? Was this or was this not a certain type of servitude in the supposedly egalitarian Erronkari community? (Otazu 1986, 184–85).

Otazu also suggests that the organization of the communal woods was controlled by the upper class: "It looks like the people who transported and traded with the timber from Erronkari were from the 'livestock owner' class" (Otazu 1986, 185).

In contrast, those who belonged to the lower class of society had no right to use the common land or any other share in its ownership. It appears that, as in Erronkari, so in Bizkaia, too, farmworkers used the common lands and the woods, were subservient to the gentry, and had to work for them:

The farmworkers in Bizkaia had the same social characteristics as those in other places, with a single exception: only the Lord is written down as their owner. Their status is mostly defined by being workers who dwell on land that was not their own; the landowner could remove them if he so wished and they also had the right to leave, as long as their departure did not mean that the landowner would lose his source of wealth. This explains why farmworkers stayed on a single piece of land or small family farm and had the right to collective items such as woods, pasture land, and the water of the communities to which they belonged. (García de Cortázar 1993, 33).

It seems to have been quite common for farmworkers to work on the nobles' and landowners' land and to pay taxes (Paul Arzak 1978, 54). An example from the Ayala *fuero* in Araba is instructive. The *fuero* denied farmworkers the possibility of having "land of their own," and, if they bought or built a house, "the landowner or any noble can enter it as his own and make it his own." In Bizkaia, things were only slightly different: farmworkers were allowed to build on and inhabit land, but the land belonged to the noble, to its owner (García de Cortázar 1966, 303). While the taxpayers' only source of wealth was work, the nobles, on the other hand, could rely on many sources of wealth: mountains, mills, smithies, farming rights, Church patronage, tools, and so on (Fernández de Pinedo 1974, 34–35). Those sources of wealth were passed from one generation to another without any difficulty; this ensured that wealthy families remained wealthy, often for centuries.

It is just a myth that farming land was divided into smaller plots (Solozabal 1975, 251). Land in the Basque Country was divided into large plots owned by the nobles, and farmworkers were obliged to work on them: "The idea that small properties predominated in Basque rural areas is one of the many myths that has so long been included in the history of the Basque Country. According to this idea, small properties were the economic base for a social structure that turned the Basque Country into a community with no large differences, in which harmony and collaboration were the components on which social relationships were based" (García de Cortázar and Montero 1983, 55). Furthermore, social classes and different attitudes to property did not disappear without trace in the Middle Ages (Solozabal 1975, 253; Otazu 1986, 302). In the eighteenth century, too, the farming world in the Basque Country was made up of large landowners and tenants (Otazu 1986, 111).

The difference between social classes was not only the extent
of their properties and their lifestyles (Otazu 1986, 331), but differences can also be seen in the different uses of common land and
woods. The belief that all members of the community, continues
Otazu, had equal access and made equal use of them is mistaken.
Furthermore, such a misleading interpretation has led to ground-
less myths such as those of "Basque democracy" and "universal
nobility." In contrast to such myths, he stresses that

> the Basque towns have always had great resources in meadows,
> pasture land, and woods as common land. This idea (in abstract)
> has led to the interpretation, which is very widely believed
> throughout the Basque Country, that these resources (as they
> were communal) were used by everybody. The reasoning was
> simple: If everything was so very democratic, why would all
> the members of the community not make use of its resources
> with the same rights? This idea has become extraordinarily
> widespread and nowadays it is very common to hear people
> talking about the use of common land as another characteristic
> of "Basque democracy." In fact, it is no more than idle talk.
> (Otazu 1986, 366–67)[5]

Other Available Evidence for Basque Notions of Property

Seeking to broaden the debate, particularly in terms of evidence
for claims related to property, we turn our attention now to a
source that is seldom used—oral literature. Oral literature (sayings, tales, songs, poems, and so on) are testimonies about any
society's past and can tell us about the speaker's attitude to property, at least to an extent (Barandiarán 1974, 309). The study of
Basque literature can draw on a variety of sources, and we could
have examined various different genres and sub-genres. However,
bearing in mind our main objective—property—we have decided
to limit ourselves to old sayings and draw particularly on sayings

5. According to Jon Juaristi, various writers, whose opinion had been biased
by a nineteenth-century pro-fuero ideology (above all Antonio de Trueba and
Fermin Caballero), do not explain the situation of Basque farmers appropriately: "although neither Caballero nor Trueba deny that most of the Basque
peasants worked the land as tenants, leasing the land from lesser nobles, they
paint a picture of absolute social harmony, with the owners' friendly kindness
and the farmworkers' willing submission" (Juaristi 1987, 35).

that have already been collected.

Having examined various different compilations, we chose Justo Mokoroa's *Repertorio de locuciones del habla popular vasca* (Collection of sayings from everyday Basque speech, 1990), which, to the best of our knowledge, has never been used before in a sociological context, never mind for the study of society's attitudes toward property. We contend that the 92,167 sayings included in the collection provide appropriate material for our objective. Furthermore, we used means of studying sayings that are well-tested and proven in the social sciences such as BRS IT computing and programming.

Our research included three steps: In the first instance, we tried to identify those subjects or people and social contexts in the sayings that were most likely related to property relations and issues. Table 8.1 lists those that appeared with greatest frequency. In the second step, we identified those objects that appeared to be most valued and those that appeared most scarce. Again, we looked for the most frequently mentioned items or objects (see table 8.2).

Finally, we isolated those sayings that mention relationships between subjects and property and examined the particular characteristics of those relationships.

Notions of and Attitudes toward Property in Justo Mokoroa's Compilation of Sayings

Having studied the relationships between subjects and property, we can distinguish between four main patterns.

Collective Durable Property Pertaining to the House or to the Community

This group's pattern suggests that property belongs mainly to *houses* and to *the people of the house*. In other words, they belong to the house or are at the house's disposal (italicized words as in the original):

> 31577 and 64301: "Ah, *our house's* woods and leafy hills! When on occasion I've gone to the Burgos area I can't tell you how sad that bare land makes me feel . . ."

Table 8.1: **THE MOST MENTIONED SUBJECTS IN SOCIAL CONTEXTS**	
WE	5793
HOUSE (Baserri, Basarri, Etse, Etxalde)	3727
MAN (Senar, Senhar)	3204
I	3024
YOU	2874
TOWN (Erri, Uri, Huri)	1997
WOMAN (Andere, Etxekoandre, Dama, Ugazabandre, Emakume, Emazte)	1852
CHILD	1778
BOY (Mutiko, Muthil, Motel)	1660
SON	1178
FATHER	1125
MOTHER (Amorde, Amaizun)	1009
GIRL	919
DAUGHTER	507

Table 8.2: **MOST MENTIONED PROPERTIES**	
HOUSE (Baserri, Basarri, Etse, Etxalde)	3727
LAND (Baztar)	1635
MOUNTAIN	833
FIELD (Baratz, Ortu, Hortu)	223
WOOD (Oihan)	316
SHEEP	346
COW (Esne-behi, Abelgorri, Buztarri-behi)	463
CAT	268
DOG (Zakur, Xakhur, Xakur)	539
DONKEY	443
WHEAT	306
MAIZE (Artho, Arthu)	292
ARDO (Arno, Ardu, Arda)	483
BREAD	499

61689: "We were afraid of midwinter and we gave the *house's* sheep grain . . ."
54711: "The *house's* maize is better than the neighborhood's."
73858: "Good cattle here? That black cow there, by the looks of it, is for your *house* . . ."

Similarly, a lot of durable property seems to belong to the *town*. The community is made up of citizens who seem to collectively own property, as can be seen in these sayings:

4645: "Then they gave the doctor food and drink at the *town* house . . ."
67272: "The farmstead that was quite close to the *town's* common land.
79586: "He started work on the *town's* common land; and of all the land worked on, he got the biggest yield."

Whether belonging to the house or to the town, most durable property is collectively owned. In other words, while there are different individuals, the town or the people of the house own the property.

It is worth mentioning that in the texts properties are never specified as belonging to the house or to the town (it should be taken into account that the suffix *-ren* is used for the genitive possessive in Basque): they belong to *etxekoak* (the people of the house), *etxerakoak* (the heads of houses), and/or *herrikoak* (the people of the town). In other words, the link between property and the house and its use by the house is underlined.

Communities, and specifically towns and houses, are linked through common property arrangements. Thus, it comes as no surprise that the *gure* (our) and *zuen* (your, in plural) appear more often than those of *nire* (mine) and *zure* (your, in singular). To compare the ideas of what is "ours" and what is "mine," *gure* appears 364 times (80.7 percent) and *nire* 87 times (19.3 percent) in relation to attitude to property (table 8.3).[6]

With respect to the subjects listed, expressions such as the following are to be found in our sayings:

1620: "We've always had somebody sick in *our house* . . ."

---

6. In relation to "your" (in singular or plural), too, *zuen* appears in 51 sayings (53 percent) and *zure* in 43 sayings (47 percent).

Table 8.3: **OUR/MY CONCEPTS IN ATTITUDES TO PROPERTY**		
	OUR	MINE
HOUSE	214	61
LAND	34	-
MOUNTAIN	21	1
WOOD	10	8
FIELD	9	2
SHEEP	10	5
COW	9	8
CAT	17	2
DOG	19	-
DONKEY	13	-
WHEAT	2	-
MAIZE	2	-
WINE	1	-
BREAD	3	-
ALTOGETHER	364	87

6840: "That man has often come late to *our farmstead* asking for a place to sleep."

4325 and 54135: "The sailors *our poor land* sent to sea had a job finding food, and often they died."

26396: "*Our hills and rocks* have never had an outsider for a boss."

5555: "Knocking trees down and not replanting them has left *our woods* empty."

5616 and 35314: "No, the sky hasn't fallen in yet. . . . Thank God. But the ram's been eating up *our best grass* . . ."

6040: "*Our sheep* have no good food and they can't fatten up at all . . ."

1358: "*Our cow* isn't well today . . ."

77678: "(It's going to rain, probably . . .)—Let it rain! It doesn't matter, '*our wheat* isn't ripe!'."

77751: "*Our maize* is drying up in the field, with reaching the storeroom. . . . And the mice are worried!"

It should be mentioned that when attitudes toward property are more precisely expressed, they sometimes change. When talking

about durable property, the "our" concept is sometimes substitut-
ed by "the people of the house" and sometimes by "the people of
the town." In terms of durable property, "the people of the house"
and "the people of the town" mean those who have come before
and those who are still to arrive. In terms of nondurable property
(farm animals and foods), however, the concept of "the people of
the house" is used less than "we." We suspect this is because the
property in question is at the disposal of the people of the house
rather than the people of the town.

Weak Private Property

In this cluster of sayings, private property is only rarely mentioned.
So while property is mentioned as belonging to "the people of the
house," "the head of the house," and "the people of the town,"
individuals' private property is also mentioned occasionally.
Expressed in linguistic terms, the genitive possessive suffix *-ren*
(*gizonaren* lurra 'the man's land', *andrearen* etxea 'the woman's
house', *mutilaren* basoa 'the boy's wood', and so on) rarely makes
an appearance (only in 9 sayings). In fact, in the whole corpus
the only connections made with the help of this suffix are those
between father(s) and house(s):

> 3.471:"You do it, Jesus, so they can go back to their father's
> house soon, so they don't starve to death."
> 69955: "I left everyone, took my stick, and walked to father's
> house . . ."
> 73350, 82890, and 88587: "They could eat all they wanted at
> father's house and now they have to eat what the pigs leave them."
> 83110 and 84887: "So many servants eat there to their hearts'
> content! And I, the son of the house, I'm almost dying of
> hunger and cold . . ."
> 24456: "He sent the third son to the father's house because he
> was worried about what would happen to him."
> 82991: "How many people will eat all the bread they want in
> my father's house while he leaves me to die!"
> 72.898: "Is there a bit left over for us among the things in our
> father's house?"
> 81079: "He took the silverware in our father's house away and
> broke it up."
> 88588: "How many workers don't bother with my father's
> bread, and here I am half dead . . ."

On examining these nine sayings and their sources, it is clear that they are literal translations from the bible or are directly influenced by the bible. Of the nine, four are taken from the parable of the prodigal son, that is, they are about returning to the *father's house*.

While the suffix *-ren* does have other uses in relation to property, it is used almost exclusively to describe a relationship between people and property. This means that the people who appear in the sayings are unlikely to be property owners. As individuals and members of society and to the extent that they are members of a "house," "local community," or "town," they have the right to use and make use of property. In fact, taking into account the weakness of the relationship between the house and property, it is clear that that relationship is based on the house's use of the property. Rather than the house belonging to the individuals, the individuals belong to the house or are the head of the house.

It is evident from the collection of sayings that such a notion of property diverges significantly from how Roman law regards it. Roman law establishes a legal connection between people and the ownership of property. Individuals have the right to use their property as they wish, both economically and otherwise. In this type of relationship, there is no place for responsibility toward property. The attitude to property is completely passive. In contrast, the Basque sayings stress the individual's duties toward the house: rather than possessing rights, the head of the household is bound by obligations.

Responsibility toward Property

The third particularity in relationships to property as expressed in our text corpus relates to *responsibility*. Rather than subscribing to notions of property that are associated with being owner, possessor, lord, head, or proprietor, it is responsibility to property that is emphasized in these sayings:

> 4640 and 55724: "The large house is for him. As well as that, my profits and food can be shared. That's for my daughter, but, even without her, there are other people to share with."
> 42066: "Even though they got on well, the house wouldn't be his until the parents died . . ."

> 6350: "The head of the house in short-sleeves, filling his pipe with grass."
> 3979: "Hearing the sound of a shot, he went to Muatz House and found the old man nearly dead."
> 25282: "When Zabala himself was the head of the house they made that church's main altar and two side altars."
> 7180: "After supper the head of the house sent them to bed."

As much as being the house's owner, leader, lord, proprietor, or possessor, the idea we are presented with here is that this is the person who is responsible for the house. In many sayings the owner, leader, lord, proprietor, or possessor comes across as the person with responsibility for the house. Rather than ownership, it is their duty toward the house that is expressed. In this sense, it must be remembered that the owner, leader, lord, proprietor, or possessor's house is never mentioned, nor is ownership; it is, rather, the house's owner, leader, lord, proprietor, or possessor who always figures in the sayings—not only in relationship to durable property, but also in connection with nondurable property. Such responsibility is expressed in the following sayings:

> 12104: "When you fancy it, you children want water. . . . But after you get married and have a wife and wine, you get used to drinking."
> 13405: "Although they [the well-behaved cows] deserved maize and wheat, the boss didn't give it to them . . ."
> 14717 and 87517: "The dog . . . if you don't want to beat it, eat all those left-overs, . . . without making the lady of the house walk around the streets ashamed."
> 12655: "I'm like a dog who's lost his master, I don't know where to go. I don't have any money . . ."
> 36486: "A dog will accept anything and give his master all his love for a piece of bread."
> 28454: "From then on, as his master gave him more food, the donkey lived a great, plentiful, and good life."

Responsibility is the most important thing in the relationship with property in these sayings. However, it seems to us that there are differences in attitude in relation to durable and nondurable properties. Responsibility for durable property means having to take care of it in an appropriate manner. In other words, the person with the main responsibility for the house's or town's property cannot do anything they want with it. This is because a lack of responsibility with regard to this type of property will affect successive generations' use of it. The attitude to nondurable property is different. The house's owner, leader, lord, proprietor, or possessor can decide how to make use of the property. Selling nondurable property does not give rise to any type of problem. In fact, nondurable property or goods or produce are regarded differently to meet the needs of the person (and his family) in charge. Thus, it is not property that is passed on from one generation to the next but responsibility.

Individuals' Responsibility toward Property

Individuals, like property, pertain to the house, so we also need to look into the question of how responsibility is linked to each individual member of the house. The woman of the house appears to have the closest relationship with the house; she is mentioned in 80 percent of the sayings that link the house to human beings. As well as underlining the connection that the woman has to the duties related to the house (10354: "On the night before the big day for slaughtering the pig, those women had a lot of work to do in our kitchen"), the sayings also tell us about the position and role of women in relation to society, something that derives from pertaining to particular farmsteads (30393: "When the lady of Bordaberri farmstead died without anybody realizing, what a feeling!").

Similarly, other members of the house are defined by their belonging to a particular house. This does not only apply to blood relations but extends to house servants and maids who also appear as belonging to the house (84093: "When we were young boys and girls we went weeding and to work in the kitchen gardens. In fact, the boys went to see how the girls worked..." 16525, 16526, and 23954: "Our *house* boy is a good girl!") So the people of the house are all connected with it in one way or another. The concept of the people of the house includes the people in the present (all the house's men, women, children, and servants), those in the past (the people buried in the house's graves), and those who will inhabit the house in the future (future generations).

People's status as societal beings is linked to the house they belong to; where they come from and which house they pertain to determines who they are. It becomes clear that the house is the main factor in determining their position in Basque society. How-ever, we should not forget that not all the house's people want to become head of the house.

In many of this corpus's sayings the house women, boys, girls, children, and daughters appear as the head of the house. Being the head of the house takes on different meanings in this corpus. On the one hand, being the head of the house means being the official successor, the person who takes on the main responsibil-ity for the house and is at the house's service (21921: "Congratu-lations, boy! You're the *head of the house*! Bravo!"). So to say that somebody is the head of the house is, in fact, to say that they are responsible for the house (3333, 55021, and 55777: "As we don't last forever, I'd like my son to be *head of the house*. To do that, I'll have to get my daughter into a good farmstead first").

Only one of the house's sons or daughters can be the head of the house (the eldest child or the one who takes responsibility for the house) (54708: "I have five children; one for the house, the eldest."). Moreover, durable property and farm animals that do not have a single person in charge of them are threatened by ruin and are often considered as lost (5472: "There are weeds on what's everybody's land." 12162: "The wolf will eat what's every-one's donkey."). For obvious reasons the head of the house should have positive characteristics such as being hard-working, diligent, trustworthy, and so on. Being the successor, the head is also the one who brings his or her spouse to the house—something one wants to get right:

> 54795: "Even though they have no dowry, I prefer skirts at our house, women workers."
> 487435: "Martin knows that girl's capable of working on the farmstead or in the town."
> 21813: "The *head of our house* is excellent (that young girl)."

A good, trustworthy, hard-working head of the house is more highly valued than any type of wealth. Leaving the responsibil-ity for the house to just anybody is a risk. For example, a head of the house with negative characteristics (obstinate, lazy, and so forth) will not take good care of the house and would be bet-ter removed from the house; on the other hand, people with the right characteristics (hard-working, kind, and so on) are wanted as the head of the house.

Responsibility for the house should not be passed on to just anybody. It has to be taken into account that housework and duties take up a lot of time and are tiring activities (46707: "Ask God to make housework as tiring as it should be."); in other words, not all individuals can carry the weight (9302 and 25389: "We aren't afraid to take our parents' house forward."). So it should come as no surprise that there are people of the house who do not want to take on such a responsibility (7885: "From now on it will be your responsibility to take care of the house. . . . Do you want that?/Oh, not that! I'm not the man for that").

In the context of Roman law the type of sayings we refer to here would make no sense. In the Roman legal tradition being a proprietor means having the right to do what you want to do with "your" property. In contrast, in the social reality reflected in our corpus of sayings the head of the house takes on responsibility for the house, a decision that involves more effort and work than rights. While the house's wealth is connected to the people who pertain to it (being *our-your* (plural) wealth), the responsibility rests on a single person; usually someone who has the most positive characteristics to be able to take on such responsibility (25064: "We had nobody better to take the house's decisions").

To sum up, who we are in society is mainly determined by the house we belong to. We belong to the house, and everyone has to take responsibility for the house in order for it to prosper. In fact, the protection that the house offers is a direct consequence of the responsibility that the people of the house take on in order to make the house prosper. Society will only survive and thrive when the people of the house and, above all, the person who takes responsibility for the house (the head of the house) fulfill their responsibilities in the right way. It is, therefore, completely understandable that positive characteristics are to be desired in the head of the house.

Validating the Results

We have pointed out some noticeable patterns with regard to attitudes and notions of property we found in the sayings. However, Mokoroa collected the sayings in a particular manner, so it could have been that our research here is of no real value. In order to validate our research, we took two Basque-speaking sources from other sources that were independently gathered and compared their speech patterns with the evidence gathered so far. We looked at Jose Azpiroz's *Arbol zarraren kimuak* (New shoots on the old tree, 1988), based on daily conversations in the southern Basque Country and a book about daily life in the northern Basque Country: Erramun Etchebarne's *Erramun harginaren oroitzapenak* (Memories of Erramun the stonemason, 1989). It subsequently became clear that the same notions and social attitudes to regulating and using property that we found in the sayings are to be found there as well: the importance of communal values and responsibility and the weakness of private property.

Conclusion

If we compare the evidence gathered from studying Mokoroa's source book with the three theoretical models discussed at the start of this chapter, it is clear that they confirm the findings of the scholars mentioned in the first group, which stresses the importance of communal values and responsibility and the weakness of private property. However, we would like to make it very clear to readers that our objective was and still is not to close the debate about traditional notions and attitudes toward property in the Basque Country once and for all. We are fully aware that there is still considerable research that needs to be done and that there are still many theoretical and empirical gaps to fill. Readers should see our argument and our evidence as a simple contribution to the subject. More light needs to be thrown on the issue of durable property, and social practices and traditions—in the Basque Country and beyond.

References

Allí Aranguren, Juan Cruz. 1989. *La Mancomunidad del Valle De Roncal*. Pamplona: Gobierno de Navarra, Departamento de Presidencia e Interior.

Angulo Laguna, Diego. 1903. *Derecho Privado de Vizcaya*. Madrid: Hijos de Reus.

Aranzadi, Juan. 1982. *Milenarismo Vasco: Edad de oro, etnia y nativismo*. Madrid: Taurus.

Arizcún Cela, Alejandro. 1988. *Economia y sociedad en un valle pirenáico del Antiguo Régimen. Baztan, 1600–1841*. Pamplona: Gobierno de Navarra, Departamento de Educación y Cultura; Institución Principe de Viana.

Azpiroz, José. 1988. *Arbol zarraren kimuak. Oroipenak*. Donostia: Etor.

Barandiarán, José Miguel. 1974. "Folklore Vasco: Necesidad de su estudio." In *Obras Completas de Barandiarán*, vol. 5. Bilbao: Editorial de La Gran Enciclopedia Vasca.

Caro Baroja, Julio. 1976. *Baile, familia, trabajo. Estudios Vascos VII*. San Sebastián: Editorial Txertoa.

———. 1978. *Sondeos históricos. Estudios Vascos VIII*. San Sebastián: Editorial Txertoa.

———. 1985. *La hora de Navarra del XVIII. Personas, familias, negocios e ideas*. 2nd edition. Pamplona: Comunidad Foral de Navarra; Institución Principe de Viana.

Celaya, Adrián. 1971. "El sentido jurídico de nuestro pueblo." In *I Semana de Antropología Vasca*. Bilbao, April 6–12, 1970. Bilbao: Editorial de la Gran Enciclopedia Vasca.

Etchebarne, Erramun. 1989. *Erramun harginaren oroitzapenak. Oroipenak*. Donostia: Etor.

Fernández de Pinedo, Emiliano. 1974. *Crecimiento económico y transformaciones sociales del País Vasco 1100–1850*. Madrid: Siglo Veintiuno Editores.

Floristán Samanes, Alfredo. 1951; 1978. *La Ribera Tudelana de Navarra*. Zaragoza: Instituto Juan Sebastián Elcano; Pamplona: Diputación Foral de Navarra; CSIC.

Galíndez, Jesús de. 1957; 1985. *El Derecho Vasco*. Buenos Aires: Editorial Vasca Ekin.

Garcia de Cortázar, José Ángel. 1966. *Vizcaya en el Siglo XV. Aspectos Económicos Y Sociales*. Bilbao: Ediciones de la Caja de Ahorros Vizcaína.

———. 1989. "Medievo y mundo urbano." In *Los Vascos a través de la Historia. Comportamientos, mentalidades y vida cotidiana*, directed and coordinated by José Luis Orella. San Sebastián: Caja de Guipúzcoa-Gipuzkoako Kutxa.

———. 1993. *Vizcaya en la alta edad media*. Colección Temas Vizcaínos 9, no. 105. Bilbao: Caja de Ahorros Vizcaina.

García de Cortázar, José Ángel, and Beatriz Arizaga. 1991. *Euskal Herria Erdi Aroan*. 2 vols. Donostia: Gaiak.

García de Cortazar, José Ángel, Beatriz Arizaga, Rosa María Martínez Ochoa, and María Luz Rios. 1979. *Introducción a la historia medieval de Alava, Guipúzcoa y Vizcaya en sus textos.* San Sebastián: Editorial Txertoa.

García de Cortázar, Fernando, and Manuel Montero. 1980. *Historia de Vizcaya*, vol. 1, *Los origenes, la Edad Media, el Antiguo Régimen.* San Sebastián: Editorial Txertoa.

———. 1983. *Diccionario de Historia del País Vasco*, vols. 1 and 2. San Sebastián: Editorial Txertoa.

García de Cortazar, Fernando, and José María Lorenzo Espinosa. 1988. *Historia del País Vasco.* San Sebastián: Editorial Txertoa.

Garmendia, Francisco. 1981. "Gure Mendiak eta Euskal Gizartearen Eraketa." In *Mendiak*, vol. 1, *Berezko eta giza-giroturiko Eusko Lurra*, edited by Enrique Ayerbe. Donostia: Etor.

Garmendia, Francisco, and Jose Luis Iriarte. 1978. "Arauketa Gipuzkoan." In *Euskaldunak: La Etnia Vasca*, vol 3. Donostia: Etor.

Idoate, Carlos. 1989. *Emigración navarra del valle de Baztán a América en el Siglo XIX. Inventario de documentos.* Pamplona: Gobierno de Navarra; Institución Príncipe de Viana.

Idoate, Florencio. 1977. *La Comunidad del Valle de Roncal.* Pamplona: Diputación Foral de Navarra.

Irala, Antonio de. N.D. *Keperin de Jemein-i idatziriko eskutitz argitaratugabeak.* Unpublished manuscript.

Irujo, Manuel de. 1945. *Instituciones Jurídicas Vascas.* Buenos Aires: Editorial Vasca Ekin.

Juaristi, Jon. 1987: *El linaje de Aitor. La invención de la tradición vasca.* Madrid: Taurus.

Juaristi, Patxi. 2001. *Euskaldunak eta ondasunak.* Iruña: Pamiela.

Lafourcade, Maïté. 1986. "El Particularismo Jurídico." In *Ser Vasco*, directed by J. Haritschelhar. Bilbao: Ediciones Mensajero.

Manterola, Ander. 1978. "Etxea." In *Euskaldunak: La Etnia Vasca*, vol. 3. Donostia: Etor.

Mokoroa, Justo. 1990. *Repertorio de locuciones del habla popular vasca oral y escrita, en sus diversas variedades. Analógicamente clasificado por categorías y conceptos a base de los cuadros e índices de A. Pinloche y F. Brunot.* 2 vols. Bilbao: Labayru.

Otazu, Alfonso de. 1986. *El "igualitarismo" vasco: Mito y realidad.* 2nd ed. San Sebastián: Editorial Txertoa.

Paul Arzak, Juan Ignacio. 1978. *Historia Del Pais Vasco.* San Sebastián: Luis Haranburu Editor.

Salinas Quijada, Francisco. 1983. *Derecho Civil de Navarra*. 2nd edition. Pamplona: Diputación Foral de Navarra; Institución Principe de Viana.

Solozabal, Juan José. 1975. *El primer nacionalismo vasco. Industrialismo y conciencia nacional*. Madrid: Tucar Ediciones.

9

Slaying the Dragon Together: Modern Basque Cooperativism as a Transmutation of Traditional Society

Joseba Azkarraga Etxagibel

> "Basques take life terribly seriously and make a religion of everything. Even politics and business, when taken on by a Basque, are addressed with religious fervor and a spirit of absolute commitment: this is very true of politics, and even more so of business. This is our problem: we tend to take things seriously, which some of the large nations around us do not."
>
> —Karlos Santamaria

The Mondragon cooperative experience (henceforth, MCE) is one of the great social innovations in modern Basque history. Beyond its impact on Basque society, it is one of the most significant examples of democracy applied to business in the world. The MCE's economic success has caught the attention of many analysts who see in this case a real possibility of conceiving alternative ways of running and setting up companies, based on the values of democracy, social solidarity, and fair distribution—in short, a significant departure from the conventional canon of capitalist business. Mondragon has even become a myth in certain circles, especially among those interested in alternative economic and organizational models.

The Mondragon Group (to give it its proper corporate name) is a complex system of businesses. It is a conglomerate consisting of 103 cooperatives from 289 different bodies (foundations, company branches, international services, social welfare bodies, etc.), most of them of medium size, and is firmly incorporated in the global market (it has established retail and production outlets on all continents).[1] The cooperatives belong to four different sectors: industrial (automotive, machine-tool, electronics, construction, home appliances, enginneering, and so on), financial (a bank and an insurance company), retail (an extensive chain of supermarkets), and knowledge (education cooperatives, which span the whole educational cycle from schools to a university, as well as fifteen technology and advanced research centers). Today, there are approximately seventy-four thousand workers, of whom approximately 40 percent are worker-owners, and it is the biggest business group in the Basque Country (and the tenth largest private firm in Spain) in both volume of business and number of workers.

The first cooperative was set up in 1956 in Arrasate-Mondragón, Gipuzkoa, but a precedent for this had been established years earlier. The cooperative idea began to take shape in the period after the Spanish Civil War (1936–1939). Those were the tough "years of hunger": the repression of the Franco regime, exile, poverty, high rates of mortality due to illnesses such as tuberculosis, the prohibition of Basque culture and language, and an economy destroyed by the war (Larrañaga 1998).[2] Distrust and tension were daily parts of a fragile coexistence.[3] In the post-civil war

---

1.   It is important to stress that this is not a usual business *holding* but rather a federation of cooperatives in which each cooperative maintains its sovereignty as decided by its worker-members' general assembly. This means that the main decision-making power comes from below. The corporate structure is designed to provide for the federated cooperatives, managing mutual funds, representing the group, and defining shared policies (which have their base in each individual cooperative's plan).

2.   The town of Arrasate-Mondragon had 7,835 inhabitants in 1933 and 3,060 in late 1936, when Franco's troops were already in the town (Altuna 2008, 98).

3.   Most Basques had been on the losing side in the civil war and Jose Maria Arizmendiarrieta himself—the driving force behind the MCE—had fought with the Basque nationalist troops against the fascist uprising (see also the next footnote). The Basque provinces of Bizkaia and Gipuzkoa (Arrasate being in the latter) were declared to be traitors by the Franco regime because of their special commitment to the democratic Second Republic. It should also be remembered that Franco's dictatorship had a policy of non-reconciliation in the

years, the ecclesiastical hierarchy sent a young priest, Jose Maria Arizmendiarrieta, to Arrasate-Mondragón, a town with a long tradition of social and working class struggle. This priest in turn became the main inspiration for the MCE.[4]

Generally speaking, Basque society was heavily influenced by the Catholic Church. Another institution was also highly influential in Arrasate-Mondragón: the Unión Cerrajera company, which was decidedly capitalist and hierarchical. The factory's daily siren marked the discipline of work and the rhythms and textures of daily life. This enterprise employed two-thirds of the population of Arrasate-Mondragón, and it had its own canteens, stores, mutual insurance funds, and even a technical school (Molina 2011). Its managers had become a real local oligarchy: they controlled not just economic power, but also the social, political, educational, and cultural dimensions of life. The historical context, then, was one of considerable asymmetric power.

The young people who initiated Mondragon cooperativism were middle managers in the Unión Cerrajera. They held posts of some importance and led the workers' demands. Finally, they helped to bring about an event that has almost been forgotten: they suggested to the directors that, within the next capital increase, the workers would subscribe to 20 percent of the capital, thus incorporating workers into the management. Arizmendiarrieta wrote the actual letter with the proposal that was then signed by the workers. The attempt at reforming a capitalist company was instantly refused, and the young activists left their jobs and founded their own enterprise, which was to become the first Mondragon industrial cooperative. Specifically, in

---

post-civil war era: its policy was one of elimination of its enemies, and some observers have commented that the post-civil war years were even harder than the war itself.

4.   Arizmendiarrieta fought with the Basque nationalists in favor of the Second Republic and was captured by Franco's troops, only miraculously escaping execution. He knew how to take advantage of the cracks in that harshly authoritarian regime, which was radically opposed to all that was dearest to him. In the 1970s the revolutionary left considered him and cooperatives to be merely reformist variants of the traditional status quo. The left argued that any practical work was just consolidating a system that had to be destroyed. At the same time, Arrizmendiarrieta was classified as a dangerous "red priest" by the Francoists.

1956 they created the first industrial cooperative (Ulgor, today Fagor), bringing about a key transformation (Azkarraga 2007a).

- A typically capitalist power structure had been turned on its head, empowering workers in three crucial areas: ownership of the company (it was the worker-members' collective property), decision-making authority (it was based on democratic power: "one worker-member, one vote"), and how profits were to be shared (equitable distribution). It was through this new organization that the workers assigned themselves a new political status and new roles, based on values of equality, democracy, and responsibility.

- As well as promoting an essential *intramural* transformation (with the introduction of democratic ways of ideas, including profit-sharing), Mondragon cooperativism also gave rise to a fundamental reworking of the company's social function (*extramural* transformation) in that it turned into an institution with social commitments, at the service of the community and its development, and aspiring to achieve social justice, thereby contributing to the whole community's moral and material progress.

- At the root of the MCE, and especially Arizmendiarrieta's thinking, was the idea to become an "active, leading community," going beyond the business world. The fundamental idea was to demonstrate that the working class was capable of managing its own affairs in all areas of public life—creating and running its own institutions in addition to the state and the market.[5]

The MCE stands for community action—mainly in, but not limited to, the economic sphere—which leads to the working class reappropriating its own life. Two dimensions are crucial in this regard: (1) *material reappropriation* by creating the necessary means and resources for daily life; and (2) *symbolic reappropriation* by activating/building the means and immaterial resources that enable the empowerment of the individual and collective: confidence, aware-

---

5. The vision of a *good society* was one increasingly self-administered and self-directed, with a responsible community being the main actor. Pursuing this aim, the Mondragon cooperatives have promoted substantial changes the way work, savings, consuming, education, research, and health are conceived. The fundamental idea was to construct a *participative society with participative citizens*, a social order in which citizens take an active, responsible part in all economic and social activities that affected their lives.

ness, effective norms of behavior, realizing the power of social relationships, and constructing social networks that enable community
self-management. This second dimension is of considerable importance: the Mondragon experience is an undeniable success in that
it achieves sufficient subjective density (shared values) and social
mass (closely knit social relationships) to make it possible to break
with the established order, and to bring about sustained change.

In this sense, the importance of education cannot be underesti-
mated (for a more detailed account see Azkarraga 2010). Approximately fifteen years went by before the first cooperative was set up,
and during those years education came to play a key role. From the
very start Arizmendiarrieta promoted study, reflection, and action
groups through the Christian workers' movement. Being a priest
in the local parish at a time when the Church had great power, he
played a very important role and was particularly influential for
the young.[6] To a large extent, the change in society was led by an
integral educational strategy: sociological and technical education;
education in social commitment; and, lastly, spiritual and religious
education.[7]

In other words, along with the *vision* for social transformation, one also has to be capable of making it happen, that is, the

---

6. This influence manifested itself through three "professorships," as Alfonso
Gorroñogoitia, the founder of the first cooperative and the most important
social leader in the Mondragon cooperative movement, notes (Gorroñogoitia
2004): he taught religious and human values at the local trade school; he participated in the Catholic Action study group; and, as a priest, he influenced
many young people through his role as confessor.

7. Arizmendiarrieta founded a social academy for studying society and contemporary thought (with particular emphasis on the relationship between
capital and labor). He also founded a technical college, which later became
a polytechnic and is now the cooperative university's engineering faculty.
The cooperative experience was created at the intersection between technological and humanistic training. Modern technical education was central to
Arizmendiarrieta's social project, because instrumental rationality provided
the necessary procedural intelligence (making market-place activities effective). However, it was regarded as being unable to analyze present conditions
in a critical fashion or to imagine alternative scenarios. For the latter, humanist
and value-oriented rationality was required. At the same time, education in
social commitment was crucial: young people were also encouraged to organize activities such as theater, hiking, sports activities, raffles in order to collect
resources on behalf of impoverished families, and so on.

subjective conditions and an appropriate mentality have to exist in order to complete the task of humanizing society. And the educational process is key to the creation of a new collective subject. However, that is not the entire explanation for the MCE's success. The MCE was founded and developed in a specific social context—Basque society—that has certain cultural and institutional characteristics that help to explain how such socioeconomic innovation was possible. I am referring here to an important social context in which, among other factors, some central features of traditional Basque society are still alive.

The Mondragon cooperatives must be regarded as one of the greatest social innovations in modern Basque history. Some authors approach the MCE as if it were a utopia realized or as a complete alternative to current capitalism. Others see it as a kind of progressive perversion of genuine cooperativism and as something equivalent to a capitalist corporation. Taking a more analytical point of view, I maintain that neither of those perceptions really stands up to reality (Cheney 2002; Azkarraga 2009). The MCE is a social and business experiment with a profound social vocation, but with necessary limits.[8]

In what follows I am going to analyze some of the conditions that made this creation possible, looking at cooperatives from the inside, that is to say, from the position I have held as a member of Mondragon for many years. More specifically, I will focus on the connection between the MCE and some key cultural, social, and institutional elements of traditional Basque society. It is difficult to explain the existence of what is considered to be one of the most important examples of business democracy and the world's largest industrial worker cooperative without taking into account the sociocultural and socioinstitutional framework in which the cooperatives emerged: a framework that had important links with premodern society.

---

8. Mondragon cooperativism has achieved a great deal: It has been an important self-administered driving force for community development. It has created considerable wealth and thousands of jobs. It also has ensured an extremely equitable distribution of the wealth that was created in the process. To date, it is the story of successful cooperativism.

The Basque Historical Context: The Cultural and Institutional Humus

It is now widely accepted that development is closely connect-ed to cultural and social factors. As Rafa Altuna and Hervé Grellier (2008) correctly point out, many studies of the Mondrag-on story employ an anthropological perspective (Greenwood and González 1990; Whyte and Whyte 1988; Bradley and Gelb 1983; Kasmir 1996; Thomas and Logan 1980). Although they are external views and interpretations, that is, without having lived the cooperative experience directly, these analyses were quite successful in highlighting factors such as Basque religiousness, its considerable industrial tradition, the democratic nature of its historical institutions, nationalism, the work ethic, attitude to savings, and social rituals such as the *txikiteo* (daily drinks with groups of friends).[9]

In other words, this is a society with strong *social capital*, to use a concept that has become very popular in the social scienc-es in recent times (Putnam et al. 1993). Social capital is connect-ed to a series of social relationships based on confidence; coop-eration and reciprocity; a sense of belonging; shared identity; the ability to build links of solidarity and cooperation; the iden-tification with collective aims; and, last but not least, the ability to found organizations in order to achieve shared aims and ob-jectives. In short, social capital is connected to everything that makes it possible for people to cooperate by relying on shared norms and values, the desire to work in collaboration in a certain location, and the capacity for self-organization. There exists, in other words, a social structure, or, as Francis Fukuyama puts it, a situation in which civil society takes hold (Fukuyama 1995).

---

9. Some nonacademic texts have also referred to the Mondragon experience in an attempt to widen the perspective. For example, British daily *The Guardian* published an interesting piece titled "Basque Country's Thriving Big Society" (Ramesh 2011). The article refers to the Mondragon cooperatives as occupying an important place in the Basque social fabric and links their democratic nature and their communitarian nature to Basque society as a whole. For the *Guardian* reporter, Basque society is a society with a tightly-knit network of relationships, symbolized in institutions such as the gastronomic societies (*txoko*, in Basque), or the unusual supporter phenomenon and infrastructure of the soccer club Athletic Bilbao (for further information on the latter, see Vaczi 2011).

Social capital has also been linked to ideological factors.[10] From a macrosocial perspective, social capital "includes factors that strengthen the organization of civil society and its integration and watchfulness with respect to actions that may be taken by the state or by private companies. Social capital helps to guide individual action and creativity not just in terms of egotistical achievement but by pointing them toward the common good" (Díaz-Albertini 2003, 248).

Putnam and collaborators (1993) identify social capital in groups, organizations, communities, or even countries.[11] In fact, they explain the development of the north of Italy and the lack of development in the south from a long-term historical perspective, referring to more than a thousand years of civic culture.[12] A long-term historical perspective may also be of use in elucidating the background to Basque cooperativism. This chapter cannot offer an in-depth discussion of all the social and cultural features of Basque society; it is therefore a necessarily limited approach. I will thus limit myself to a discussion of a few aspects of its singularity—a few snapshots in other words—that may help us just to

---

10.   One of the basic dimensions of trust is sharing a similar view of the world and having certain shared beliefs about what a good society consists of; in other words, sociocognitive material, shared interpretations that help to produce a collective identity, give an experience meaning, and enable communication among members of the group.

11.   From such a perspective, the key to founding strong institutions is "civic commitment" in terms of participation in different organizations (cultural and sports associations, clubs, churches, choirs, etc.). Organizations such as those mentioned above integrate individuals into society by using a wide range of types of collaboration, encouraging coordination and communication, contributing to good governance, and, in general, to economic progress through relying on reciprocity and cooperation.

12.   Northern Italian regions, so the argument goes, generally take greater interest in public matters and in community organizations. They seem to respect the law, trust public institutions, horizontal social networks, and so forth. In other words, social capital is a factor that is allegedly in a better position to explain communities in the north. From this point of view, social capital is also an asset accumulated over time thanks to the organized activity of members of society in the past (whether individuals or collectives). These organized activities are based on certain *social norms* that encourage cooperation, taking on central values (solidarity, confidence, reciprocity) and the existence of "networks of commitment." All of these lead to greater levels of welfare (Putman et al. 1993).

consider the importance of the historical, cultural, and institutional background to the creation of the MCE.

A Historical Foundation for Community Practices

Mythology may in fact be taken as the starting point. Etymologically, the name Mondragón means "The Dragon's Hill." The dragon in question is the well-known creature of myth that brings misfortune, destruction, hunger, and unhappiness to the community. In the conventional version of the myth, it is Saint George, the young prince, who kills the dragon and frees the community.[13] There is, however, a significant variation in the Mondragón version, also highlighted by the anthropologist, historian, and linguist Julio Caro Baroja: the story does not reflect the archetype of the individual hero because the townsfolk themselves vanquish the monster. More specifically, the legend talks of collective intelligence, strategy, and cohesion: foundry workers (there have been foundries in the Mondragón Valley since the thirteenth century), so the story goes, carved a beautiful girl out of wax. The dragon devoured her and his heat melted the wax, which stuck his jaws together, leaving him at the mercy of the townsfolk's lances. In this way, overcoming misfortune occurs through collective action, with no need for either superheroes or aristocrats. The singularity of this Basque myth underlines a communitarian sense and strategy for achieving well-being; a sense and a strategy that are, in fact, at the basis of Mondragon's modern cooperative experience.

From an anthropological perspective, the myth condenses the experience of the community through images and stories. Andrés Ortiz-Osés, the founder of symbolic hermeneutics, contends that "*Basque mythology*, along with the Basque language (*Euskara*) is the most important cultural monument in Basque tradition," and while "Euskara represents the ancient Basque language, mythology represents ancient Basque thought" (Ortiz-Osés 2007, 11–12).[14]

13. From a deep psychological perspective, this myth is the outward projection of the fight within each human being, between the hero/ine and his/her shadow. Symbolically, the hero-prince represents the urge for a superior awareness that will overcome the inertia of the unconscious (the dragon) and thus be able to restore the psychic balance.

14. The Basques are often referred to as the only pre-Indo-European people

According to Ortiz-Osés and Luis Garagalza, the version that we have mentioned is an "interesting reference to the Basque communalist background" (Ortiz-Osés and Garagalza 2007, 226–27). [15] In question is the extent this type of tale—which, in fact, is not very well known in Arrasate-Mondragón—molds people's self-representation and experience in modern times. It would probably be foolhardy to suggest that there is, in fact, any influence.[16] However, I believe that the existence of such a tale and its unusual mythological characteristics are significant in themselves.

A second important feature needs mentioning: during the ancien régime, and in many parts of the Basque Country, *hidalguía universal* (universal nobility) was introduced. The inhabitants of the Basque provinces were recognized as nobles as long as they

---

in Europe; in other words, they were there prior to the Indo-European invasions that took place between 6,000 and 3,500 BC (those invasions formed the demographic and linguistic basis for what Europe is today). Mythologist Andrés Ortiz-Osés stresses the profound differences that exist between the Basques and the Indo-European peoples: "Today indigenous Basque culture is the last bastion standing against Indo-European patriarchal-rationalist culture. Indigenous Basque culture is, in fact, pre-Indo-European and pre-patriarchal: the Basques, who came from an autochthonous Pyrenean Cro-Magnon evolution, existed as a distinct ethnic group before the famous patriarchal Indo-European invasions" (Ortiz-Osés and Mayr 1980, 105). Basque mythology does not belong to the group of mythologies with a Father God; the main God is a goddess named Mari (Ortiz-Osés 2007, 12). Christianity was introduced relatively late and, with regards to pre-Christian archetypes, the mythical-cultural tendency is matriarchal. There are, additionally, naturalist and communalist connotations (in contrast to what has been termed "rationalist," patriarchal, and individualist mythologies, which spread all over Europe, along with the mentioned invasions). We should make clear that when "Basque matriarchalism" is talked about, this is usually a reference to a psychosocial structure based around the matriarchal-feminine archetype. Ortiz-Osés, with caution, chooses to describe this by coining the term *"matrial"* (Ortiz-Osés 2007, 12).

15. There is another significant variation in the Navarrese town of Urdiain. In this case, it is the damsel who kills the dragon, being a woman who limits the power of the traditional medieval male hero (Ortiz-Osés and Garagalza 2007, 226–27).

16. Although it is important to note that renowned ethnographer José Miguel Barandiaran was still compiling Basque myths in the first half of the twentieth century, which means that the oral transmission reached down to the heart of modern industrial times. For more about the historical construction of Basque identity and the role of archetypes and myths, see Beriain (1998).

could prove that their families came from a farmstead (*baserri*). This "equaling upward" might have had a considerable impact on the relationships and institutions in traditional Basque society. This is of interest to our topic because it might mean that, to some extent, political institutions were founded among equals (a basic principle in cooperative organization). This "universal nobility" was a social reality that undermined the stratified order of society and introduced a proud collective self-perception. While this does not mean that traditional Basque society was completely egalitarian in structure, in contrast to other traditional Western societies Basque society was at least not organized in the same stratified manner, and socioeconomic differences were probably not as wide as in other Western societies. Furthermore, work became compatible with being noble.[17]

It is well known that the Basque Country also had a singular normative and legal tradition, known as Pyrenean or Navarrese law, which differed from Roman law and Germanic law in having a much wider understanding of public law (Urzainqui 1987). The structure of property was also unusual in that most peasants were owners of their own land (and had a degree of liberty that probably did not exist in Europe). Furthermore, there was a characteristic understanding of property: the basis for property, the house,[18]

---

17. As Caro Baroja states, "During the ancien régime in Castile, it was inconceivable for a nobleman, even a mere *hidalgo*, to dedicate himself to industry or commerce. The only acceptable positions for him were in public administration, in the militia, in the priesthood, or in managing agricultural properties. But in the Basque provinces our ancestors, gentlemen of noble orders with titles, not only themselves worked in foundries and shipyards but also bought and sold merchandise and did business with outsiders. Thus one can say that by the middle of the eighteenth century there existed in Gipuzkoa and Bizkaia a social class that did not resemble the great aristocracy of Castile and Andalusia, who held sway over immense estates. Nor did they resemble the impoverished *hidalgos* so familiar to us in the classical literature. Rather this [social class] could be compared to what in England was called 'the gentry', constituted by wealthy families of more or less obscure or mixed ancestry, which increased its wealth generation after generation and lived very comfortably, taking advantage of all the opportunities and fashions of the moment" (Caro Baroja 1974, 161).

18. The farmstead (*baserri* in Basque) was a self-sufficient unit of production with its own land for crops and, additionally, rights to use communal pastoral lands.

was indivisible and the owner-inheritor could not use it as they wished, being its mere manager and having the obligation to pass it on, in its entirety, to the following generation (the proprietor, in fact, is the family; the house belongs to the current generation, but also to past and future generations). In other words, property rights in the Basque Country were collective and it was guaranteed that resources would be used so the collective good would benefit.

For centuries the fundamental idea behind Basque public law was to serve and to uphold a traditional form of democracy (Lafourcade 2003). One of the most important institutions in traditional Basque society was the parish assembly. In each town, the owners of each house decided by majority vote about matters concerning the community. In this traditional conception of democracy, each house—rather than one individual—had a vote and each group of houses chose a representative to the *biltzarra* (general assembly).

Thus, the basic ingredients of a cooperative, such as collective ownership and democratic practice, have a long history in the Basque Country. It is worth noting in this context that there was even a very early proto-industrial experience in the Basque Country, in fact in the home valley of the MCE, in the Upper Deba region. In his analysis of the sixteenth century, the Basque historian and anthropologist José Antonio Azpiazu (2002) points out that what has been called the Golden Century for Spain could well be called the Platinum Century for the Basque Country, not least because of the considerable development and trading relationships of the Upper Deba Valley (Mondragón Valley) with the rest of Europe. As this example shows, in the Basque Country the industrialization process should be dated to much earlier than the end of the nineteenth century and it surely points at some of the early roots of Mondragon's strongly industrial cooperativism.

Many studies confirm that the local economy in Upper Deba region (the Mondragon cooperatives' home valley) in the sixteenth century was not limited to agriculture. On many farmsteads farming was not enough to guarantee the survival of the whole family (due to lack of land or the inappropriateness of the land for cultivation). It therefore had to be supplemented with proto-industrial work such as, for example, making bladed weapons and light firearms or using forges and iron taken from mines (Caro Baroja 1974, 1986; Azpiazu 1999, 2002). When the demand for arms fell, iron tools for rural use were manufactured instead. The farmstead has always been an important production unit, but as Altuna and Grellier suggest, perhaps it has been more important than commonly believed. It was certainly more than just an idyllic spot connected to agriculture and herding (Altuna and Grellier 2008, 37).

Azpiazu also maintains that there are indications of early co-operative activity in sixteenth-century Basque social organization. It was

> a considerable industrial area. It covered several dozen towns and villages, organized in a genuinely cooperative manner in which each center of population, each profession and type of work connected a series of jobs and services whose efficiency and productivity should be enough to shatter the skepticism of anyone who doubts the importance of the Basques in supplying the most powerful armies at the start of the Modern Age. (Azpiazu 2002, 17)

He adds that, as a consequence of having to survive in a narrow valley with poor natural resources, people had to rely on each other, working together, and trying to bring individual and collective interests into harmony in order to make the most of the available natural resources.

Reciprocal relationships and institutions, which formed part of the traditional rural world, endured well into the twentieth century, some of them lasting until the present day. This is of particular interest because both Arizmendiarrieta, the charismatic priest who inspired Mondragon cooperativism, and the founding nucleus of people came from this same rural world: in other words, they were the prolongation of the social, cultural, and institutional set-up of the traditional Basque world. In fact, the industrialization model of Gipuzkoa was specific: it took place in small towns like Arrasate-Mondragón, with small firms (producing paper, arms, textiles, and locks), and focused on local and skilled workers who remained culturally and socially connected to an agrarian environment. A leading activist from the Upper Deba Valley, raised in a farmstead located in Arrasate-Mondragón and now in his seventies, expressed it this way: "It is a special valley. We learned at the same time to milk cows and melt iron." (Altuna 2008, 7).

Reciprocal relationships and institutions in the traditional Basque world included the following features (some typical features of rural societies in general):

- mutual assistance in terms of work (in cases in which there was too much work for one family or household to cope with);
- neighborhood work known as *auzolan*, that is, collaboration between houses or family farmsteads in order to collectively manage services and resources shared among several households (taking care of local shrines, paths, bridges, wells, and so forth);
- other traditional forms of informal assistance—many of them held by women—and communal safety networks that guaranteed some form of welfare infrastructure, (syndicates, fire insurance associations, friendly societies for funerals, and so on).

Obviously, this brief, selective, and inevitably limited historical picture of premodern Basque society remains incomplete. It serves only to illustrate the point that the Basque historical framework provides a rich background of symbolic, social, and institutional experiences that apparently helped to bring about and maintain the MCE. The historical picture serves only to highlight that if the Basque Country had not had this background of community resources, it would certainly have been much more difficult to build an experience like Mondragon.

Contemporary Communitarian Practices

The cultural and institutional *humus* that I referred to is not confined to premodern history but continues in the modern urban setting. This can be seen in various kinds of sociability that any observer can easily detect also in today's daily life: in features such as the *txoko* (gastronomic society) and *koadrila* (tightly knit groups of friends), and in social rituals such as txikiteo.

In fact, the koadrila and txoko continue to affect social life considerably.[19] These groups of friends have been described as the

---

19.   The groups of friends are made up of a wide range of people who are of the same age and sex, from the same neighborhood, or who went to the same school. A kuadrila is not just marked by friendship; relationships are egalitarian, based on shared attitudes, mutual respect, and trust (Heiberg 1989), with

basic support for social and public life in its most local and daily dimension (Arpal Poblador 1985; Pérez-Agote 2006). In Jesús Arpal Poblador's opinion, the group of friends is at the same time the institutionalization of communitarian forms of life in opposition to the social division created by modernization and also a public practice in contrast to the indivisibility of the family unit. In other words, the koadrila exceeds the domestic community but it counters the "lonely crowd" of city life (Arpal Poblador 1985).

The phenomenon of the koadrila was strengthened under Franco's regime and still creates important interpersonal links, although there have been important transformations in recent years, such as a move from its affiliative nature to a more acquisitive character. Txikiteo is one of the tightly knit groups of friends' most important rituals (Pérez-Agote 2006), at first a very masculine habit, but later also practiced by women: meeting daily, normally after work, to go from bar to bar drinking small glasses of wine. Today, the txikiteo custom is not an everyday ritual, although it is still important on weekends (Martínez 2005). But the importance of this social custom in the creation of cooperatives is greater than one might initially think. First, its underlying logic is very similar to the logic of cooperative activity, at least at a micro level: "To go on txikiteo or *poteo*, the members of the group have a kitty. They all put in the same amount of money. In rotation, one of them looks after the kitty, orders the drinks for everyone. . . . This member is trusted by the group; he accounts for the purse and usually reminds the others when the funds have to be topped up" (Altuna and Grellier 2008, 46). On the other hand, Alfonso Gorroñogoitia himself, a founder of the MCE, states the importance of this mainly male social custom, as it established the local communicative infrastructure through which the cooperative idea could spread:

> Once it got around in Arrasate-Mondragón that we were going to set up a company, many people who trusted us and who wanted to make a change in their professional career joined us. You have to bear in mind that Unión Cerrajera [the capitalist company] was still fairly prosperous. . . . That's why it's surprising that the first hundred members joined out on the street, practically during the txikiteo, and they were qualified workers.

---

significant psychosocial effects.

Likewise, a remarkable network of relationships emerged around Basque gastronomical societies. The txoko is a physical place (dining area and kitchen) in which the member-owners meet to eat and socialize (during Franco's dictatorship, txokos were one of the few places Basques could legally gather, sing songs, and speak in Basque). So how are relationships formed? One can usually encounter some diversity among the txoko members in terms of social upbringing, hobbies, and political tendencies. However, they usually share the same cultural and linguistic background. Furthermore, being a member provides each and everyone with the same rights and obligations, which are specified by statutes and approved by all members of the assembly. Txokos are owned by their members, traditionally men, and run democratically: one member, one vote. The members take turns in a democratic way in order to share fundamental roles (treasurer, president, secretary, chair, and so forth) and to ensure that the society works properly. After the collective space has been used, a detailed expense form is filled out and each participant pays pro rata. In these gastronomical societies, the custom of doing things together and its egalitarian structure are a more formal representation of the social and cultural characteristics of the koadrila. Most gastronomical societies are actually the coming together of several groups of friends or a koadrila, each one making use of the txoko, which belongs to everyone (Homobono 1994; Hess 2007).

In fact, cooperatives rely on organizational principles that are close to those mentioned: relationships based on trust, shared capital, autonomy, collective administration, responsible administration of shared goods, rotating responsibilities, the harmonization of individuals and groups, democracy, equality, reciprocity, cooperation, a cultural and social relationship with the terrain or location, and so on. In the Basque setting the *lifeworld* has been well structured by communicative processes that help to develop and foster social relationships and networks. Thus, the cooperatives themselves have become a well-structured public space—an area of social action—in terms of communication and in which it is possible to reach a consensus about shared meanings and practices.[20]

---

20.   This was particularly apparent in the early phase of Mondragon cooperativism. The testimonies of the founders show a type of business meeting,

In summary, contemporary Basque society is well structured in terms of sociability. As Ramón Zallo points out, this characteristic has also had significant political effects:

> While now weaker, the resources of sociability that were so efficient in delegitimizing the Franco regime still exist: in fact, they enabled the whole country to respond to the regime quickly and as a whole, something that did not happen anywhere else in the Spanish state. Naturally, this involved the closely knit network of public areas and "routes" for socialization such as the groups of friends, associations that meet at txokos and other social activities and movements such as the *ikastolas* (schools in which teaching is done in Basque), mountaineering and hiking, recreational clubs, [traditional Basque] dance groups, movements to encourage adults to learn Basque, the scouts, parish social activities. This network was also based in relation to family ideology and influence as transmitters of the historical memory of a nation that suffered terribly during the Franco years. (1995, 37–64)

We have discussed the tightly knit social network that forms the backbone of much of public and local life, something that has made it possible for larger scale experiences to emerge in other areas, such as economic activities.

In conclusion, as with other experiences of social and solidarity economy, the Mondragon experience emerged out of a particular human ecosystem, a specific cultural and institutional framework, which together with its physical setting forms a complex sociohistorical configuration: traditions; particular social relationships; specific cultural resources; social customs; identi-

---

or workers' assembly, with two characteristics. On one hand these meetings lasted many more hours than today's shorter and probably more effective meetings. On the other, they served to recreate continuously the cooperative values. In fact, all cooperative meetings were in the first instance also educational experiences that served the purpose of reproducing the values of the cooperative experience. Furthermore, the cooperatives' exterior world in Arrasate-Mondragón was a prolongation of that inward integration, thanks to communal local life and social rituals such as the txikiteo, in which the cooperative's members met (for the cooperative managers it was morally imperative not to move away from the cooperative members' social world and to take part in local social customs). Consequently, the cooperative rationality continued unfolding in the town.

ty and identities; a history of production; technological characteristics; administrative structures; and, in general, the psychosocial, normative, and community characteristics of the Basque
people. The Mondragon story is one of a considerable reserve of
social capital that has been built up over the centuries, although
it is also a product of the specific time in which it emerged. The
Basques' collective experience, despite its traumatic episodes and
violent ruptures has left a *humus* that made it possible for social
innovation to evolve.

Developing Communitarian Kind of Companies

In the following sections I will go into more depth on the development of communitarian kinds of companies, including institutional and cultural dimensions.

The Institutional Dimension: Practical Solidarity

The MCE was founded by a tightly knit network of committed people with communitarian principles, what could
be called a *community of meaning*. Their main inspiration
lay in Arizmendiarrieta and his communitarian approach.[21]
Arizmendiarrieta began with the notion of *social priesthood*,
which was a well-established concept in the Basque Catholic
Church: this all-embracing idea included not only the path to
individual salvation but also responsiveness to social problems
and people's material needs. His main approach consisted of
strengthening communities by focusing on the individual and
collective acceptance of responsibility, in order to change the
structures of power. Arizmendiarrieta wanted to move beyond the capitalist paternalism practiced by Unión Cerrajera

---

21. Arizmendiarroieta's ideological formation came not from one but a number of sources: the Catholic Church's social doctrine, the communitarian per-
sonalism of French religious philosophers Emmanuel Mounier and Jacques
Maritain, cooperativist thought, socialism (especially that associated with
the British Labour Party and Toribio Etxebarria's Basque socialism), and the
Basque social tradition. He also read critical thinkers of the time, such as Paulo
Freire and Herbert Marcuse. For further information about Arizmendiarrieta's
intellectual development see Azurmendi (1992). For his biography, see Molina
(2005).

in the form of schools, workers' mutual associations, company stores, and so forth. He wanted to create a new social order in which labor had primacy over capital. Self-management and self-government were the key ideas. The working class had to demonstrate its own maturity by taking responsibility for itself, constructing its own structures, particularly at a time of a repressive dictatorship that made it difficult to consider any alternatives.[22]

To a large extent, Mondragon cooperativism is the result of an attempt by Christian social justice thinking to provide an answer to the problems created by capitalist society and its inherent class conflict. As Robert Oakeshott remarks, this "oasis of democracy" was constructed through a peculiar "alliance between Church and technology" (Oakeshott 1973). The Basque economist Antxon Pérez de Calleja explains it as follows:

> At the beginning of the twentieth century, the Church, or part of it, began to feel that it was part of a class war. Its way to address this was to be either acting in determined, practical ways in favor of the forces in power of the right, or—given that the opposite was unthinkable—looking for a third way through the self-organization of a working class that still had some sympathies for the Church, particularly when it came to cooperatives. (Pérez de Calleja 1989, 10)

Both the creation of study group—in which the founders of the MCE received their education—and setting up technical colleges after the Civil War—which the founders also went to—were activ-

---

22. Arizmendiarrieta promoted a "new social order" and a "new man." For Arizmendiarrieta, neither liberal capitalism nor state socialism led to human dignity: people did not seem to him to be the primary objective in either model. As an alternative, he suggested taking on both individual and collective responsibility in order to improve communities morally and socially. This necessarily also extended to business efficiency. It required, for example, taking the code of conduct that is based on economic and market calculations and the planning of business activities more seriously. Arizmendiarrieta studied at the main seminary in Vitoria-Gasteiz, which put him in contact with modern strands of Christian thought of the time, both in social and theological terms. He was a disciple of the social anthropologist and priest Barandiaran—considered the patriarch of Basque culture in the twentieth century—and his group of followers.

ities supported by the Church's more liberal and modern wings.[23] In the Basque Country many priests participated and supported the founding of cooperatives. The Mondragon movement just stands out because of its size and success. Faced with the advance of "de-Christianizing forces" such as socialism, anarchism, and communism, the Church saw it necessary to intervene and to offer the apparently increasingly secularized working class a convincing solution. This provided the larger theological context in which Mondragon cooperativism emerged and later developed.

Mondragon shows that it is crucial to analyze reality critically: Which field exactly is ready for action? How can one turn large-scale and ambitious concepts such as solidarity into practice? From the outset the MCE has been a highly practical laboratory with diverse pragmatic mechanisms for mutual support, cooperation, and reciprocity.

A solution was found by creating mechanisms for "intra-cooperative mutual support" (inside each cooperative). The reduced yet egalitarian scale of profit distribution was in particular helpful in this respect. Of course, there were differences in terms of payments and salaries, but these were solved by introducing limits: during the first three decades, the income of the highest earner (for example a bank manager), could not exceed three times that of the lowest (for example a production line worker). The cooperative members' lifestyles, especially during the first generations, were based on a strict moral code. A narrow range of payment scales was one of the mechanisms to incentivize moral behavior. For many years social differences among cooperative strata was thus reduced in objective terms: the Mondragon moral culture prevented the possibility of the more able members to distance themselves or to "take off."[24]

---

23. "The most efficient instrument in the fight against atheism was the study groups, whose main objective was to train an elite among the working class in order to spread Christian social ideas" (Rivera and de la Fuente 2000,70).

24. Arrizmendiarietta was deeply concerned about the "structural consolidation of individualist positions" in society (Azurmendi 1992, 712) and postulated that cooperativism would lead to a social order in which communal wealth would be of prime importance compared to that of the individual. Cooperativism tried to create a classless society, but not a society without differences. In fact, any society that offered such mutual support on a large scale would have to accept differences, making use of them for the common

"Inter-cooperative mutual support" (among cooperatives) is probably one of the MCE's most important innovations and had been one of its most remarkable characteristics from the start:

- The whole Mondragon project started as a single cooperative that helped other smaller units until they could function properly for themselves, usually by helping out and transferring all types of resources to the smaller, more needy unit: capital, human resources, experience, knowledge of technical, social, and business management, and so on.
- The cooperatives eventually federated into groups, joining forces in a partially decentralized grouping that enabled economies of scale to be constructed without excessive bureaucratic control (namely, each cooperative remains independent, with power always remaining with the workers; the cooperatives' members delegate certain powers to higher organisms but under the rule of subsidiarity).[25]
- Groups have also created shared (intercooperative) economic resources to respond to periods of crisis, for example, by starting new initiatives or achieving economies of scale.
- The cooperatives have created a second-degree superstructure, enabling access to shared and effective resources: the cooperative bank, a social welfare system (the state left cooperative members outside its own social welfare structure), technical and research centers, a university, and so forth.
- Such mutual aid schemes among groups have allowed for the creation of mechanisms such as workers' reassignments and "relocations": when a cooperative is in difficulty, its workers can be relocated to join other cooperatives that need more workers. This means that employment is guaranteed.[26]
- Other key mechanisms have been created, such as "reconver-

---

good. The belief was that all people are equal in dignity but different in their talents; and that it is important to value those differences that stem from personal merit. The idea of having equal opportunities was an essential part of such thinking. The ideal outcome would be a society in which differences are progressively reduced, yet without falling for unfair, antisocial, non-mutual, and inefficient egalitarianism.

25. Initially, the groupings were based on sociological-geographical criteria; in other words, being located in the same local area. Later, they were based on industrial sectors (on business criteria, belonging to the same type of business).

26. It is not always easy to use this mechanism because the receiving cooperatives have to accept the arrival of members whose skills do not always match their needs.

sion of results": cooperatives with profits use some of those profits to cover losses in other partner cooperatives. At present, there is hardly a single cooperative in the Mondragon group for which the support of others has not been important or even decisive. In other words, a powerful sociobusiness and communitarian resilience has been created to function as an insurance against market uncertainties and other challenges that may lead to situations of vulnerability.

Solidarity with the community and the local area are additional features.

- The Mondragon culture understands that essential mutual support consists of creating further employment (especially cooperative employment), that is, it aims at increasing the number of members of the community in the cooperative project.[27] Originally, the Mondragon experience was built around just a small group of people; however, its inclusive strategy meant that it extended its "social contract" to currently include thousands of people.[28]
- With regard to profits obtained, the Mondragon culture demands the "total capitalization of results": that is, the reinvestment of profits. Reinvestment rather than the monetarization of profits has been an essential requirement. The cooperatives were not set up to fill private pockets but rather to advance the collective good. Hence also the maxim of "work a lot and consume little" for the first couple of generations—a combination of a strong work ethic and an attitude of sacrifice—giving priority to community rights. This means that on the one hand the accumulation of capital and economic expansion has been possible; and on the other hand that the whole community has advanced in economic terms thanks to the creation of more employment (to the detriment of the idea of making private profit).

27.   Throughout history there have been many cooperative experiences that, because of their business success, have decided to put a limit to their number of members or change their organizations' social and legal structure in order to continue growing by contracting salaried workers and thus avoiding the possibility of sharing their profits among a greater number of people.
28.   Unlike the traditional work contract, the cooperatives' social contract favors a social relationship that transcends the economic dimension and, additionally, establishes a social connection, allowing people to integrate fully into the work community. A social relationship is more complex and is based on members' rights and obligations as member-owners.

- Last but not least, each cooperative is under a legal obligation to give part of its profits to the community to help to finance various activities ranging from sports to cultural events and community activities.

Cultural Dimensions: Communitarian Culture and Substantive Rationality

Material factors have certainly been important to the MCE's success. For instance, and paradoxically, Mondragon would have been hardly possible without the Franco dictatorship, since this regime was characterized by a kind of economic autarky in which the competitive pressure was very low and cooperatives could sell everything they produced. Later, with the "technocratic phase" of the regime in the 1960s and with economic liberalization, Spanish per capita income grew. This particular type of modernization process was crucial for Mondragon because the household appliances produced by cooperatives—washing machines, refrigerators, and gas stoves—became goods that every home demanded.

However, going beyond material factors, there were also other "subjective" factors that also played an important role in the development of the MCE, such as cultural norms and a moral infrastructure that made it possible to construct the complex institutional framework described above (Azkarraga 2007a, 2007b). Education was key to this. The MCE is a product of both a kind of naivety (as one of the founders pointed out, "we did it because we didn't know it was impossible") and the result of a carefully planned and conscious decision and strategy, embedded in an educational strategy.

In addition to paying attention to the all-important material conditions, Mondragon cooperativism also tried to get the link between business and ideology/morality right. I refer here particularly to the sense of always having contained a mystical component in many members that reaches out beyond Mondragon, by remaining committed to a "project for society."

Intersubjectively shared and morally binding beliefs amounted to a specific attitude to life, an *ethos*, a particular moral code. Professional commitment became a style of life: work became almost a form of redemption—human work is the way to cooperate with God in order to complete nature—and life was ruled by frugality, savings, selflessness, hardworking, service to the community, sacrifice, self-discipline, and, consequently, business success.[29] It is somewhat paradoxical: Mondragon members were at the same time trying to live a Spartan life based on hard work and, in such a developmentalist context, they were promoting a growing consumerism through the consumer goods that they produced (Azkarraga 2007b; Molina 2011). Mondragon cooperatives grew thanks to a consumerist-oriented lifestyle and a materialistic society that was in many ways contrary to their values. Besides, it is this modernization process that has also led to a rapid secularization and loss of religious values in society, also in the cultural space of Mondragon, and it has been highly painful and anomic for the founders.

Nonetheless, this body of beliefs tied business activities to religious values in the first generation and, by doing so, created the structures of personality and subjective conditions needed in order to operate effectively in the market.[30] However, the cooperative ethical project is not just a pragmatic mechanism designed to adapt to market conditions. It is, rather, a communitarian ethic that has given work and business activities a deep moral meaning. Not complying with this ethos would probably have led not only to economic failure but for many of the participants it would have been a violation of ethical duty above everything else.

These values existed as an end in themselves, particularly for the first generation involved in the MCE, but not only the founders. Progressively, they have metamorphosed into a more utilitarian idea of cultural support. In fact, current cooperative members have moved further toward material well-being and individualism, a set of values that somewhat contradicts the traditional mor-

---

29.   As Molina points out, "The rigid culture of work implanted in the new enterprise was Spartan: ten- to twelve-hour days with a forty-minute break for lunch, Monday through Saturday, and ten days of vacation in August" (Molina 2011, 23). For further reading on the historical relationship between Basques and the work ethic see Cerrato Allende (2011).

30.   Clearly there are noticeable similarities to observations made by Max Weber in his famous work *The Protestant Ethic and the Spirit of Capitalism* (1965). However, I believe that there is one considerable difference: Mondragon cooperativism's (Catholic) keystone is communitarian development rather than individual wealth or salvation (which were the driving forces for Calvinist individuals in Weber's analysis).

al motives. The austere, Spartan, self-sacrificing, and committed way of life has ceded to a more consumerist and hedonist life-style, more interested in material possibilities.[31]

For a long period business activity had been accompanied by a particular moral culture with the effect of making the former more efficient. Particularly in its Christian version, pursuing a moral path became a "cause" for many people. It offered something close to participation in humanity's redemption in exchange for daily self-sacrifice, austerity, discipline, and the renunciation of individual interests. The objective was to develop a communitarian experience in which, according to Peter L. Berger (1975), the concept of "development" was not simply the objective of some rational actions in the economic-business sphere; it was also, at a deeper level, the center that radiated hope, including the expectation of redemption or, in more secular terms, liberation. The cooperative ideology offered a perspective of meaningful behavior and life. Because of that, during the founding period and the early years, there was an ultimate ratcionality that could give work a much deeper meaning. It provided a "transcendental link" (in the Christian sense of the word) by being able to found business action on values and a vision of good life and good society.

However, one should bear in mind that the cooperative commitment draws on an amalgam of sources and inspirations, not all of them Christian (Azkarraga 2007a):

- I have already pointed out the Christian commitment and support, particularly the link to the Church's social values, which favor cooperativism as a way to solve the "social question."
- Cooperative secularization began in the late 1970s and the gap left by religion was filled by a substantial secular support. Some of it has been socialist in origin (Arizmendiarrieta himself

---

31. Picking up on Weber's idea (1965), perhaps it is instrumental-economic action itself that has decided to do without a package of values that it no longer needs. Traditional values have stopped being essential or have become simply dysfunctional or are without purpose to the overall economic performance. To put it another way, the business mentality and lifestyle required to be able to guarantee successful adaptation to market conditions (hard-working workers and a culture of efficient management) are reproduced mechanically without any need for ideological legitimation or substantial axiomatic roots (Azkarraga 2007a, 2007b).

referred to Mondragon cooperativism as the main reference for Basque socialism, meaning non-Marxist socialism).

· Last but not least, Mondragon feeds into the nation-building project of Basque nationalism. [32]

As a consequence, the MCE relies on three main pillars: religion, class, and nation. Christianity, Basque nationalism, and social progressivism, together with business pragmatism, make up the ideological constellation and basic driving force of this particular type of cooperativism, with different combinations for each individual participant and generation. [33] This ideological constellation has been the basis for its legitimation, drawing on a stable frame of reference for its main participants' feelings, actions, coordination, and direction.

Mondragon culture has been based on the successful combination and continual feedback between two types of rationality: formal-instrumental and substantive (drawing on a Weberian distinction, the latter referring to the degree to which economic action serves ultimate values). The relationship between economy (economic rationality) and morals (democratic-social rationality) has been, to put it another way, symbiotic: the more progress is made in business terms the more progress is made in terms of collective self-management and the democratic community development project. In this way, it has overcome the antinomies and contradictions that have marked so many experiences of the social and alternative economy over the years. The cultural model in which efficiency and meaning have come to rely and even enrich each other has been one of the main keys to Mondragon's success.

However, the MCE's success has made the experience ambivalent. On the one hand, cooperative culture has no reticence

---

32. In the modern history of the Basque Country there is, in addition to co-operativism connected to socialism, a tradition of Basque nationalist cooperativism dating back to the very origins of modern Basque nationalism. Indeed, cooperativism was taken to be one of the keystones of the future independent Basque nation's socioeconomic organization (Arrieta et al. 1998, 156).

33. The first generation's belief in Christianity gave way to following generations' more secular ideas, which emphasized socialism and Basque nation-building. With globalization, an erosion of ideological commitment has been noticeable; pragmatic attitudes and modern theories of management seem to prevail.

concerning economic-business activity. For that reason, it has become part of the first rationalizing wave of the cooperative phenomenon through which economic action has acquired its own legitimacy: business laws are treated as autonomous and must be complied with. This part of cooperativism's logic is pragmatic and breaks with other more moral or idealistic models: it distances itself from traditional economic ethics or from economic traditionalism as described by Max Weber (1965).

On the other hand, the strength and success of the Mondragon cooperatives' business activities derive from their connections with criteria and maxims that cannot be regarded as being merely instrumental. On the contrary: Mondragon cooperativism has always been based on the connection between business and a sense of collective purpose and attachment. It is partly due to this very logic that the MCE has maintained a certain reluctance to fully accept capitalist modernity, that is, to accept that economic reasoning and modern individualism become the more powerful criteria and all other ways of thinking accept such commanding power.[34] The MCE rebels against this idea not by questioning economic rationality and instrumental action but rather by attempting to harmonize them with a set of values (such as democracy, equality, social justice, solidarity, and so on). As the economist Robert Oakeshott observes, the oasis of democracy called Mondragon was the product of a particular "alliance between Church and technology" (Oakeshott 1976).

It could well be argued that economic rationality has never been a problem in itself; it is just that its deregulation and limitless expansion have created an increasingly unstable world (ecologically, culturally, and socially). As Basque sociologist Imanol Zubero states, "the main problem of capitalist society is not and has never been the existence of economic rationality; it is, rather, the problem of marking and respecting the *limits* within which it can

---

34. Capitalism may be understood as follows: throughout history, economic reasons have removed the restraints put on them and destroyed ways of thinking that obstruct its expansion (from moral, religious, family, ecological, or social perspectives). In the same way, and bearing in mind Karl Polanyi's classic definition, all socialism can be understood as an attempt to tame economic activity: it is necessary to put economics at the service of society and subordinate economic objectives to social objectives, the economy being a means and not an end in itself (Gorz 1989).

and must be practiced" (Zubero 1998, 128). Or, as Michael Walzer expresses it, "the morality of the bazaar belongs in the bazaar. The market is a zone of the city, not the whole of the city" (Walzer 1983, 109).

Cooperativism has provided one of the possible historical answers to the question of how to address the problem of poverty created by capitalism and unemployment; but cooperativism is also a wider, moral reaction against a type of human relationship that springs from modern economic life and instrumental rationality.[35] A communitarian outlook and its efforts to redefine economic action by taking into account noninstrumental action and meaning have been crucial to challenging modern capitalism (while breaking with traditional economic values).

Conclusion

Perry Anderson once remarked that Marxism seeks "subjective agencies capable of effective strategies for the dislodgement of objective structures" (Anderson 1983, 105). This probably also holds true for Mondragon cooperativism: a collective subject is created that effectively transforms the capitalist company's organizational structure and creates a working class self-managing experience.

Creating a subjective agent is a historical process of considerable complexity. I have already pointed out some of the factors involved in such a process (see Azkarraga 2007a, 2007b): traces of the Basques' millenary ancestral culture; rural culture; the Basque democratic tradition; the important proto-industrial and industrial culture that existed in the valley long before Mondragon cooperativism was founded; the worldview and work ethic of a whole generation and modern industrial society; the message of Christian social justice; and the educational process that accompanied the cooperative movement. As I have pointed out before, the historical, relational, institutional, and cultural framework

---

35. One of its main theorists even speaks of "moral upheaval" understood as "a reaction against the excesses of private property, the injustices of capitalism, the immorality of the business world. A reaction against things as they are in the name of a certain social morality, the working class's morality, which is very different to that of the managing classes that have gone before: the nobility and the bourgeoisie" (Laserre in Dionisio Aranzadi's (1998), in Arrieta et al. 1998, 25).

both creates and rests on a model of subjectivity and identity, on an *ethos* and a form of self-government.

Basque society makes for an interesting case: despite important transformations in recent decades (Gatti et al. 2005) there still exist basic beliefs, rites, and institutions, in short, considerable community-based attitudes and traditional roots, not to mention important cultural characteristics such as the Basque language that feature largely. Basque society is also a heavily industrialized and modern urban society. In more ways than one it seems to have been reticent about modernity without actually rejecting it (Hess 2009). It seems to have adapted to modern forms without breaking with some older ways and customs. That is perhaps why there are still today relationships and institutions based on reciprocity that are closely related to the traditional, communitarian world despite being a heavily industrialized society. To put it another way, Basque society seems to have found a configuration truly of its own making, somewhere between tradition, modern, or postmodern ways, with a late preponderance toward traditional practices.[36]

Mondragon is not an ode or a throwback to traditional society. On the contrary, there is in Mondragon a profound will to join modernity, including an intense attachment to development and a deep devotion to technology. Basque cooperativism may be interpreted as an amalgam: at its base we encounter a kind of sociability and a worldview that contains considerable traditional aspects (this can be seen in the religious worldview, for instance, at the beginning and among the first generation); at the same time it connects with modern narratives such as class, nation, people, and development/progress; and in its current form it embraces postmodern or late modern phenomena such as loss of ideology (along with the pluralism and individualism typical of our times).[37]

---

36.   The use (until recently) of political violence to achieve self-determination/independence and socialism for the Basque Country is an example of a society that has maintained a (nonpostmodern) narrative of liberation and transformation until well into the twenty-first century; an experience of sacrifice and martyrdom (Zulaika 1988) that coexists with postmodern symbols such as titanium (I refer here to the main building material used in famous Guggenheim Museum Bilbao) and the typical characteristics of a consumer society.
37.   Furthermore, the (relative) loss of cooperative identity is not just ideological. Corporate internationalization has developed within Mondragon over the past two decades along largely *non*cooperative lines: for example, produc-

In other words, Mondragon cooperativism can be seen as the modern transmutation of certain institutional characteristics of traditional Basque society. On one hand, we find a tightly knit network of reciprocity, cooperation, and mutual support that subverts the capitalist model of company and alters power relations. On the other, we see a specific cultural framework that breaks with economic traditionalism but puts in its place a model in which economic action becomes again related to meaning, especially in the religious model.

If we analyze the evolution of the MCE from the perspective proposed by Peter L. Berger and Thomas Luckmann (1995), Mondragon's development has led to a breakaway from the *superordinate* value system (especially its religious manifestations), but also from other ideological motivations, in which economic action was part of a more general system of meaning. Once the last references to a unitary understanding of the world subsided, the MCE moved closer to a community of meaning in a minimalist sense: cooperatives comply efficiently with objective meaning connected to the sphere of economic-business action. In other words, economic action—instrumental action—becomes autonomous and frees itself from its place in a more general value system (inherited by tradition/religion or constructed through modern narratives). Berger and Luckmann speak about the modern crises of meaning and link it to modernization, pluralism, and—particularly in Europe—secularization. Something similar can be said about the MCE. For those people of the first generation it was possible to integrate one's own life into a superordinate system of meaning. In a sense, its members could interact in the instrumentally rational sphere of action while at the same time remaining attached to a strong value system (religion especially offered robust rational-value categories for conducting one's life). But this cultural model became more and more difficult and the crises of meaning began to spread (Azkarraga 2007a, 2007b): in the first

---

tion plants of a conventional capitalist nature have been set up in other countries and on other continents. The changes that have taken place have raised concern owing to certain practices not in keeping with basic cooperative principles (see, for example, Altuna 2008; Azkarraga 2007a, 2007b; Azkarraga et al. 2012; Bakaikoa et al. 2004; Cheney 2002; Errasti et al., 2003; Kasmir 1996; Miller 2002; Redondo et al. 2011; Sarasua 2010; Williams 2007; Winther and Sørensen 2009; Heras-Saizarbitoria 2014; Flecha and Ngai 2014).

instance, the religious wrapper melted away; then, during a second phase, economic action split away from the secular wrappers of class and nation. Finally, and especially in the context of globalization, values going beyond instrumentally rational objective meaning have come into conflict with its specific instrumental rationality.

The global interest in Mondragon has to do especially with evaluating how to replicate it in other countries. The reflections I have offered here may not be very helpful for that task, since I contend that the emergence of such an experience is most likely connected to longer historical processes, the particular features of a given society, and/or the specific characteristics of the period of time in which cooperatives emerge (the cooperatives' foundational culture and material conditions). However, we can draw interesting lessons from Mondragon, some of which are valid for other locations. I will mention only one particularly interesting example: The social innovation that the MCE has brought about was based on weaving certain traditional and communitarian characteristics into the modern economy, industrial urban culture, and the fabric of modern life in general. This is one of the general lessons that can be learned from the Mondragon experience: to innovate means to "create" something new, but this modernization does not necessarily imply that one has to renounce the past. Things and thoughts have, and still are, created from something else. Although it may seem paradoxical, there is a connection between the inheritance of our innovative capability and intelligent adaptation. We just need to take care of the past and transmit it, rather than challenging creative culture and the past, as has been so often the case. The snobbery that is so typical of modernity, such as its emphasis on the conquest of the future, the canonization of individual liberty, its hedonism, and the glorification of the immediate present have left modern societies with a weaker historical referential framework. It has devalued past experiences and thereby minimized people's capacity to make sense of all this.[38]

---

38. Critics such as Christopher Lasch (1978) see this radical devaluation of the past as one of the main symptoms of our current cultural crisis. What at first sight seemed like a progressive attitude may, in fact, embody societies' incapacity to face up to the future. It is our relationship with others that makes

The past and experiences of the past can contribute and serve as aspirations that produce meaning. They provide a sense of continuity and give the collective self a sense of strength that is extremely helpful in the formation of personal identity and collective projects aimed at humanizing society. In fact, it is difficult to create a collective identity exclusively from the present, and solely from the here and now. All human groups with the ability to influence their own existence need some type of heritage, collective memory, and a historical background to construct their identity and to make the best of it. The MCE is a good example of that: how to create significant social innovation by using past/traditional positive resources that enable and empower people, in order to make history—despite not choosing the historical conditions—rather than to suffer it.

References

Anderson, Perry. 1983. *In the Tracks of Historical Materialism.* London: Verso.

Altuna, Larraitz, coordinator. 2008. *La experiencia cooperativa de Mondragon: Una síntesis general.* Eskoriatza: LANKI-Mondragon Unibertsitatea.

Altuna, Rafa, and Hervé Grellier, H. 2008. "Bases culturales e institucionales del desarrollo empresarial cooperativo de Mondragón." In *El fenómeno cooperativo en el mundo. Casos de Argentina, Brasil, Italia, País Vasco y Países Nórdicos,* coordinated by Rafa Altuna, Hervé Grellier, and Eguzki Urteaga. Mondragon Bilduma no. 1. Arrasate-Mondragón: Mondragon Unibertsitateko Zerbitzu Editoriala.

Arpal Poblador, Jesús. 1985. "Solidaridades elementales y organizaciones colectivas en el País Vasco (cuadrillas, txokos, asociaciones)." In *Processus sociaux, idéologies et pratiques culturelles dans la société basque,* edited by Pierre Bidart. Pau: Université de Pau et des Pays de l'Adour.

---

us what we are: our relationship with our contemporaries, those who came before us and are no longer with us. Because of that, and in the same way that each individual's personal biography is a powerful factor in explaining their current situation and potential future, the pasts of human collectives can also be a store for resources that enable and potentially empower members of those collectives.

Arrieta, Leyre, Miren Barandiaran, Alazne Mujika, and José Antonio Rodríguez Ranz. 1998. *El movimiento cooperativo en Euskadi (1884–1936)*. Bilbao: Sabino Arana Kultur Elkargoa.

Azkarraga, Joseba. 2007a. *Mondragon ante la globalización: La cultura cooperativa vasca ante el cambio de época*. Cuadernos de LANKI, no. 2. Ezkoriatza: Mondragon Unibertsitatea.

———. 2007b. *Nor bere patroi: Arrasateko kooperatibistak aro globalaren aurrean*. Vitoria-Gasteiz: Eusko Jaurlaritzaren Argitalpen Zerbitzu Nagusia.

———. 2009. "El cooperativismo como conciencia crítica." *Nexe: Quaderns d'autogestió i economía cooperativa* 25. Available at www.nexe.coop.

———. 2010. *Educación, sociedad y transformación cooperativa*. Eskoriatza: Gizabidea Fundazioa; Mondragon Unibertsitatea.

Azkarraga, Joseba, George Cheney, and Ainara Udaondo. 2012. "Workers Participation in a Globalized Market: Reflections from and on Mondragon." In *Alternative Work Organizations*, edited by Maurizio Atzeni. London: Palgrave.

Azpiazu, José Antonio. 1999. *El acero de Mondragón en la época de Garibay*. Arrastate-Mondragón: Ayuntamiento de Mondragon.

———. 2002. *Picas vascas en Flandes. Historias de armas de Euskal Herria*. Donostia: Ttarttalo.

Azurmendi, Joxe. 1992. *El hombre cooperativo. Pensamiento de Arizmendiarrieta*. Aretxabaleta: Otalora.

Bakaikoa, Baleren, Anjel Errasti, and Agurtzane Begiristain. 2004. "Governance of the Mondragon Corporación Cooperativa." *Annals of Public and Cooperative Economics* 75, no. 1: 61–87.

Berger, Peter L. 1975. *Pyramids of Sacrifice: Political Ethics and Social Change*. New York: Basic Books.

Berger, Peter L., and Thomas Luckmann. 1995. *Modernity, Pluralism and the Crisis of Meaning: The Orientation of Modern Man*. Gütersloh, Germany: Bertelsmann Foundation Publishers.

Beriain, Josetxo. 1998. *La identidad colectiva: Vascos y navarros*. Pamplona: Universidad Pública de Navarra; Alegia: Ediciones Oria-Haramburu.

Bradley, Keith, and Alan Gelb. 1983. *Cooperation at Work: The Mondragón Experience*. London: Heinemann Educational Books.

Caro Baroja, Julio. 1974. *Vasconiana*, vol. 3, *Obras Completas*. San Sebastián: Ed. Txertoa.

——. 1986. *Introducción a la historia social y económica del Pueblo Vasco*, vol. 6, *Obras Completas*. San Sebastián: Txertoa.

Cerrato Allende, Javier. 2011. "Culture and Social Representations of Work among Basques: Implications for Organizational Commitment and Cooperative Attitudes." Translated by Jennifer Ottman. In *Basque Cooperativism*, edited by Baleren Bakaikoa and Eneka Albizu. Reno: Center for Basque Studies, University of Nevada, Reno.

Cheney, George. 2002. *Values at Work: Employee Participation Meets Market Pressure at Mondragón*. Updated Edition. Ithaca, NY: Cornell University Press.

Díaz-Albertini, Javier. 2003. "Capital social, organizaciones de base y el Estado: Recuperando los eslabones perdidos de la sociabilidad." In *Capital social y reducción de la pobreza en América Latina y el Caribe: En busca de un nuevo paradigma*, compiled by Raúl Atria and Marcelo E. Siles. Santiago de Chile: CEPAL.

Errasti, Anjel Mari, Iñaki Heras, Baleren Bakaikoa, and Pilar Elgoibar. 2003. "The Internationalisation of Cooperatives: The Case of the Mondragon Cooperative Corporation." *Annals of Public and Cooperative Economics* 74, no. 4: 553–84.

Flecha, Ramon, and Pun Ngai. 2014. "The Challenge for Mondragon: Searching for the Cooperative Values in Times of Internationalization." *Organization* 21, no. 5: 666–82.

Fukuyama, Francis. 1995. *Trust: Social Virtues and the Creation of Prosperity*. New York: Free Press.

——. 2003. "Capital social y desarrollo: La agenda venidera. In *Capital social y reducción de la pobreza: En busca de un nuevo paradigma*, coordinated by Raúl Atria and Marcelo E. Siles. Santiago de Chile: CEPAL.

Gatti, Gabriel, Ignacio Irazuzta, and Iñaki Martínez de Albeniz. 2005. *Basque Society: Structures, Institutions, and Contemporary Life*. Translated by Cameron J. Watson. Reno: Center for Basque Studies, University of Nevada, Reno.

Gorz, André. 1989. *Critique of Economic Reason*. Translated by Gillian Handyside and Chris Turner. London and New York: Verso.

Gorroñogoitia, Alfonso. 2004. "Nuestras cooperativas son producto de una sociedad rural." Interview by Zuriñe Velez de Mendizabal for *Euskonews*, January 16–23. Available at www.euskonews.com/0238zbk/elkar_es.html.

Greenwood, Davydd, and José Luis González. 1990. *Culturas de Fagor: Estudio antropológico de las cooperativas de Mondragón.* San Sebastián: Txertoa.

Heiberg, Marianne. 1989. *The Making of the Basque Nation.* Cambridge Studies in Social Anthropology, no. 66. Cambridge: Cambridge University Press.

Hess, Andreas. 2007. "The Social Bonds of Cooking: Gastronomic Societies in the Basque Country." *Cultural Sociology* 1, no. 3: 383–407.

———. 2009. *Reluctant Modernization: Plebeian Culture and Moral Economy in the Basque Country.* Oxford: Peter Lang.

Heras-Saizarbitoria, Iñaki. 2014. *"The Ties that Bind?* Exploring the Basic Principles of Worker-Owned Organizations in Practice." *Organization* 21, no. 5: 645–65.

Homobono, José Ignacio. 1994. "Grupos amicales y asociaciones: La sociabilidad en el País Vasco." *Revista Vasca de Sociología y Ciencia Política* 8: 231–53.

Kasmir, Sharryn. 1996. *The Myth of Mondragon: Cooperatives, Politics, and Working-Class Life in a Basque Town.* Albany: State University of New York Press.

Lafourcade, Maïté. 2003. "A l'heure actuelle une université de plein exercice en Pays Basque Nord est une utopie." Available at www.euskonews.com/0215zbk/elkar21501fr.html.

Larrañaga, Jesús. 1998. *El cooperativismo de Mondragón: Interioridades de una Utopía.* Aretxabaleta: Otalora.

Lasch, Chistopher. 1978. *The Culture of Narcissism: American Life in an Age of Diminishing Expectations.* New York: Norton.

Martínez, Zesar. 2005. "The Associative World: *Cuadrillas* and Peer Groups." In *Basque Society: Structures, Institutions, and Contemporary Life*, edited by Gabriel Gatti, Ignacio Irazuzta, and Iñaki Martínez de Albeniz. Translated by Cameron J. Watson. Reno: Center for Basque Studies, University of Nevada, Reno.

Max-Neef, Manfred, Antonio Elizalde, and Martin Oppenhayn. 1986. *Desarrollo a escala humana. Una opción para el futuro.* Santiago de Chile: CEPAUR; Fundación Dag Hammarskjöld.

Miller, Mike. 2002. "Mondragon: Lessons for Our Times." *Social Policy* 32, no. 2: 17–20.

Molina, Fernando. 2005. *José María Arizmendiarrieta (1915–1976). Biografía.* Bilbao: Caja Laboral-Euskadiko Kutxa.

————. 2011. "The Spirituality of Economics: Historical Roots of Mondragon, 1940–1975." Traslated by Jennifer Ottman. In *Basque Cooperativism*, edited by Baleren Bakaikoa and Eneka Albizu. Reno: Center for Basque Studies, University of Nevada, Reno.

Oakeshott, Robert. 1973. "Mondragon: Spain's Oasis of Democracy." *The Observer.* January 21.

————. 1976. "Grass roots' Enterprises Thrive amid the Basques." *The Financial Times.* July 9.

Ormaetxea, José María. 2004. *Didáctica de una experiencia empresarial. El cooperativismo de Mondragón.* Aretxabaleta: Otalora.

Ortiz-Osés, Andrés. 2007. *Los mitos vascos. Aproximación hermenéutica.* Bilbao: Universidad de Deusto.

Ortiz-Osés, Andrés, and Luis Garagalza. 2007. *Euskal mitologia. Izena duen guztia omen da/Mitología vasca: Todo lo que tiene nombre es.* Donostia-San Sebastián: Nerea; Kutxa.

Ortiz-Osés, Andrés, and Franz-Karl Mayr. 1980. *Matriarcalismo movasco. Reinterpretación de la cultura vasca.* Bilbao: Universidad de Deusto.

Pérez-Agote, Alfonso. 2006. *The Social Roots of Basque Nationalism.* Translated by Cameron Watson and William A. Douglass. Foreword by William A. Douglass Reno: University of Nevada Press.

Pérez de Calleja, Antxon. 1989. *Arizmendiarrieta, el hombre de acción.* Arrasate: Gizabidea Fundazioa.

Putnam, Robert D., Robert Leonardi, and Raffaella Y. Nanetti. 1993. *Making Democracy Work: Civic Traditions in Modern Italy.* Princeton: Princeton University Press.

Ramesh, Randeep. 2011. "Basque Country's Thriving Big Society." *The Guardian.* March 30.

Redondo, Gisela, Ignacio Santa Cruz, and Josep Maria Rotger. 2011. "Why Mondragon? Analyzing What Works in Overcoming Inequalities." *Qualitative Inquiry* 17, no. 3: 277–83.

Rivera, Antonio, and Javier de la Fuente. 2000. *Modernidad y religión en la sociedad vasca de los años treinta.* Leioa: Universidad del País Vasco-Euskal Herriko Unibertsitatea.

Sampaio, Carlos Alberto Cioce, Joseba Azkarraga, Larraitz Altuna, and Valdir Fernandes. 2010. "Pensando la experiencia de cooperativismo de Mondragón bajo la mirada de la ecosocioeconomía de las organizaciones." In *Cuestiones practices en la economía social globalizada*, coordinated by Rafa Altuna, Hervé Grellier, and Eguzki Urteaga. Oñati: Mondragon Unibertsitatea.

Sarasua, Jon. 2010. *Mondragon en un nuevo siglo: Síntesis reflexiva de la experiencia cooperativa.* Cuadernos de LANKI, no. 3. Eskoriatza: Mondragon Unibertsitatea.

Thomas, Henk, and Chris Logan. 1980. *Mondragón: An Economic Analysis.* London: George Allen & Unwin.

Urzainqui, Tomás. 1987. "Repercusión de la conquista de Navarra en el campo del derecho y sistema jurídico propios." Available at http://www.euskomedia.org/PDFAnlt/vasconia/vas11/11037058.pdf.

Vaczi, Mariann. 2011. "Subversive Pleasures, Losing Games: Basque Soccer Madness." *South African Review of Sociology* 42, no. 1 (April): 21–36.

Walzer, Michael. 1983. *Spheres of Justice: A Defense of Pluralism and Equality.* New York: Basic Books.

Weber, Max. 1965. *The Protestant Ethic and the Spirit of Capitalism.* Translated from the German by Talcott Parsons. London: Allen & Unwin.

Whyte, William Foote, and Kathleen King Whyte. 1988. *Making Mondragon: The Growth and Dynamics of the Worker Cooperative Complex.* Ithaca, NY: ILR Press.

Williams, Richard C. 2007. *The Cooperative Movement: Globalization from Below.* Aldershot, UK: Ashgate.

Winther, Gorm, and Michael Kuur Sørensen. 2009. "The Mondragon Co-operatives Going Global?" In *Globalization & Transnational Capitalism: Crises, Opportunities and Alternatives*, edited by Li Xing, Gorm Winther, and Li Jizhen. Aalborg, Denmark: Aalborg University Press.

Woolcock, Michael. 1998. "Social Capital and Economic Development: Toward a Theoretical Synthesis and Policy Framework." *Theory and Society* 27, no. 2: 8–9.

Zallo, Ramón. 1995. "Nacionalismo, etnicidad y democracia." In *Coloquio sobre Nacionalismo vasco, un proyecto de future con 100 años de historia.* Vitoria-Gasteiz: Fundación Estadio.

Zubero, Imanol. 1998. *El trabajo en la sociedad. Manual para una sociología del trabajo.* Leioa: Universidad del País Vasco-Euskal Herriko Unibertsitatea.

Zulaika, Joseba. 1988. *Basque Violence: Metaphor and Sacrament.* Reno: University of Nevada Press.

10

Plebeian Culture, Moral Economy, Reluctant Modernization: An Attempt to Understand Basque Egalitarianism Differently

Andreas Hess

In his study *El "igualitarismo" vasco: Mito y realidad* (1986) Alfonso de Otazu attempts to deconstruct the idea that since time immemorial a notion of egalitarianism has prevailed in the Basque Country. Against the idea that every Basque was a *hidalgo*—a nobleman—Otazu shows that some people were not only more noble or more equal than others but also that the very idea of equal and widespread noble origin usually served those in the ascendancy looking for power; at other times it helped those who were already in power defending their privileged positions. Against the idea that Basque society and culture were somehow less bound by class distinctions, and against Basque nationalist tendencies to idealize a glorious past, Otazu describes the many historical layers of class conflict that arise when a country embarks on the long transition from traditional forms and features to modern capitalism.

Otazu should be commended for his study, particularly since it led to a number of important investigations that took the issue of social inequality and class and how it related to the Basque nationalist cause seriously. However, while showing that Basque society has always been subject to stratification (like any other region or nation), and that social stratification is not just something that is simply imposed from the outside world (namely, the Spanish state), two specific points were somehow obliterated. First, Otazu and those historians and social scientists who accepted the logic of his argument, look only at objective dimensions and historically verifiable data that supported their claim. The collective-subjective and moral dimensions of and responses to past and present conflicts disappeared and fell under or off the social scientists' or the historians' radar screen. Second, studying specific Basque motives and occurrences such as the obvious and easily identifiable appeal to the common good and the prevailing egalitarian and subjective sense of justice—all that which the English historian E. P. Thompson has called plebeian culture and moral economy—drifted somehow into the background or were forgotten.

I will argue in this chapter that a better observation point exists and that it will allow us to interpret the available historical, social, and anthropological material not only differently but even better. More specifically, and to the point of a paradigm change, I propose that the conceptual approach of E. P. Thompson and the insights of other social scientists, such as Albert O. Hirschman, are of primary relevance here. Applying Thompson's work on plebeian culture and moral economy allows us to look into how the egalitarianism ethos emerged, why it was maintained for such a long time, and whether those historical-institutional expressions of plebeian culture and moral economy that were "invented" a long time ago have survived and are still operational or whether they are in crisis or are even in danger of becoming extinct. Such a historical evaluation and reinterpretation would allow us to study in more detail the subjective-collective dimensions that emerged out of unique class-constellations. Furthermore, a paradigm change would allow us to study class conflict in the context of local, regional, and even national constellations, yet without denouncing them as mere attempts to find an answer to "objective" historical expressions of ruling class behavior or as a mere historical "consolidation processes" of new ascending classes striving for elevated and distinguished positions. In other words, a new approach would allow us to take a deeper look into what has been called Basque peculiarities or singularities, yet without running into the danger of essentializing them and without reducing them or narrowing them down to purely Basque nationalist discourse.

In his writings on late eighteenth-century England, Thompson has suggested that plebeian culture and moral economy were intrinsically linked. "Plebeian culture" was an auxiliary term that Thompson used to describe a situation in which class was not what classic Marxist theory assumed it to be. Thompson proposed a shift away from the objective notions of class and class consciousness, and moving toward studying subjective-collective dimensions such as the active contribution that the "plebs" make to the common culture and customs. In his own writings Thompson preferred to see these older preindustrial classes in terms of "fields of gravity," that is as heterogeneous constellations consisting of many dimensions and layers in which traditional popular customs played a major role. It was these "customs in common" that also helped to keep a moral economy alive—an economy that could take on various and different meanings for the plebeian crowd such as common rights, norms, or obligations, day-to-day habits or practices, but which, taken together, in many ways constituted a force that was alien or opposed to the powers that be (Thompson 1980, 1991).

Thompson was not the only scholar to write about plebeian culture and moral economy. The economist Albert O. Hirschman has provided us with an interpretation that I think fits perfectly well with Thompson's concerns. As Hirschman demonstrates in *The Passions and the Interests* (1977), early political economy was motivated by a strong moral impetus. Hirschman's interpretation of political economy found a more concrete application in the study of modes and behaviors such as "exit," "voice," "loyalty," and "commensality" (see his *Exit, Voice, and Loyalty* [1970]; *Shifting Involvements* [1982]; and *Crossing Boundaries* [1998]). They allow for a closer look at the microlinks that exist between political economy, customs, and morals (Hess 1999). I maintain that such an approach could produce new insights into what so far has remained a "black box" for the historians, sociologists, and anthropologists who have studied the Basque Country.

More specifically, I will try to discuss some of Thompson and Hirschman's conceptual tools by looking at three particular institutions: (1) the *baserri* (the Basque farmstead), (2) the *cofradía* or *kofradia* (the fishermen's fraternity) and (3) the *txoko* or *sociedad gastronómica* (gastronomic or cooking society, often just shortened to *sociedad(es)*). Each of these institutions occupies a unique place in Basque history, society, and culture, including partly also the Basque diaspora. While the investigation of baserri culture allows one to study the countryside and the changes that occurred with industrialization, the cofradía allows the researcher to see the connection that the Basque Country has with the sea; finally, the sociedades gastronómicas are not as old as the two aforementioned institutions and differ in that they clearly represent a more recent and urban phenomenon and represent an effort to come to terms with urbanization and the more anonymous forms of modern life. In describing how these three institutions work I suggest that they must be seen as expressions of a plebeian culture and institutional expressions of a related moral economy. Together they create a social *habitus* and a cultural disposition that is reluctant to modernization.[1]

The Baserri: An Exit Model of Plebeian Moral Economy

E. P. Thompson has described the unique class constellation that the observer can encounter in eighteenth century England, just before capitalism's triumph (Thompson 1980, 260ff). What the historian finds, according to Thompson, is not the existence of a prototype or otherwise easily identifiable industrial working or middle class. Instead, he suggests, we encounter a constellation consisting of a small oligarchic gentry and a numerically larger rural and small town plebs. Latent conflict and occasional open confrontation existed between the two but these were also always mediated by the existence and occasional political and social intervention of the lower "Whiggish" gentry, the press, an insistence on rights, and the occasional and almost always spontaneous protest movements that could, on occasion, bridge social differences and mobilize people—from the poor to the lower

---

1.   For a more detailed account of reluctant modernization in the context of the Basque Country see Hess (2009). For a discussion of the Basque gastronomic society see Hess (2007), and for a discussion of the Basque fishing fraternity Hess (2010).

gentry. Thompson points out that most of the craftsmen and traders who made up the small town and rural plebs had what can be
called a rather "vertical" and more individualistic consciousness
in the sense of a high esteem or pride in their particular trade
or craft. Thompson contrasts this with the modern, more "horizontal" collective notion of consciousness that one can encounter when studying modern industrial working class behavior.
However, from the existence of a "vertical" notion one should not
conclude that the plebs was under the total spell of the patrician
land-owning elite or that they followed every order from above
without questioning it. In contrast, particularly when it came to
defending traditional rights and customs, latent disquietude and
dissatisfaction could easily lead to massive, often spontaneous
protest and reactions (ibid., 262).

Thompson argues further that it is wrong to reread or reproj-
ect contemporary and modern notions of class struggle back into
preindustrial times. He suggests instead paying more attention to
what the multitude of plebs actually did, particularly in relation
and reaction to the hegemonic class in power. Labeling such conflicts "class struggles without class," Thompson observes that in
the historical process forms of collective consciousness usually
come about at the end of the struggle. In other words, collective
consciousness is the result of a struggle not its starting point. Class
is about how people experience their condition and how they
react when the social equilibrium is being threatened. Class consciousness can only be a result of this—not a precondition. Thus,
while the patrician gentry and oligarchy acted in a paternalistic
way and expected to be followed, the plebs in turn demanded to
be treated with respect (ibid., 270ff). One must not imagine this
constellation as an open confrontational conflict or struggle but
rather as two operating gravity fields trying to maintain a balance.

During a period of transition toward the later eighteenth
century, the societal equilibrium came under new pressure. This
was mainly due to the rise of a new market economy that clashed
with an older sense and practice of moral economy. The old moral
economy, rich in its traditional symbolic values, was, according to
Thompson, a unique expression of plebeian culture. Thompson
suggests looking particularly at symbolic rituals and notions, such
as the pride of being a free-born Englishman (ibid., 281). Such
"natural" notions of identity with their implicit calls for equality,

justice, and fairness, help to explain the struggles for symbolic authority. Conflicts over common rights and traditional customs were conflicts over hard-won entitlements. To understand them is crucial because it helps the historian or social scientist to conceive of the nature of patrician hegemony and power not as being total but rather resembling an unwritten preliminary contract, which the plebs could always call into question when the equilibrium threatened to come off balance and tip toward the side of the patrician oligarchy.

Using mainly historical anthropological material and ethnographic sources, Thompson has investigated behavior in preindustrial and precapitalist marketplaces. He argues that it is mainly in this context that a moral economy can be fully investigated. Thompson notes that the old economy—that is, the economy before capitalism's victory—still knew moral rules and regulations (Thompson 1980, 80ff). Developed from traditional subsistence production, the produce and the products of the farm or the sea were exchanged in direct face-to-face interaction and exchanged in local or regional markets. Everybody still knew each other; trade was conducted in the shortest way possible between producer and buyer and did not involve any intermediaries. There was no "chain" of trade to speak of. If one purchased from Farmer X (or Fishing Crew X), one usually knew what to expect and what the quality of the product was, who produced it, and how it got to the market. The purchasing price was usually seen as just or fair in the sense that the buyer thought that the product was worth the value and amount of labor paid for. Additionally, production and consumption in the same small town, village, or region led to a certain confidence or trustworthiness. Beyond that, the marketplace also became a scene for interaction and transaction of a more general type in which news was traded and conversations took place. It was a meeting place in which not only goods were traded or sold, but it was a truly "universal" experience in its own right. It was universal in the sense that the crowd got a sense of its own multitude, size, and power, as can be demonstrated by studying the early collective protests against rising bread prices, which the authorities often arbitrarily introduced without any prior warning or sometimes without having consulted the direct producers or buyers (ibid., 128). In contrast to the older moral economy, the universalizing trend of modern capitalist market conditions and trade are more anonymous in character and normally do not allow for such direct chains of interaction and notions of worthiness and fair exchange. Thompson finally points out that the writing of history all too often implies working with two ideal type models only—the fully developed capitalist market and its nonindustrial, noncapitalist predecessor. According to Thompson, this does the complexity of historical processes and particularly complex transitory periods little or no justice.

Thompson's account provides many productive insights; however, it may also appear to have its limitations when applied to the Basque context. While it is right to stress the processual dimension of complex class constellations such as the constant power play between plebeian culture and patrician gentry, there are also microinstitutional dimensions that one can look at. However, apart from the preindustrial and precapitalist marketplace, surprisingly very little is said about the rather sluggish nature of other plebeian institutions than the marketplace. Thompson also leaves open the question of whether independent farmers and small landholders played a significant part in the plebeian struggle.

It is my contention here that Hirschman's suggestions for studying aspects of moral economy and particularly its institutional dimensions by looking at various available options such as exit, voice, and loyalty provides an additional and useful element and helps partly to explain what sometimes remains a black box in Thompson's view on moral economy.[2] It seems to me that the exit option that Hirschman posits is of particular relevance to the analysis of the crisis the baserri finds itself in today. In *Exit, Voice, and Loyalty* Hirschman describes the three options that individuals have in relation to economic, political, or social institutions. "Voice" stands for protest or speaking out; literally, it means voicing one's discontent. Only if the "voice" option has become exhausted, either because it is simply disregarded, not heard, or otherwise unsuccessful, does the "exit" option of leaving appear as a radical alternative. "Loyalty" links the two together and describes the ideal situation: it is usually loyalty that allows for voice and keeps exit at bay.

---

2. For a more general overview of Hirschman's contribution to the critique of political economy see Hess (1999).

I pointed out earlier that I am convinced that Thompson's and Hirschman's descriptions can, with some important qualifications, be productively applied to the Basque context and generate some interesting results, if not a new interpretation. It is particularly with reference to the history and function of the baserri as an institution that we can now try to put the ideas of the existence of a plebeian culture and moral economy to use and perhaps see the survival struggle of the baserri in a different light.

Taking at first a broad-stroke view and seeing the Basque baserri in a more general and European context, during transitory periods from feudal to modern times, the available historical material shows that, by comparison, the rural Basque *baserritarra* (farmer) and his farmstead stand out in terms of being relatively free from personal dependencies from masters or other forms of direct interference and control. While rural folk and peasants of other countries and regions were serfs and suffered from complete personal dependencies while working the soil they did not own, the same cannot be said for the Basque case. I am not referring here to a rare exceptional decade or a century but I am actually pointing toward an exceptional long time period, ranging from the beginning of the sixteenth century to the nineteenth century.

To be sure, there were considerable regional differences within the Basque Country; there were also numerous changes in the political structures until the Basque provinces emerged in their modern form. There were, particularly in premodern times, periods of great insecurity such as the bandit wars. Moreover, the countryside witnessed conflicts about power and control in which the rural folk and small town plebs played a considerable part in providing a counterbalance to the *jauntxos* (local bosses and powerbrokers, something akin to squires) and the political oligarchies. There were shortages that threatened the livelihood of rural folk and there were disasters such as the plague, which were more threatening in urban areas and towns but which also had an impact on the countryside. Finally, the Basque provinces were subject to wars and foreign invasions, which produced some significant crises.

However, having briefly mentioned the political, social, and sometimes natural intervening forces and constraints, it is also safe to say that for a time period of almost three hundred years the Basque baserri and its occupants could develop almost in an organic fashion and were, again comparatively speaking, relatively free from direct dependencies or forms of direct oppression. More specifically, it is during this long period that Basque nobility became a common tradition. It may well be the case, as Otazu says, that notions of egalitarianism helped the patrician oligarchy and the jauntxos in their attempt to either gain access to or stay in power, or benefit from being close to power. Bearing this in mind there is, however, another plebeian side to the story. The conflicts of the nineteenth century between the new regime of mainly urban liberals and rural Carlists (who were trying to maintain the *fueros* and the old order), and the support that the latter received from the rural countryside and the baserritarrak (plural form), demonstrates that the sense of tradition in combination with a sense of egalitarianism may have been more widespread and firmly established than some historians and social scientists are willing to accept.

Similarities between a notion of being a noble Basque and Thompson's notion of the *freeborn Englishman* can easily be detected. As in the case of the English *crowd* or plebs, the Basque Country was likewise not free of contradictions. In the case of the baserri they were obvious: the baserri as an institution provided first and foremost for its occupants. It did so through heavy demands on the individuals who occupied the baserri. Hard labor and the land ownership of the *etxekojaun* were sometimes contentious issues. So was the manner in which control and power of the baserri as an institution were passed on (in most cases on primogeniture, the passing on of the baserri to the eldest son or daughter and the exit of the younger siblings).

To be sure, there was a reason for following this primogeniture model. Only having access to four to six hectares on average, it was necessary not to fragment the landholdings. The only way of doing so was not to break up the land and the baserri. But as we have seen, the individual price that was paid was enormous; many people emigrated and sought their luck in the Americas or somewhere else; military or naval services were also options, as were religious orders. With increased urbanization and industrialization other exit models became important such as leaving and looking for employment in the city or the next new industrial town.

Despite all these complications, exit allowed the traditional baserri to survive for a very long time, before finally the arrival of modern industry, urbanization, the limited profit perspectives of the baserri itself, and the reluctant response to modernization and the new markets—actually supported as late as the 1920s by unrepentant Basque nationalists including academics—put so much pressure on the baserriak that they could not survive in their traditional form. From then onward, it was almost as if the traditional baserri was living on borrowed time. The call for historic rights and the old, independent institutions, first during the two nineteenth-century Carlist Wars, then later in the form of twentieth-century Basque nationalist claims, seemed to provide merely an ideological compensation for nonexisting practical solutions.

If all of this sounds too negative, one must also see what the baserri and its occupants had to lose. In contrast to other countries, the subsistence model of the baserri provided for its occupants and even beyond for the rural town or village (until demographic changes and the growth of towns and cities shifted the demand side beyond what the baserri could provide). The form of practical help and solidarity that one could expect from the *auzoa* (neighborhood) even took on an organized solidary form, as we see in Douglass's studies (Douglass 1969, 1975). The Church in the Basque Country did not, at least in the countryside and in the auzoak, appear as an oppressive force. It was, rather, an institution that provided practical help through local parish and community contacts (almost in a bottom-up fashion through action within the auzoa), relevant knowledge (religious organizations suggested practical reforms on more than one occasion), and political deliberation (the rural *anteiglesias* or districts of the valleys and the numerous confraternities that were formed are the prime examples that come to mind here). Free of oppressive landlords and masters, the baserritarrak were, comparatively speaking, living in satisfactory conditions. There was no hunger or malnutrition and people did not work like serfs or slaves but owned (in most cases) their land. In many ways the plebeian exit model of moral economy had a price—but it also worked.

The traditional baserri and the moral economy it represented worked as long as the plebeian culture with its small towns and rural environment functioned. Once the settings began to change it fell behind. Even as early as the third decade of the nineteenth century the traditional baserri went into crisis. Limited land holdings with little hope of expansion (including the commons) simply did not suffice and were not made for catering for an always expanding and demanding modern market. That the baserri actually survived for another hundred years is due to compromise and concession (employing more intensive farming methods, changing the produce, and so on); but even this long survival struggle is a miracle and can only be explained by cultural embeddedness and a strong sense of community and cultural belonging. That culture was rural, small town-based, religious, proud to be Basque, oral, mainly Euskara-speaking, proud of an egalitarian ethos, and free (whether it always delivered fully on the last two promises is, as we have seen, indeed questionable).

The baserri and the culture it represented are in many ways illustrations of Thompson's plebeian culture and moral economy. However, it differed maybe from the English model in that it was more rural and even more embedded, had more Basque customs in common than the communities Thompson referred to in his historical account. The baserri as an institution was also for a very long time successful because it was based structurally on the exit of large numbers of people. While all this sounds like a huge contradiction, it should be stressed here, first, that societal reality is full of contradictions and that it is, second, also a reality that Europe knows very few examples of in which its peasants or farmers were actually free for such long time periods. In relation to Hirschman's discussion, I would like to suggest here that the traditional baserri, its functioning, and even its demise can best be understood as representing a certain *modus vivendi* within plebeian culture. I call this the "exit model of moral economy."

Facilitating Voice: Moral Economy and the Cofradia

The sea demands a very different organizational form of social and economic life when compared to that of the rural world. The fishermen's social interaction and market-related exchange are activities that are separated and combined sea-and-land affairs; while rural communities are, socially speaking, soil-to-soil based encounters that are only occasionally interrupted by market-day encounters in the town or village. Out at sea the crew of a boat or vessel works separately from their families, town, and community, forming—for the time being but often also beyond the time at sea—strong bonds among seafaring companions. While the men are "working the waves," the women remain on land preparing for and dealing with almost everything that has to do with the landing (picking nets), buying, selling, and further distribution of fish, and/or the preparation for the next fishing trip (such as flicking and repairing nets). It is the woman who runs the household and takes care of the children. In contrast, the rural and soil-based baserri and its occupants rely much more on a joint effort that is less physically separated (although, as we have seen, some differentiation of labor also prevails in the rural world). The differences between the rural and the seafaring world are mainly explicable by their respective unique physical environment that in each case demands different social communication skills and leads to different economic activities. However, the traditional cofradía and its moral economy could only develop and function properly because they were also an expression of a mainly urban or semiurban environment and culture out of which a plebeian culture would emerge eventually.

Coastal communities founded in the early Middle Ages were established with a purpose in mind. The harbors functioned not only as communication posts between coast and the interior but also as communication posts along the coast, directed mainly toward the sea and the people who made a living from it. In contrast to Mediterranean harbor settlements, those on the Cantabrian coastline developed less "organically"; they were planned settlements and establishments and, as pointed out above, very much of an urban or semiurban character or type. This distinguishing feature can only partly be explained by geographical conditions such as the steep coastline. The dense settlements allowed for a concentrated effort; it created a critical mass and functioning infrastructure devoted to specific social-economic aims. Fishing, trade, and emerging small-scale industries (iron, shipbuilding) were the main economic activities. Fishermen, artisanal laborers such as carpenters, hook-makers, cofradía employees, and small-scale tradespeople were its main players and, together with their families, formed the biggest part of the working population. Other powerful players in the town did emerge or were present, though, such as the Church or local administrators and other town officials.

One feature stands out, however, and that is that at no point can we encounter the development of an elite or stratum that occupied and maintained a powerful position, at least not in the sense that it determined or controlled the daily life of the harbor town over sustained periods. If one studies historical accounts of Basque coastal communities during the last five hundred years, it is impossible to identify something like a local ruling class that reproduces itself over centuries. What one does encounter, though, are the aforementioned three key institutional players, who are all in one way or another an expression of or connected to the plebeian majority of the local community: the cofradía, the mayor's office or town hall and administration, and the local church. It was this institutional constellation and its supporting social network that allowed a plebeian culture and a stable moral economy to emerge.

It would be wrong to think of this plebeian culture as one of complete equality of conditions and this is not what the term refers to. What the term signifies in our context is, first, that there is a working majority in the town and that this population mainly depends on seafaring and fishing and related activities and industries; second, that this population knows also some internal distinctions and a certain division of labor to remain functional; third, that it is a working population in which one can hardly encounter extremes, be it in the form of either a significant and powerful super-rich stratum or a segment or layer of entirely deprived people; and fourth, that a stable institutional infrastructure is there to support the working majority in their economic efforts and social and cultural lives. These four circumstances or conditions helped and contributed to the development of a local civic spirit, culture, and economy, something that is unique and that one hardly encounters in such a developed form in other traditional fishing communities in Europe.

In order to function properly and to have a lasting effect, the solidarity aspects that have developed must take on an institutionalized form and must be suitable to the environment in question. Thus, while the rural environment demands particularly strong relationships with the next-door neighbor, especially in time of need (harvest) and emergencies (births, deaths, essential repairs), being out at sea and working the waves is much more hazardous than working on the farmstead and demands a different common effort. Out at sea there are always conditions that cannot be fully controlled and against which one is not fully protected. There are real risks that one might never return and the great number of fishermen's lives lost at sea speaks of the risks involved. It is therefore not surprising that fishing communities have, from the early Middle Ages onward, done everything to protect fishermen and to organize mutual help, first by forming strong bonds among the crew and, second, by institutionalizing solidarity in the form of the cofradía.

Once in place, such institutional forms of solidarity evolved slowly but steadily over centuries and over time became more and more sophisticated in the way they operated. The institution began as a Christian confraternity and mutual-aid society and was in most cases founded around the same time that official status was given to the respective local town or harbor. In the beginning, the cofradía was an association without any great infrastructure or built environment. It evolved eventually into a guildlike institution with its own proper facilities, gaining considerable power and control in the local village or town and amounting to what could be described as a local monopoly-like corporation. What mainly symbolized the beneficial activities of the cofradía was the sale and marketing of fish. In order to fully appreciate the functioning of what was new about the market and what made it work it is again useful to refer briefly to how Thompson has described market and related social activities before the arrival of the modern capitalist relations.

In his essay on moral economy and the English crowd, Thompson notes that the old economy, that is the economy before capitalism's victory, still knew certain moral rules and regulations (Thompson 1980, 80ff). Developed at subsistence level production, the produce and the products of the farm (or from the sea) were usually exchanged directly and without mediation; only later did local or regional markets come into play. But even when markets began to develop everybody still knew each other; the chain of trade was the shortest way possible between producer and buyer and involved few if any intermediaries. If one purchased from Farmer X (or Fishwife Y), one usually knew the quality of the product one was purchasing and the price was typically seen as just or fair in the sense that the buyer thought that the product was worth the amount paid. Additionally, production and consumption in the same town or village was based on direct interaction and with that developed trustworthiness. The marketplace was a space in which not only goods were directly traded or sold, but it became a unique experience in its own right in the sense that the crowd that frequented this public space could also experience a sense of its own power, as can be demonstrated by studying the early days of protest against new conditions such as rising bread prices. Because of its direct communication and interactive patterns, there was also a sense of still being interested and being aware of each other's circumstances and condition (ibid., 128).

Thompson's description applies mainly to the rural small town and its market, but one just has to add a few specific features from fishing communities and his description could easily be applied to any cofradía's fish auction. The main features would hardly change: the prevalence of face-to-face interaction and personal trustworthiness, and regarding the market not only as an economic exchange mechanism but also a place in which other forms of social interaction can take place such as trading news, chatting, the common and sociable consumption of food and drink, and so on. Even the mentioning of near-subsistence production in Thompson's description would apply to the early fish market. One of the most striking features would be that the market itself was run without middlemen. If we had to find an overall characterization of the activities taking place we would have to say that economic activities were a crucial feature but that these were always still embedded in other forms of social interaction.

Although the cofradía as an institution was founded to benefit all members and their family relations we must not imagine it as an idyllic place in which everything just worked to perfection. There has never been complete equality among associates in the confraternity. Between owners (*maestros*), captains, and the working crews there were always differences in terms of opinion and interests, which also found their expression institutionally, particularly when it came to distributing the share or when it came to occupying the most powerful positions in the cofradía. While those differences were real, there was no rule or invisible glass ceiling that would in principle prevent individual fishermen from becoming either small owners or shareholders and occupying one of the more attractive positions in the cofradía. For a very long time, until the arrival of industrialization to be precise, fishermen could always make their voice and concerns heard, either individually or collectively, and this sense of "having a voice" would also naturally extend to economic activities such as the market and the fish auction. No reality matches better Hirschman's formula that it is a sense of loyalty (and one could add in this context, solidarity, and common experience fostered under the often extreme conditions of the sea) that allows for "voice" to be heard and keeping protest and "exit" at bay.

With the emergence and differentiation of different types of modern fishing such as industrial trawling and large fish-processing industries, the internal cohesion and solidary aspects of the crews and the cofradía eroded. Principally because of the change in labor practices and the sheer scale of the new fishing expeditions, the cofradía could no longer hold on to the traditional forms of solidarity. A split became manifest: on one side, the workers and their rather mechanical work patterns—trawling is considerably less artisanal than traditional fishing—and, on the other side, capital, either in the form of an absent shipowner or in the form of a corporation. Since trawling relies less on individual or collective experience and more heavily on technical infrastructure and knowledge that is concentrated in one person (the captain or the owner), it is unlikely that such solid solidary bonds emerge between captain/*maestro* and crew as they did before the arrival of trawling and industrial labor relations. The crew on a trawler can be hired at any harbor and are usually treated like industrial employees, that is, their labor power is regarded as a mere commodity. The men are less likely to stem from the same town or village or even from the same family. These circumstances make communication more like that of a floating factory or shop floor than that between buddies or family relations.

The industrialization of working practices at sea and on land, the increased division of labor, and new market conditions changed the fishing sector and the decision-making processes of the cofradías totally. Canning factories, processing plants, better transport, new forms of refrigeration, and the internationalization of the fish market also brought in outside players; and while new investments helped the fishing sector to expand, industrialization and the involvement of outside capital also meant new class differentiation not just in terms of the split between captain and crew but also in terms of responsible and responsive ownership. In the past and for centuries there had been small and medium-sized companies, usually family-run, which together with the fishing crews and their dependents determined the policies and politics of the local cofradía. This changed considerably at the turn of the twentieth century when the monopoly for landing and selling fish that the fishing fraternities held onto was abolished, mainly due to the demands of a new free market, which was influenced heavily by the new incoming capital and its interests.

However, the old monopoly rights and traditional forms of solidarity did not go quietly. There was indeed a widespread reluctance to modernization, industrialization, and capitalization of fishing. For example, in the Bizkaian towns of Bermeo and Ondarroa—for a long time the two largest fishing communities on the Basque coast—conflict over the issue of who had the right to speak and decide ("voice") had been a major feature of life there, and fervent disagreements over the types of fishing, the right to land fish, and the right to market the sale (or to be exempted from it) led to faction-building and finally even organizational splits. Both Bermeo and Ondarroa had developed a significant trawling sector and eventually the disagreements over the type of fishing, the timing and length of the fishing seasons, landing and selling rights, and so on, led to the founding of new cofradías. It meant the end of traditional forms of loyalty and solidarity and the idea that the cofradía represented all fishermen and all interests.

Ever since the split emerged, there had been attempts to stay together and reunite the different interests again under the roof of one cofradía—yet only with limited success. The industrialization process and the demand of market liberalization that went with it appeared to be unstoppable. In the 1920s Basque nationalist attempts under the aegis of Eusko Ikaskuntza (the Society of Basque Studies) tried to appeal to all the factions and interests and argue for more unity and a more coherent approach toward the controlled exploitation of the sea. Such efforts were more an attempt at a broader enlightenment and had little real consequences. Under the Franco regime (1939–1975) the monopoly was somehow artificially prolonged, mainly for political motives and reasons. Francoist fishing policies tried to secure the support of and misused the cofradía as corporatist institutions over which they had full political and social control. However, while the monopoly of the cofradía was thus artificially kept alive, the continuing economic changes kept eroding the very institution itself.[3]

At the present time, not much is left of loyalty, the "voice" of fishermen (collectively or individually), and the former egalitarian ethos of the old-style cofradía. The uncontrolled freedom and exploitation of the sea together with the centralization of decision-making processes—first in the form of the local provincial government, later in that of the Basque and Spanish government, then followed by the European Union—eventually led to a situation in which the seas were seen as a limitless resource base to be exploited as if there was no tomorrow. In the end, this had disastrous consequences. After years of "open seas" talk and free market ideology there is now a new awareness and a more protective rhetoric that speaks of ecological balance and sustainability, limited quotas, and stricter control. Yet, while ecological rhetoric has now become the talk of the day, the very institutions that could have guaranteed such policies are in a moribund state.

To be sure, there cannot be any going back in time, not least because the entire social-economic environment of the old harbor towns has changed. While nowadays one can still detect a sense of old civic "plebeian" pride and the presence of a rich tradition in the small Basque towns and harbors, symbolic gestures can hardly be substitutes for the more fully developed plebeian spirit and a related moral economy that now belong firmly to the past. In that past, the plebeian culture and moral economy dimension was able to develop because of the existence of common identities stemming from or derived from similar or identical working environments such as seafaring, fishing, and related activities. Today, this is no longer the case. At present, only a minority of the population works in the fishing sector and maintains a symbolic presence there. Furthermore, harbor towns in the Basque Coun-

---

3.   In an informative anthropological account of and reflection on maritime fishing on the Basque coast, Juan Antonio Rubio-Ardanaz (2006, 30) describes the long twentieth-century struggle between *pesca artesenal* and *artes menores* (traditional fishing that is economically less profitable) and *pesca capitalista* and *artes mayores* (capitalist and economically more profitable fishing). Rubio-Ardanaz refers mainly to the port of Santurtzi, at the mouth of the Nervion River (now part of Greater Bilbao), but his description could, with minor variations, also be easily applied to the harbors of Bermeo, Ondarroa, and Pasaia (Gipuzkoa).

try have, demographically speaking, changed dramatically over the last few decades. A process that started at the end of the nineteenth century has led to what seems to be an almost unstoppable drive toward urbanization. Nowhere has this process become more visible than in the moribund state of the cofradías, which once had lent voice to the fishermen.

Creating Loyalty through Commensality

As noted before, "Plebeian culture" was an auxiliary term that Thompson used to describe a situation in which class was not what classic Marxist theory assumed it to be (Thompson 1980, 1991). Rather than forming nascent prototypes of the industrial working class, the English historian preferred to see classes in terms of "fields of gravity," that is, as heterogeneous constellations consisting of many dimensions and layers and in which traditional popular customs played a major role. It was these common customs that also helped to keep a moral economy alive—an economy that could take on various and different meanings for the plebeian crowds such as common rights, norms or obligations, day-to-day habits, customs, and practices, but which, taken together, in many ways constituted a force that was alien and opposed to elite classes.

Today, any close look into the stratification structure of the Basque Country will reveal that, apart from the metropolitan region of Bilbao, its industrial environs, and a few industrial towns and industrial development zones such as Durango, Eibar, Elgoibar, Ermua, and Hernani, clear-cut, visible class structures are barely noticeable. In many ways, the Basque Country seems to be a prime illustration of Thompson's main notion of plebeian culture. Indeed, the work of social historians and historical anthropologists confirms the existence of such a plebeian cultural macroconstellation and the place cooking societies play in its moral economy (Luengo Teixidor 2002; Homobono 1987, 1989, 1990, 1997; Arpal 1985).

While historians and social scientists have hinted at and analyzed macroconstellations such as plebeian cultures and the moral economy that goes with them, the political economist Hirschman looks at the micro level of institutions. In his seminal book *Shifting Involvements: Private Interest and Public Action* (1982) he addresses the problem of periodic shifts that have occurred in modern society. He argues that the retreat into privacy and the inclination toward public action happens in "wave-like" appearances. Here, the main motive behind both private retreat and public action is viewed as a sense of disappointment. Hirschman does not discuss social practices in which public concern mingles with private activities and thereby helps to maintain a civic equilibrium in civil society. To go a step further, merging the two spheres, the private and the public, was regarded as a potential threat to civil society. However, in a later essay on commensality Hirschman reexamines some of his previous arguments. There might be, he contends, occasions on which the merging of the two spheres can actually have positive results. Indeed, far too long, so his argument goes, have "economists [and other social scientists] looked at the consumption of food as a purely private and self-centerd activity" (Hirschman 1998, 28).

Hirschman stresses that the function of the common meal of commensality can, and indeed does, vary. He reminds us in particular of Heinrich Mann's novel *Der Untertan* (The Subject), in which the main character Diederich Hessling is drawn into a form of beer-drinking and pretzel-eating commensality that can only be described as reactionary in terms of the later outcome, National Socialism. Against such negative examples and experiences, Hirschman now reveals the great potential of commensality, that is, not means-centered but ends-related. It is exactly at this juncture that the Basque cooking society comes into play. It seems that in the case of the txoko we are dealing with a positive example of how commensality—at least when organized collectively and when sensibly institutionalized—can have a positive function in providing loyalty through contributing to the maintenance of a civic equilibrium in society. In other words, when such commensality emerges, human beings are not treated just as means toward certain ends but as ends in themselves.

Providing the microinstitutional framework for such ends-centered interaction, the txoko contributes to the maintenance of the social equilibrium. Txokos are an institutionalized measure and increasingly an interclass phenomenon against the divisions of modern society, or, in other words, an attempt at life-world integration (Luengo Teixidor 2001; Arpal 1985; Habermas 1962). Combining aspects of tradition and modernity, they are attempts to provide answers to purely instrumental and systemic rationalization or system integration. However, in contrast to the roles of public institutions and the public sphere that Habermas emphasizes and promotes, txokos are neither purely public nor purely private institutions; rather, they occupy a unique space somewhere in the middle of the continuum between the public and the private sphere. It is this very middle position that contributes to the txokos' success and popularity.

Yet one must also note that the txoko does not only have progressive social functions; it also reproduces existing age and sex/gender constellations, and often treats societal aspects as if they were community aspects (Arpal 1985, 140ff). In this context, some commentators have interpreted the txoko as a communal institution that functions as a compensation device by exercising a "cooling" effect on an overheated personality type and lessening tensions in a collective group therapy, almost resembling a psycho-dramatic setting. This interpretation suggests that the txoko provides a communal escape route from the grindings of societal life, implicitly suggesting a shift toward a communal "exit" strategy and thus somehow limiting the positive impact on society as a whole (Aguirre Franco 1983; Wijck 2000).

However, it would be wrong to perceive the nature of the txoko solely in light of such suggestions. As an institution it is as good (or as bad) as the society and the members who constitute it. The fact remains that eating at the txoko, particularly during the fiestas, interrupts daily life and routine, and is clearly an expression of what Georg Simmel termed "conviviality" (Homobono 1987). The txoko as an institution is also a symbolic reproduction of Basque society and identity and particularly supportive in terms of accommodating the transition from rural to urban life, thus providing an example of a historic reformulation of the community-society divide (Arpal 1985). As a potential reproduction cell for Basque nationalist discourse, both the *cuadrilla* (group of friends) and txoko can also be seen as nationalist models of sociability and commensality that are not bound by rigid class structures but rather bridge across class distinctions and positions (Pérez-Agote 1986; Luengo Teixidor 2001).

Whatever the details and the individual and collective enjoyments in the sociedades are, it is obvious that this institution has indeed become a cultural backbone of modern Basque society.

Here, in the example of the Basque cooking societies, we find a form in which the public and the private actually enrich each other. It seems indeed wrong to me to degrade them as part of an "invented tradition" (Hobsbawm and Ranger 1983) or regard them as "terrorist recruitment cells," as is sometimes implicitly suggested by commentators like Jon Juaristi (1987). The opposite is true: the sociedades gastronómicas are relatively modern institutions, which actually allow the Basque Country to overcome some of the tensions that arise when an old civilization meets the modern societal conditions of the twenty-first century. The relationship between the private and the public is a delicate one, and has not always worked out well in modern times. The txoko, which uniquely connects both spheres, appears to be indeed the Basques' most genuine and beneficial contribution to the question of how a plebeian culture with a long history can survive under modern conditions.

Plebeian Culture, Moral Economy, Reluctant Modernization

Barrington Moore's *Social Origins of Democracy and Dictatorship* (1967) was the first study that hinted at the paradoxical and sometimes contradictory forms of modernization processes. Moore was soon to be joined by other critics. Like Moore, Thompson criticizes the hidden sociological metaphysics of the structural functionalist approach of Talcott Parsons (1968) and Neil J. Smelser (1963) and the way they describe the historical process of modernization (Thompson 1987, 238ff and 267ff). Pointing out that "history knows no regular verbs," he reminds social theorists and sociologists that history has never been a process without a subject in which human agency, moral problems, and ambiguous decisions simply disappeared or became buried in structures or differentiation processes (Thompson 1978, 267f).

Similarly, Hirschman dislikes the contradiction-free, almost "smooth"-appearing descriptions of modernization processes. In *The Rhetoric of Reaction* (1991) he points out that modernization was never a straightforward unilinear process but instead a paradoxical, uneven process that included major historical digressions and detours. For Hirschman the road to modernity was full of ambiguities, contradictions, ambivalences, and often even outright resistance (Hirschman 1991; Hess 1999, 350ff). Taking a look at the various commentators that have accompanied and commented on the long journey toward modernity, he distinguishes three approaches. The first approach is one in which normal meaning is turned upside-down and any reform project is rejected. Any expressed desire for improvement can only lead to worsening the present condition or state. Antimodernist thinkers are aware of human limitations and unforeseen circumstances, but what appears at first sight to provide genuine insight into the human condition is in the end rendered completely meaningless because the idea that there can be anything new in this world is simply dismissed. The second approach Hirschman criticizes is similar to the first but has an additional critical edge, in the sense that it is assumed that underlying social structures have always been beyond the reach of collective human action and that throughout history it has only been a small elite that made the far-reaching decisions, while the masses only followed. To change these eternal conditions and iron laws would be futile. What this approach denies is the existence of any form of meaningful collective agency and subjectivity. The third approach that is subject to Hirschman's criticism argues that change can only threaten what has already been achieved. Here, past reforms are being played out against new ones. That increased democracy threatens an already achieved liberty is one of the standard complaints of this peculiar form of status quo-defending, reactionary rhetoric.

Hirschman is concerned that all three forms of the rhetoric of reaction limit our understanding and possible vision of what has been and what is still possible and within human capacity and capability for change. Only by changing perspectives and keeping the lines of communication open between what often seem to be contradicting messages will we be able to conceive of the ambiguities, contradictions, and ambivalences of the process of modernization.

Thinking about modernization started out first with the description of ideal types (Durkheim 1893, Tönnies 1878, Weber 1922). These sociological classics were then deconstructed and reinterpreted by a new generation of system thinkers who argued that modernization was a unilinear and progressive paradigm and process (as, for example, in the structural-functionalist thought of Parsons [1937] and Smelser [1963]). Against such clinical contradiction-free attempts, both classic and modern, Moore, Thompson, and Hirschman have voiced their concern and criticism. To these names we can add one other pioneering attempt to conceive of tradition and modernity differently: that of Joseph R. Gusfield. Referring to and reflecting on twentieth-century examples from India and elsewhere in Asia, Gusfield argues that it is plainly wrong to conceive of tradition and modernity as polar opposites in the linear theory of social change (Gusfield 1967). He also dismisses the presuppositions that there is a track leading to success called "rational economic behavior" and a final aim called modernity, to which all roads lead, as being plainly one-dimensional. In contrast to such claims, Gusfield points out that the experiences of new nations such as India have clearly shown that the old and the new, tradition and modernity, are much more entwined than had been previously thought. It is by no means always the case that the old is completely replaced by the new. Instead, mixed forms or fusion models encompassing the old and the new can regularly be encountered. Furthermore, the development of new practices, norms, and values are by no means limited to what he terms the "great tradition" of urban areas and cities (ibid., 353). The "little tradition" of rural small towns and villages can equally develop norms and values, particularly when new modern circumstances demand some form of adjustment. Traditional skills can be used and applied to pursue new ends, a selection of traditional values and norms can easily sit beside new values and norms, extended families, traditional trust, and obligation can also supplement and help to get over the birth pangs of modern industrialized society. In short, "tradition and modernity are frequently mutually reinforcing, rather than systems in conflict" (356).

In his critique, Gusfield refers mainly to the experience of and examples from Asia, where out of an old civilization and various traditional local cultures new nations emerged. However, Gusfield's critique of a one-dimensionally perceived modernization process can also be applied to the history of multiple speeds and experiences of various Western roads to nationhood and can help to fine-tune crucial arguments concerning modernization, such as creative fusion and the mixing of traditional and modern elements.

As I have tried to explain, the Basque Country is a case study that illuminates and illustrates some of the points raised above. With particular reference to the three institutions discussed in greater detail, I have tried to point out that the Basques have been modernizers for a long time. To be more precise, they have been reluctant modernizers but modernizers nevertheless. More specifically, my case study reveals three modes of adjusting to changing circumstances: two of them (the baserri and the cofradía) were successful for centuries but are now in terminal decline or already history; one, which is less old (the txoko), remains very much alive and finds itself in a healthy condition, actually to such an extent that it can be called a remarkable success story.

I termed the three modes of reluctant modernization "exit," "voice," and "loyalty" (after Hirschman). I have tried to see them also as expressions of plebeian culture and a related moral economy (after Thompson). To be sure, the three modes of exit, voice, and loyalty do not each appear exclusively and on their own, neither in the baserri, nor in the cofradía, nor in the case of the txoko. As a matter of fact, all three are institutions in which all three modes can be found. However, historically speaking, in each institution one mode prevailed over the others in the end. As we have seen, exit conditions were the main mode that prevailed and dominated in the baserri. The extended families of the baserri created a loyal core and managed to institutionalize a moral economy. However, the voice option in the baserri remained structurally limited and in the end massive exit from the farm and the rural world prevailed, leading to an institutional crisis—partly induced from outside—from which the baserri would never recover. In the case of the cofradía the situation was different. Creating a voice for all the fishermen lies at the heart of the cofradía. For centuries, the unique working environment that is the sea has helped to create this institutionalized form of loyalty. This only functioned as long as the institution remained balanced in the sense that the internal differentiation of labor and capital remained limited. Once modern market forces arrived (mainly in the form of modern trawling and the internationalization of the fish market), bringing a qualitative change to working and sales practices, the cofradía in its traditional form steered into crisis. To be sure, the cofradía managed to mix the old with the new for almost another century but, toward the end of the twentieth century, really become defunct and is now moribund. The txoko, in contrast, remains the most successful institutional form in which an older plebeian culture and moral economy has managed to survive, mainly because creating friendship and loyalty became the main features. If Hirschman is right about the formula of a successful moral economy—namely that it is loyalty that enables voice and keeps exit at bay—then the txoko can serve as a prime example. As we have seen, loyalty is created through commensality, an intersubjective form of communication in which the end product (food and drink) is consumed collectively. Almost by definition and design it renders instrumental means-ends rationality and communication meaningless—a key argument for the txoko's success. Indeed, its main purpose is not to care for immediate needs and survival—as the baserri and the cofradía have to—but exactly its opposite, the pleasure and joy created through the consumption of good food and drink that is the txoko's main raison d'être.

Over the course of half a millennium the baserri and the cofradía and for almost 120 years the txoko have been very successful in adjusting to the circumstances and the environment they have found themselves in. Changes there have been plenty, particularly from the late nineteenth century onward. Often the Basques' response to these changes have been reluctant, but we have to understand that such reluctance was based on the conviction that change only makes sense if it leads to long-term improvement and security of the whole group. In other words, there has indeed been a collective dimension to responses to modernization challenges. This means that the individuals and social groups involved were not mere dupes of objective social structures. Instead, they were to a large extent the makers of their own fortune. In this context, the rhetoric of egalitarianism has indeed been a major tool, not just as a kind of gut reaction to modern challenges but as a moral force, a rallying call around which plebeian culture could gather and gain momentum. Such rhetoric helped people to make history, even if that kind of history-making rarely made it into the annals or the history books. To sum up the argument, reluctant modernization is a hybrid form that has helped to mediate and negotiate between traditional and modern forms of life. It is a specific—or perhaps more accurately, adequate—expression of the collective-subjective dimensions of plebeian culture and moral economy that some participants in debates about the origins of Basque nationalism and the allegedly forgotten social inequality to which I referred above never address and discuss.

That individuals and groups can make and indeed have made history is the central message here. That they have made history under particular circumstances and in a special environment is the second part of the message. In doing so, they have found their own answer—an attitude that can be described as being reluctant to modernization and taking on the particular institutionalized form of exit, voice, or loyalty.

References

Aguirre Franco, Rafael. 2006. *Las sociedades populares, Donostia 1870–2005*. Donostia-San Sebastián: Hiria.

Apraiz, Juan Antonio, and Aingeru Astui. 1987. "La pesca en Euskalerria: La pesca de litoral." In *Itsasoa. El mar de Euskalerria, la naturaleza, el hombre y su historia*, vol. 2, directed and edited by Enrique Ayerbe. Donostia: Etor.

———. 1989. "La pesca en Euskalerria: La pesca de bajura." In *Itsasoa. El mar de Euskalerria, la naturaleza, el hombre y su historia*, vol. 4., directed and edited by Enrique Ayerbe. Donostia: Etor.

Arpal, Jesús. 1979. *La sociedad tradicional en el País Vasco (el estamento de los hidalgos de Guipúzcoa)*. San Sebastián: L. Haranburu.

———. 1985. "Solidaridades elementales y organizaciones colectivas en el País vasco (cuadrillas, txokos, asociaciones)." In *Processus sociaux: Idéologies et pratiques culturelles dans la société basque*, edited by Pierre Bidart. Bayonne: Maubec.

Barruso Barés, Pedro, et al., eds. 2004a. *Historia del País Vasco: Edad media (siglos V–XV)*. San Sebastián: Hiria.

———. 2004b. *Historia del País Vasco: Edad moderna (siglos XVI–XVIII)*. San Sebastián: Hiria.

———. 2005. *Historia del País Vasco. Edad contemporánea (siglos XIX–XX)*. San Sebastián: Hiria.

Bikandi, Juan José. 1989. "Aspectos sociales de la actividad pesquera: Ciclos laborales y compañias." In *Itsasoa. El mar de Euskalerria, la naturaleza, el hombre y su historia*, vol. 4, directed and edited by Enrique Ayerbe. Donostia: Etor.

Canal i Morell, Jordi. 1992. "La sociabilidad en los estudios sobre la España contemporánea." *Historia Contemporánea* 7: 183–205.

———. 1993. "El concepto de sociabilidad en la historiografía contemporánea (Francia, Italia y España)." *Siglo XIX* 13 (January–June): 5–25.

Caro Baroja, Julio. (1944) 1986. *De la vida rural vasca (Vera de Bida-soa)*. San Sebastián: Editorial Txertoa.

———. 1985. *Los vascos y el mar*. San Sebastián: Editorial Txertoa.

———. 1986. *Introducción a la historia social y económico del pueblo vasco*. San Sebastián: Editorial Txertoa.

———. 1990. *Los vascos*. Madrid: Ediciones Istmo. Published in English as *The Basques*. Translated by Kristin Addis. Reno: Center for Basque Studies, University of Nevada, Reno, 2009.

Douglass, William A. 1969. *Death in Murelaga: Funerary Ritual in a Spanish Basque Village*. Seattle: University of Washington Press.

———. 1975. *Echalar and Murelaga: Opportunity and Rural Exodus in Two Spanish Basque Villages*. London: C. Hurst.

Durkheim, Émile. (1893) 1984. *The Division of Labour in Society*. 2nd edition. With an introduction by Lewis Coser. Translated by W.D. Halls. London: Macmillan.

Enríquez Fernández, José Carlos. 1994. "El pensamiento agrario durante la Ilustración Vasca." In *Pensamiento agrario vasco. Mitos y realidades (1766–1980)*, edited by Instituto Vasco de Estudios Rurales-Nekazal Ikasketarako Euskal Institutoa. Bilbao: Universidad del País Vasco-Euskal Herriko Unibertsitatea.

Etxezarreta, Miren. 1977. *El caserío vasco?* Bilbao: Fundación C. de Iturriaga and M. de Dañobeitia.

Erkoreka, Josu Iñaki. 1991. *Análisis histórico-institucional de las Cofradías de Mareantes del País Vasco*. Vitoria-Gasteiz: Gobierno Vasco-Eusko Jaurlaritza.

Garmendia Larrañaga, Juan. 1979. *Gremios, oficios y cofradías en el País Vasco*. San Sebastián: Caja de Ahorros Provincial de Guipúzcoa.

Garmendia Larrañaga, Juan, and Luis Pedro Peña Santiago. 1982. *El mar de los vascos*. 2 vols. San Sebastián: Txertoa.

Gracia Cárcamo, Juan Antonio. 1985. "Los conflictos sociales en la cofradía de pescadores de Bermeo a través de sus ordenanzas." In *Congreso de Estudios Históricos. Vizcaya en la edad media*. San Sebastián: Eusko Ikaskuntza.

———. 1992. "La evolución de las actividades pesqueras y de la Cofradía Marítima." In *Lekeitio*, edited by Juan Manuel González Cembellín. Bilbao: Bizkaiko Foru Aldundia-Diputación Foral de Bizkaia.

Gracia Cárcamo, Juan Antonio, et al. 1983. *Historia de la economía marítima del País Vasco*. San Sebastián: Editorial Txertoa.

Gusfield, Joseph R. 1967. "Tradition and Modernity: Misplaced Polarities in the Study of Social Change." *The American Journal of Sociology* 72, no. 4: 351–62.

Hess, Andreas. 1999. "The 'Economy of Morals' and its Applications: An Attempt to Understand Some Central Concepts in the Work of Albert O. Hirschman." *Review of International Political Economy* 6, no. 3 (Autumn): 338–59.

———. 2007. "The Social Bonds of Cooking: Gastronomic Societies in the Basque Country." *Cultural Sociology* 1, no. 3: 383–407.

———. 2009. *Reluctant Modernization: Plebeian Culture and Moral Economy in the Basque Country*. Oxford: Peter Lang.

———. 2010. "'Working the Waves': The Plebeian Culture and Moral Economy of Traditional Basque Fishing Brotherhoods." *Journal of Interdisciplinary History* 40, no. 4 (Spring): 551–78.

Hirschman, Albert O. 1970. *Exit, Voice, and Loyalty: Responses to Decline in Firms, Organizations, and States*. Cambridge, MA: Harvard University Press.

———. 1977. *The Passions and the Interests: Political Arguments for Capitalism before Its Triumph*. Princeton, NJ: Princeton University Press.

———. 1982. *Shifting Involvements: Private Interests and Public Action*. Princeton, NJ: Princeton University Press.

———. 1991. *The Rhetoric of Reaction: Perversity, Futility, Jeopardy*. Cambridge, MA: Harvard University Press.

———. 1998. *Crossing Boundaries: Selected Writings*. New York: Zone Books.

Hobsbawm, Eric, and Terence Ranger, eds. 1983. *The Invention of Tradition*. Cambridge: Cambridge University Press.

Homobono, José Ignacio. 1987. "Comensabilidad y fiesta en el ámbito arrantzale: San Martin de Bermeo." *Bermeo* no. 6: 301–92.

———. 1990. "Fiesta, tradición e identidad local." *Cuadernos de Etnología y Etnografía de Navarra* 22, no. 55 (January–June): 43–58.

———. 1997. "Fiestas en el ámbito arrantzale: Expresiones de sociabilidad e identidades colectivas." *Zainak* no. 15: 61–100.

Imaz, José Manuel. 1944. *La industria pesquera en Guipúzcoa al final del Siglo XVI. Documentos de la época*. San Sebastián: Imp. de la Excma. Diputación.

Iturbe, José Angel, and Francisco Letamendia. 2000. "Cultura, política y gastronomía en el País Vasco." In *Cocinas del mundo.*

La política en la mesa, edited by Francisco Letamendia and Christian Coulon. Madrid: Editorial Fundamentos.

Juaristi, Jon. 1987. *El linaje de Aitor: La invención de la tradición vasca.* Madrid: Taurus.

Luengo Teixidor, Félix. 2001. *San Sebastián. La vida cotidiana de una ciudad.* San Sebastián: Editorial Txertoa.

Martínez, José. 1994. "La vida rural vasca desde la antropología social." In *Pensamiento agrario vasco. Mitos y realidades (1766–1980)*, edited by Instituto Vasco de Estudios Rurales-Nekazal Ikasketarako Euskal Institutoa. Bilbao: Universidad del País Vasco-Euskal Herriko Unibertsitatea.

Martínez, José, and José Ramón Mauleón. 1994. "Sociedad rural tradicional y crisis del caserío en los años 1950–60." In *Pensamiento agrario vasco. Mitos y realidades (1766–1980)*, edited by Instituto Vasco de Estudios Rurales-Nekazal Ikasketarako Euskal Institutoa. Bilbao: Universidad del País Vasco-Euskal Herriko Unibertsitatea.

Moore, Barrington, Jr. 1967. *Social Origins of Dictatorship and Democracy: Lord and Peasant in the Making of the Modern World.* London: Penguin.

Otazu, Alfonso de. 1986. *El "igualitarismo" vasco: Mito y realidad.* 2nd ed. San Sebastián: Editorial Txertoa.

Parsons, Talcott. (1937) 1968. *The Structure of Social Action: Study in Social Theory and Special Reference to a Group of Recent European Writers.* 2 vols. New York: Free Press.

Pérez-Agote, Alfonso. 1986. *La reproducción del nacionalismo: El caso vasco.* Madrid: Centro de Investigaciones Sociológicas.

Rubio-Ardanaz, Juan Antonio. 1994. *La Antropología marítima subdisciplina de la antropología sociocultural.* Bilbao: Universidad de Deusto.

Rubio-Ardanaz, Juan Antonio. 2006. *Lemanes, sardineras y pescadores: Realidades marítimas en perspectiva antropólogia.* Santurtzi: Editorial Grafema.

Rubio-Ardanaz, Juan Antonio, ed. 2003. *La pesca y el mar: Cambio sociocultural y económico. Zainak* special issue. Donostia-San Sebastián: Eusko Ikaskuntza.

Sesmero Cutanda, Enriqueta. 1997. "Aproximación a las relaciones intracomunitarias de los pescadores bermeanos a mediados del siglo XIX." *Zainak* 15: 219–32.

Smelser, Neil J. 1963. *The Sociology of Economic Life.* Englewood Cliffs, NJ: Prentice-Hall.

Thalamas Labandibar, Juan. 1935. *Aspectos de la vida profesional vasca. El campesino, el pescador, el obrero.* Donostia : Beñat Idaztiak.

Thompson, E. P. 1980. *Plebeische Kultur und moralische Ökonomie.* Frankfurt: Ullstein.

———. 1991. *Customs in Common.* London: Merlin Press.

Tönnies, Ferdinand. (1878) 1955. *Community and Association.* Translated and supplemented by Charles P. Loomis. London: Routledge & Kegan Paul.

Urzainki Mikeleiz, Asunción. 1994. "Pensamiento social agrario en las ponencias y lecciones de los primeros congresos de estudios vascos." In *Pensamiento agrario vasco. Mitos y realidades (1766–1980),* edited by Instituto Vasco de Estudios Rurales-Nekazal Ikasketarako Euskal Institutoa. Bilbao: Universidad del País Vasco-Euskal Herriko Unibertsitatea.

Van der Loo, Hans, and Willem Van Reijen. 1992. *Modernisierung: Projekt und Paradox.* Munich: Deutscher Taschenbuch Verlag.

Weber, Max. (1922) 1968. *Economy and Society: An Outline of Interpretive Sociology.* 3 vols. Edited by Guenther Roth and Claus Wittich. Translated by Ephraim Fischoff and others. New York: Bedminster Press.

———. 1946. *From Max Weber: Essays in Sociology,* translated and edited by H. H. Gerth and C. W. Mills. New York: Oxford University Press.

Wijck, Anke van. 2000. *Basque Male Cooking Societies.* Unpublished MA dissertation, Boston University.

Zulaika, Joseba. 1996. *Del Cromañón al Carnaval: Los vascos como museo antropológico.* Donostia: Erein.

About the Contributors

José Angel Achon is Professor of History at the University of Deusto, Bilbao.

Xavier Arregi teaches Philosophy at a Donostia-San Sebastián college.

Joseba Azkarraga teaches Sociology at the University of the Basque Country, Leioa

Margaret Bullen is Professor of Social Anthropology and Director of the Department of Values and Social Anthropology at the University of the Basque Country, Donostia-San Sebastián.

Francisco Garmendia was Professor Emeritus at the University of Deusto, Bilbao.

Patxi Juaristi is Professor of Political Science at the University of the Basque Country, Leioa.

Jone Miren Hernández is Professor of Social Anthropology at the University of the Basque Country, Leioa.

Andreas Hess teaches Sociology at University College Dublin (Ireland) and is a Faculty fellow at the Center for Cultural Sociology at Yale University.

Maïté Lafourcade is Professor Emerita of the University of Pau and the University Pays de L'Adour, France.

Anne-Marie Lagarde teaches modern literature and Basque Studies in Iparralde.

Oihane Oliveri teaches at HABE, the Basque Language Institute.

Coro Rubio is Professor of Contemporary History at the University of the Basque Country, Vitoria-Gasteiz.

Index

marriage law in, 72; medieval, class structure in, 200–201; partial autonomy of, 4, 5; political structures in, 133n4; preservation of ancient government and culture in, 5; property ownership traditions in, 193; and Spanish Civil War, 218n3; universal nobility in, 108, 109, 111

Biscay, *fueros* in, 52, 67; nineteenth-century arguments in defense of, 122–23; removal of, 115; survival under Bourbon rule, 121

Bloch, Marc, 49

Bonaparte, Joseph, 116

Borrow, George, 107–8

Bruni, Leonardo, 14

Bullen, Margaret, 162n5

business innovation of Mondragon Group, replicability of, 247–48

Butler, Judith, 183–84

Caballero, Fermin, 202n5

Calatrava, Francisco, 22

Cambridge School, 2, 27–28

Campbell, Joseph, 164

Cantabri, and matriarchal culture, 135

Capdevielle, Marie-Josée, 142n13

capitalism, importance of balancing with social goals, 243–44

capitalist democracy, systemic crisis of recent years, 2

Carlists: rural support for, 263; and Spanish Civil War, 7–8

Carlist War, First (1833-1839): and Basque attachment to *fueros*, 115; and effort to remove *hidalguía* privileges, 117

Carlist Wars (1833-1840 and 1872-1876): and collapse of house system, 264; and triumph of forces of modernization, 6–7

Caro Baroja, Julio, 21n9, 144–45, 165, 166, 193, 225, 227n17

Castile: establishment of, and subordination of territorial rights to royal rights, 50, 55; legal status of women in, 94

Catalonia, abolishment of *fueros* in, 121

Catherine (queen of Navarre), 67

Catholic Church: and Basque language, 177; in Basque matriarchy myth, 165; efforts to impose political structures, 73; Gipuzkoa, *hermandad* and, 37; influence on Basque society, 219; and Machiaviellianism, 52; and Mondragon Group, 219, 221, 235–36, 244; and practical help to community, 264; response to twentieth-century de-Christianizing forces, 236, 236n23

Celaya, Adrian, 18–19, 22

Centenero de Arce, Domingo, 37

Cervantes, Miguel de, 21

(fishermen's fraternities) and, 271; impact on Basque region, 233; and Mondragon Group founding, 235, 239; and Spanish cultural conflict, 7

freedom. *See* liberty

fueristas, and Basque egalitarianism as political tool, 121, 122, 126

Fuero de hidalguia ad Pragmaticas de Toro & Tordesillas (Poza), 14n3

Fuero general de Navarra (c. 1237), 66

fueros: abolition of in Carlist Wars, 6, 14n1; appearance in written form, 138; as autochthonous, 20; Basque elite's resistance to removal of, 115; and Basque republican tradition, 10; and Basque rights as majorat, 52–54; Bourbon rule and, 121; as central to Basque identity, 13–14n1, 22; commentators on, 17–18; as complex and dynamic, 18–19; critiques of idealized treatments of, 13–16, 25–26; debate on origin of rights given in, 44–45; decentralization of power in, 18–19, 33; definition of, 6n2, 13n1; durability of, 22; early records of, 66–68; and egalitarianism as political myth, 120–23; egalitarian rights recognized by, 18, 20; emphasis on self-government in, 18; foundation

in European humanism, 16, 17–18, 23–25, 32–33; as framework for legitimate behavior, 95; fundamental principles of, 19; habeas corpus tradition in, 22; historical origins of, 19–22; and humanist republicanism, 14n1; legitimacy of, Tubalian myth as basis of, 51–52; limits on taxation in, 19–20, 21–22; and mountain republicanism, 18, 18n6, 33; nineteenth-century efforts to remove, 114–19, 121; as non-state form of government, 22; prioritization of custom over law in, 13n1, 19, 24, 33; quasi-autonomy granted by, 17; recording of marriage traditions in, 137–38; rural support for, 263; in Spanish Basque provinces, survival into nineteenth century, 114–19; Spanish Constitution and, 115, 116–17; tradition of defending, and development of republican tradition, 56

Fukuyama, Francis, 223

Gallastegui, Elías, 175
Garagalza, Luis, 226
García de Cortázar, Fernando, 199
Garibay y Zamalloa, Esteban de, 40, 52
gender: as analytical tool, 158–59; characteristics assigned to, and reproduction of

side of province, 100
Gipuzkoa, women in: economic role of, 142; male authority over, 94, 96, 97; restrictions on political involvement, 94; universal nobility (*hidalguía*) and, 93–94
Goizueta, Jose Ma., 124
Gorroñogoitia, Alfonso, 221n6, 231
Gramática vascongada (Añibarro, Pedro Antonio), 149n21
The Great Chain of Being (Lovejoy), 29
Grellier, Hervé, 223, 229
gudariak, and Spanish Civil War, 7–8
Guipúzcoa. *See* Gipuzkoa
Gusfield, Joseph R., 278

habeas corpus, in *fueros*, 22
Hautes-Pyrénées: titles of house members in, 148; and *toka/noka* system of gender distinction, 148
Hegoalde. *See* Southern Basque Country
Henry III (king of France), 67
Henry IV (king of France and Navarre), 67
hidalguía, universal. *See* universal nobility
Hirschman, Albert O.: on commensality, 274; on "exit," "voice," and "loyalty" responses to dominant culture, 257, 261, 279; on modernization process, 276–77, 278; on periodic oscillations between

private retreat and public action, 273–74; on plebeian culture and moral economy, 256, 257, 280
historical determinism, and current conception of equality, 2
Historical Territories, establishment of, 49; autonomy of, as anomalous, 50; Catholic basis of legitimacy in, 50, 51–54; and development of provincial institutions, 50; and development of universal nobility concept, 50–56; similar processes throughout Europe, 50. *See also* Gipuzkoa, founding of
Hornilla, Txema, 165, 166
house(s) (*etxe*): as basic structure of Basque society, 21, 65–66, 67–68, 131; European debate on wise domestic management and, 96–97; extended families associated with, 65, 71, 96; gender equality in, 140; in Gipuzkoa, status hierarchies in, 96; in larger political structure, 73, 141; in Mokoroa's *Repertorio de locuciones*, analysis of terms related to, 203–7; political representation of, 66; responsibilities of members of, 210–12; roles in, 132; as source of social identity, 210–11
house societies, Lévi-Strauss on, 134

house system: and adjustment to modernization, 279, 280; and Basque democratic tradition, 228; and Basque rights as majorats, 52–54, 54–55; challenges faced by farmers in, 262, 263; collapse of, 263–64; eldest child's inheritance of family estate at marriage, 70, 72, 95–96, 133, 137, 138, 142, 142n13; equality of houses in, 66, 74, 77, 79, 150*t*; equal rights of married couple (*coseigneurie*) in, 70–73, 96, 132–35, 149–51; and exit model of Plebeian moral economy, 261–65, 279; and family property, as indivisible, 68, 71, 95–96, 137, 192; and family property, master of the house as caretaker of, 192–93, 208–10, 212, 227–28; and neighborhood, mutual aid within, 141, 264; obligation to protect extended family, 96; origin of, 65; and *pater familias* model, 96, 97, 100, 101; relative freedom and prosperity of farmers in, 262–63, 264; required single status of unmarried children living at home, 144; as theologically-based, 54; titles of house members in, 148, 152*t*; and universal nobility in Gipuzkoa, 90, 93, 95–96, 97. See also *coseigneurie* (co-ownership); family

property; master of the house (*etxerakoa*); property ownership; younger children, exogamy of

Humboldt, Wilhelm von, 16, 111–12

Ibarretxe, Juan José, 9
Idiáquez, Juan de, 99
Idoate, Florencio, 194, 195–97, 198
idyllic rural Basque society, myth of, 158; and matriarchy myth, 166; nineteenth-century literary amplification of, 124–25; as nineteenth-century political tool, 121, 122–23, 125–26; origins of, 121
El "igualitarismo" vasco (Otazu), 255–56
Imízcoz, José María, 41
individualism, atomistic: binary opposition to collectivism, alternatives to, 26–32; as current model of equality, 2; as failed model, 27; linear conception of history in, 26–27; principles of, 26
inheritance law: Lévi-Strauss on types of systems for, 133–34; in matrilineal and matriarchal societies, 134, 135–36
inheritance law, Basque: eldest child's inheritance of family estate at marriage, 70, 72, 95–96, 133, 137, 138, 142, 142n13; and house as owner of jointly-held assets, 192;

basis in custom, 66; early
records of, 66–69; efforts
to remove *hidalguía* privileges, 114–19; elite control of, 97–99, 101, 111–19;
French Revolution as end
of in France, 66, 77, 81, 86;
groups excluded from, 68,
73; house system as basis of,
66, 67–68; and *pater familias* model applied to gov-
ernment, 100, 101; public
officials, 75–76, 77; resistance to Church-imposed
structures, 73; resistance to
French regulation efforts,
79; survival in Spain, 66.
See also General Assemblies
(*Biltzar Orokorra*); Gipuzkoa, political structures in;
local town councils; parish
assemblies
political theory, contextual
approach to, 27–28
Poumarède, Jacques, 138
Poza, Andrés de, 14, 14n3, 18,
20, 109
precapitalist economy, in Biscay, impossibility of return
to, 8
press, Basque: gender ideology in, 186; and women's
movement, 177–78
Primo de Rivera, Miguel,
175n13
private property, as Roman
legal concept, 191, 192, 208
property ownership in Basque
society: broad base of, as
myth, 201; different ac-
counts of, 191; donations

to monasteries in Middle
Ages, 195–96; and durable
vs. nondurable property,
209–10; expansion of pri-
vate ownership over time,
195n2; forms of, 21, 21n9;
and master of the house
as administrator of joint
assets, 192–93, 208–10, 212,
227–28; oral literature as
source of information on,
202–3; political significance
of, 21; property-related
terms in Mokoroa's *Repertorio de locuciones*, analysis of,
203–13, 204t, 206t; restrictions on sale of, 198; rules
and restrictions for use of
common land and woods,
195, 196–99, 200–201, 202;
scholars reporting commu-
nal ownership, 191–94, 213;
scholars reporting mixed
communal-private own-
ership, 194–99; scholars
reporting predominance
of elite private ownership,
199–202; weak form of,
196–99, 207–8, 213. *See also*
collective ownership; *coseigneurie*; family property
provincial assemblies, elite
control of representation
to, 113–14
Provincias Vascongadas: adop-
tion of universal nobility,
108; census-based electoral
system, introduction of,
119; class hierarchy in,
110–11; elite control of
political process, survival

into nineteenth century, 114–19; under French rule, abolishment of nobility requirement for government office, 116; loyalty to crown, as argument for Basque exceptionalism, 122, 123; municipal government, elite control of, 115–16; nineteenth century challenges to *hidalguía* privileges, 115–17; political structures in, control by wealthy elite, 111–14; universal nobility in, as more cliché than reality, 107–8, 111–14, 120; universal nobility in, as tool to establish provincial jurisdiction, 109

Putnam, Robert D., 224

Pyrenees, Central: *coseigneurie* in, 140; marriage and gender equality in, 150t

Pyrenees, Hautes-. *See* Hautes-Pyrénées

Repertorio de locuciones del habla popular vasca (Mokoroa), analysis of property-related terms in, 203–13, 204t, 206t

republican tradition: commonalities with communitarian model, 30; of early modern period, scholarly debate on, 14

republican tradition, Basque: as alternative tradition to modern state, 22; commentators on, 17–18; debate on, 37; evolution of

univeral nobility concept into, 54–56; foundation in European humanism, 16, 17–18, 23–25, 32–33; loss of, 8–9; need for balanced approach to, 14; and republican language, loss of, 9; return of, social change as obstacle to, 9; as subject of this book, 9–10; and universal nobility, 9–10, 19–20. *See* also *fueros*

The Rhetoric of Reaction (Hirschman), 276–77

Rivadeneira, Pedro de, 52

Roman law: influence on *fueros*, 138, 165; and inheritance laws, 133; legal incapacity of women in, 70; as patriarchal, 71, 138; as source of private property concept, 191, 192, 208; as threat to Basque legal system, 66, 138, 165

Rosanvallon, Pierre, 1, 2

Roussean, Jean-Jacques, 16

Rubin, Gayle, 159

Rubio-Ardanaz, Juan Antonio, 272n3

Salinas Quijada, Francisco, 192–93

Sánchez Carrión, Jose María, 162–63n7, 177

Sancho VII (king of Navarre), 66

Sandel, Michael, 2

Sanjurjo, José, 3n1

San Sebastián, and effort to reform *fueros*, 117–18

Santamaria, Karlos, 217

symbolic law (laws of prohibition): and Basque marriage practices, 143, 152*t*; compatibility with social equality, 145–49; Lévi-Strauss on, 133–34

taxation: communal property and, 199; of peasant class, 201; universal nobility as means of escaping, 91, 92, 109

taxation in traditional Basque culture: assessment and collection of, 76, 80; hierarchies of wealth and, 97–98; limits on, 19–20, 21–22; parish assemblies and, 75; royal taxes, 76, 80; taxable items, 75; uses of funds from, 75–76

Theobald I (king of Navarre), 66

Thompson, E. P.: on modernization process, 276, 278; on plebeian culture and moral economy, 256–57, 258–59. *See also* plebeian culture; plebeian moral economy

Tocqueville, Alexis de, 1

town councils. *See* local town councils

town guards, duties of, 75

Trabudua, Polixene, 170n10, 181, 183

traditionalism, ongoing battle with modernization, 6–8

Tratado de la religión y virtudes que debe tener el príncipe cristiano (Rivadeneira), 52

troncalidad, inalienable family property as, 137

Trueba, Antonio, 125, 202n5

Tubalian myth, as basis of legitimacy for Basque liberties, 51–52, 90

Tully, James, 28

txikiteo (daily drinks with groups of friends), 223, 230, 231, 233n20

txoko (gastronomic societies): and Basque adjustment to modernization, 274–75, 279–80; and Basque nationalism, 275; and communitarianism in Basque culture, 230–31, 230–31n19, 232; cultural functions of, 275; and "exit," "voice," and "loyalty" responses to dominant culture, 280; and middle space between public and private, 274–75, 276; as plebeian moral economy, 259–65; and social equilibrium, 274–75

tyranny of the majority, as potential consequence of egalitarianism, 1

Ugalde, Mercedes, 173, 181

Unión Cerrajera Co., 219, 231, 234–35

universal nobility (*hidalguía*): as autochthonous, 90, 109; as basic status recognition, 21; basis in Catholic Tubalian myth, 51–52, 90; basis in residence status, 90, 93, 112; and Basque egalitarian tradition, 226–27, 227n17;

www.ingramcontent.com/pod-product-compliance
Lightning Source LLC
Chambersburg PA
CBHW020336270326
41926CB00007B/210